SECRETARIAT

UPDATED EDITION

RAYMOND G. WOOLFE JR.

FOREWORD BY RONALD TURCOTTE, SECRETARIAT'S JOCKEY

THE DERRYDALE PRESS

LANHAM • NEW YORK • PLYMOUTH, UK

With the exception of those mentioned below, all photographs in this book were taken by Ray Woolfe, Jr. and Ray Woolfe, Jr./Daily Racing Form, reproduced through the courtesy of Daily Racing Form.

The Blood Horse, 11; Bob Coglianese, 76 L; Jerry Frutkoff and Jim McCue, 58; Bob Hart, 27, 28 Top; Sheet Meadors, 14 Top; Bert and Richard Morgan, 14 Bot., 23 Bot. L; J. Noye, 100, 101; NYRA 46 Top, Bot. 48, 49 L,R, 56; Stuart Allen Sup, 108–109; T.R.R.A., 66 Top L,R; Photo Communications, 192; John Crofts, 194; Anne M. Eberhardt, 195.

To All Who Love Horses
and with
Special Thanks to George Worthington
and Merrilyn Smith

THE DERRYDALE PRESS

Published by The Derrydale Press
An imprint of The Rowman & Littlefield Publishing Group, Inc.
4501 Forbes Boulevard, Suite 200, Lanham, Maryland 20706

Estover Road, Plymouth PL6 7PY, United Kingdom

Distributed by NATIONAL BOOK NETWORK

Copyright © 1974 and 1981 by Raymond G. Woolfe Jr.
First Derrydale Printing 2001

Library of Congress Cataloging-in-Publication Data Available

ISBN 978-1-58667-067-2 (alk. paper)
ISBN 978-1-58667-117-4 (pbk. : alk. paper)

ACKNOWLEDGMENTS

I wish to express my gratitude to those who helped me make this book happen.

To Penny Chenery, Lucien Laurin, Ron Turcotte, Elizabeth Ham, Howard Gentry and all the people of Meadow who gave me so much of their time and made me at home in their shed row.

To the DAILY RACING FORM for its courtesy in making available copyrighted material regarding Secretariat.

To Elisabeth Jakab, whose infinite patience and editing ability got this book out of me. To DAILY RACING FORM columnist Charlie Hatton for his wisdom and wonderful humor and to librarian Steve Haskin for his assistance with research and technical details.

To Peter Schults for humoring me.

And, last but not least, to my friends who got a lot of race track mud in their shoes operating my additional cameras and riding herd on my often absent mind.

Thank you all.

Contents

ALLAH CREATES THE HORSE

When Allah willed to create the horse, He said to the South Wind: "I will that a creature should proceed from thee—condense thyself!"—and the wind condensed itself. Then came the Angel Gabriel, who took a handful of this matter and presented it to Allah, who formed of it a dark bay or a chestnut horse (*koummite*—red mingled with black) saying: "I have called thee horse, I have created thee Arab, and I have bestowed upon thee the colour *koummite*. I have attached good fortune to the hair that falls between thy eyes. Thou shalt be the lord of all other animals. Men shall follow thee wheresoever thou goest. Good for pursuit as for flight, thou shalt fly without wings. Upon thy back shall riches repose and through thy means shall wealth come."

Then he signed him with the sign of glory and of good fortune, a star in the middle of the forehead.

EMIR ABD-EL-KADER
1807–1883
Letter to General E. Daumas, 1857

Foreword

Besides being a gifted photographer and writer, Raymie Woolfe is also a thoroughly knowledgeable, lifetime horseman. He comes from a racing family and has all the necessary credentials to tell Secretariat's story, both in words and through pictures.

I first met Raymond Woolfe Jr. in the jock's room in 1964 while I was riding at Delaware Park, and Raymie was a steeplechase jockey at the same track. We quickly became friends, and Raymie was instrumental in my moving on to Saratoga after the Delaware race meeting ended. Steeplechase racing was very popular in New York at the time, and Raymie was going up to Saratoga to ride for the month of August. Saratoga was also the toughest race meeting in North America. All the top jockeys would go to Saratoga for the meet, and although I was leading rider at Delaware, I had some doubts about going up to Saratoga to compete against all the big name riders. Raymie convinced me I could compete with the best.

Although Raymie subsequently stopped riding races and went on to other things, both in and outside racing, we have remained friends through the years. I have always appreciated his confidence in me and have honored his friendship.

When first Riva Ridge and then Secretariat came along, Raymie's race-riding days were over and he was working for the Daily Racing Form. He was impressed with both horses from the beginning, and I can assure you that he never missed a thing that was happening around Mr. Lucien Laurin's barn at Belmont Park. Raymie's father, a well-known and respected trainer, and Mr. Laurin had been friends from way back, so of course Raymie was already well known to Mr. Laurin and felt very much at ease with him. Raymie would always be welcome around the barn, and Mr. Laurin would speak freely to him about Big Red and his training schedule. Raymie also became close friends with Secretariat's groom, Eddie Sweat. He would visit with him often, talking about the big horse and his ways. Being around the barn so often, he of course had many opportunities to speak with Mrs. Tweedy. This often gave Raymie an edge over other photographers as he would know exactly what we were going to do every morning, and he could then position himself to take the best action shots possible.

Raymie thoroughly did his homework in writing this book. He was able to draw upon his own vast experience in horse racing and his tremendous amount of time spent at Belmont Park with the big horse at Barn 5. His knowledge and dedication have been an asset throughout, and his skills as a photographer and writer speak for themselves.

Raymie Woolfe's book *Secretariat* brings back in detail many a memory of that great time in American racing to all of us. The racing world will forever be grateful and richer for the experience of reading it.

Ron Turcotte

Ron Turcotte
Secretariat's jockey

ONE

On the Toss of a Coin

I: Courting Chance

In the fall of 1969, a small group of people assembled in the offices of Alfred Gwynne Vanderbilt at the Belmont Park racetrack. They had gathered in the inner sanctum of the chairman of the Board of Trustees of the New York Racing Association to toss a coin.

These were not ordinary people, and the occasion was not an ordinary game of chance. On one side was Mrs. Helen "Penny" Tweedy, daughter of the noted Virginia horse breeder Christopher T. Chenery. For the last year and a half, she had been attempting to learn the horse business and manage her ill father's Meadow Stable at the same time. Giving her priceless advice and moral support was her father's good friend, Arthur Boyd "Bull" Hancock, Jr., himself a legend in the thoroughbred breeding world. On the other side were Ogden Phipps and his two children, Cynthia and Ogden, Jr. "Dinny." Phipps was the owner of the great sire, Bold Ruler.

The coin toss was to determine who would have first choice of foals from two of Chenery's mares that had been bred to Bold Ruler under a unique agreement. Since breeding to their famed champion was no casual matter, Phipps and his mother Mrs. Henry Carnegie Phipps, had devised a shrewd arrangement which maximized the potential of their great horse. Breeders would send two approved mares to Bold Ruler on a two-year contract. The fee was one foal each year. First choice the first year was determined by the coin toss; the loser got first choice the second year. Since Meadow Farm's mares and their produce had become synonomous with excellence in racing, Chris Chenery's participation was welcomed.

9

Ogden Phipps, owner of the great sire, Bold Ruler.

Penny Tweedy once observed, "It was a great deal for the Phippses because they would end up with the offspring of the best mares in the country." It had been the kind of gamble that appealed to the enterprising Chenery. But over the years, fortune, and the coin toss, had favored the Phippses, and they had won the most promising foals.

This was to be the last coin toss for Meadow.

When she took over Meadow, Penny Tweedy had decided to terminate the arrangement. However, honoring her father's word, she had, in 1968, sent two of Meadow's prized broodmares, Somethingroyal and Hasty Matelda, to Bold Ruler.

That spring, Somethingroyal had dropped a filly and Hasty Matelda a colt. Somethingroyal was in foal again to Bold Ruler, but Hasty Matelda was barren. Thus, whoever won the coin toss would only get one foal; the loser would get two.

"We were joking," Penny Tweedy recalled, "because we both said we wanted to lose."

Little did she or the others in that room know then that this simple toss of silver was to decide the ownership of one of the greatest racehorses the world has ever known.

Phipps had decided to call tails on the toss before he even entered the room. He had opted for tails the last time, too.

Alfred Vanderbilt, as the neutral party, flipped the coin, a fifty-cent piece. As it rose into the air, Phipps called out "Tails!" The coin landed on the floor. Bull Hancock, the tallest person in the room, leaned over. "Tails it is," he said. Phipps had won the toss.

It was Phipps's habit to take fillies in a toss with Meadow, and so he took Somethingroyal's filly. Meadow was left with the

Bold Ruler, sire of Secretariat.

11

Hasty Matelda colt and whatever Something-royal would produce the following spring.

The filly won by Phipps that day was named The Bride. She raced four times and was never better than sixth. The colt left to Penny Tweedy was named Rising River. He had soundness problems, and Meadow eventually sold him for $50,000 on his bloodlines. On the last coin toss, Fortune had finally smiled on Meadow Farm. The foal being carried by Somethingroyal was Secretariat.

At the time of the coin toss, Penny Tweedy had already spent almost two years attempting to cope with the affairs of Meadow. But Meadow, unlike most of the great racing stables, which are nourished by regular infusions of private capital from their owners, had to support itself. Her father decided to incorporate his horse operations in October 1958. "If Meadow can't stand on its own," he said, "I don't want it." But Meadow not only proceeded to pull its own weight; it made an enviable profit. This made it fairly unusual in the topsy-turvy economics of racing where many owners run their stables at a loss, or at best break even, with a modest gain every five years to satisfy their tax status as a viable business.

Christopher Chenery himself was an unusual man. A native Virginian and a self-made millionaire, he decided in 1936 to buy back Meadow, his old family homestead at Doswell, Virginia, twenty miles north of Richmond. Built in 1810 by an ancestor, Charles Dabney Morris, the Meadow had passed from family hands in the dark days following the Civil War. Long an enthusiastic polo player and fox hunter, Chenery rode daily until his health failed him in 1966. His mounts were almost always thoroughbreds, and his great love for them made him determined to gear his ancestral home to the production of fine horses.

Well meaning critics pointed out that the 2600 acre farm was unfashionably located, too swampy, and the grass too poor to raise thoroughbreds. But the redoubtable Chenery, fifty years old when he decided on this venture, had a talent for seeing possibilities that other people didn't. First an engineer, then the owner and manager of several utility companies, he had gone on to finance the first offshore oil drilling in the coastal waters of the Gulf of Mexico. He proceeded to apply his various skills to the farm's problems. About 225 acres of his best lowland pasture were pure floodland. But Chenery had noticed that along the edge of the meadow's bowl-shaped bottom was the ruin of an old pre-Civil War levy about three-quarters of a mile long, built to hold back the waters of the North Anna River. He had it reconstructed and drained the Meadow of its swamps. He renovated and added to the buildings and supervised the careful planting of good pasture grass. Soon the old farm bloomed with rich mixtures of blue grass, orchard, fescue, and clover. He was ready to acquire the horses that were to complete his dream for the Meadow.

Chenery's premise was that the most important element of such a farm was the quality of its mares. With his great instinct for a good deal, he proceeded to acquire a series of foundation mares that were to make the Meadow famous by their offspring. His first buy turned out to be an incredible bargain that has probably never been equaled in the horse world. At a dispersal sale in January 1939, Chenery acquired Hildene, a yearling filly by Bubbling Over out of Fancy Racket for $750. She never raced, but her offspring and her daughters' offspring were to earn over $3 million. She was a classic example of what horsemen call a "blue hen."

Chenery had purchased Hildene on the advice of Arthur Boyd Hancock of the fabulous Claiborne Farm in Kentucky, a friend whose family ties with Chenery had begun in Virginia's antebellum days when another Chenery ancestor, Major Thomas W. Doswell, drew Captain Richard Hancock into the thoroughbred business. The Hancocks were, like the Doswells and Chenerys, Virginia horsemen until 1910 when Hancock's wife inherited 1300 acres of the best land in Kentucky's Bourbon County. This was the nucleus of today's 5700 acre Claiborne Farm.

The friendship continued with Hancock's son, A. B. "Bull" Hancock, Jr., who was born on January 24, 1910. The younger Hancock was destined to become one of the most formidable figures in the horse world. His intuition about horses and their bloodlines, coupled with an amazing ability to do the right thing at the right time, was to make him a living legend.

Success was not just handed to Bull Hancock. In 1945, returning from his service in the Air Corps, he found not a flourishing breeding empire, but a crumbling dynasty. That year, his father suffered the first of a series of heart attacks. Claiborne's renaissance was brought about by the talent and tireless effort of this man and the able employees with whom he surrounded himself.

It was easy to understand why A. B. Hancock, Jr. had been dubbed Bull. The combination of his size, strength, and personality were almost overwhelming. Six feet two inches tall and heavyset, he spoke with a deep, resonant voice and would genially extend a gentle ham of a hand that could as

Christopher Chenery loved to ride the wild places.

13

Bull Hancock and his father, A. B., Sr., at Clairborne.

Helen and Christopher Chenery at the races in Saratoga. August, 1960.

easily crush a rock as shake a hand. Although he was a fierce competitor in anything he undertook, he possessed that intangible and captivating air of gentle grace that is carelessly referred to as "southern charm."

Bull Hancock ran the biggest thoroughbred operation in the world, and he ran it to perfection. He knew every mare at Claiborne on sight, what she'd been bred to, and what she was worth. He could recognize a stud prospect anywhere, and he could put together a multimillion-dollar horse syndicate with one swing through the Saratoga box section. Once asked what his secret for success was, he is reputed to have replied, "We just try to do the usual unusually well." One of the usual things Bull Hancock did was bring to Claiborne the two stallions who were to be the source of Secretariat's lineage. The first was Princequillo, the Irish-bred son of a Belgian sire and a French dam who raced exclusively in the United States. An outstanding stakes winner, Princequillo went on to beget daughters who had an amazing propensity for producing winners earning over $250,000 each—in all, 238 of them. His most famous daughter was Somethingroyal, the dam of Secretariat. Later, Hancock paid $340,000 for the Aga Khan's great Nasrullah, who was to sire Bold Ruler, the sire of Secretariat.

Hancock's operation emphasized the "classic" horse—one who can compete in the best races against the best horses in the world. With such perfection as a constant goal, the most important part of breeding horses is selecting stallions. Considering the rate of elimination through poor racing performance, genetics, gelding, and injuries, only about 12 out of every 10,000 registered colts become successful sires. With these odds, most breeders conclude that the choice of good stallions is mostly luck. But when a man selects not just one or two successful sires, but a steady succession of them, as Bull Hancock did, it is more than chance. His approach was the straightforward premise that good runners are the best candidates to be good sires. Statistics show that one successful stallion will come from every two colts who are racing champions. This theory was supported by the fact that of the twenty-six stallions at Claiborne when Secretariat was sired, sixteen of them were champion race horses both here and abroad.

While Bull Hancock had been turning Claiborne Farm back into the foremost thoroughbred breeding establishment in America, Christopher Chenery had been steadily building the quality of the horses at Meadow Farm. In 1947, he bought his second great blue hen, the mare Imperatrice, a proven stakes performer, for whom he paid $30,000. She was to be the most significant buy he ever made. The mare was nine years old and had already produced—although this was unknown at the time of her purchase—what was to be a stakes-producing mare, Imperieuse, as well as two stakes winners, Scattered and Imperium. Just what a fantastic bargain Meadow had acquired began to be evident the following June when Scattered won the Coaching Club American Oaks, one of the most important races for three-year-old fillies in the country.

It was all uphill for Meadow after the purchase of Imperatrice. She was to provide four stakes winners for Meadow. But her most historic offspring, ironically, was one of only two foals she produced which never

Bull with one of his Clairborne runners.

II: Transition

Christopher Chenery's health began to fail seriously in the mid-1960s. For the first time, there was a whisper of concern for Meadow's future, for as its guiding genius began to fade, so did its fortunes.

In October 1967, Chenery unaccountably agreed to sell four of his best bred stakes mares. Penny decided something had to be done, and quickly. She stepped in and stopped the sale of one mare. Even though she knew that there was an element of unfair advantage in the transactions, she honored the sale of the other three. In November, another blow descended on the Chenerys: Mrs. Helen Chenery died. It was a time of sadness and transition for the Meadow.

A family meeting was called. It was also a meeting of the Board of Directors of the Meadow Stud Corporation. Heretofore, Penny's participation in the affairs of Meadow had consisted of attending the board meeting. Now, it was decided that she should undertake Meadow's management.

Neither her older brother, Dr. Hollis Chenery, chief economist of the World Bank in Washington, D.C., nor her older sister, Mrs. Margaret Carmichael, who operated a secretarial and book editing service in Tucson, were in a position to take on this responsibility.

Thus, the duties of management were left to Penny Tweedy, the youngest of the three Chenery children, and to her father's executive secretary of more than thirty-five years, Elizabeth Ham, who probably knew more about the Meadow than anyone else.

Penny began a crash program of self-education. Her every moment was spent devouring racing literature of all kinds. She read the

raced in the money. This was a bay filly by Bull Hancock's great Princequillo, foaled in 1952. Named Somethingroyal, she made only one start and was promptly retired. Her first foal to race was a stakes-placed filly, who made her debut in 1960. In the next twelve years, Somethingroyal's offspring were to earn $1,187,153.

In 1965, Somethingroyal was sent to Bold Ruler for the first time. This initial match produced Syrian Sea, one of the top two-year-old fillies of 1967.

16

Somethingroyal,
dam of Secretariat.

Meadow's floodlands.

Morning at the Meadow.

Meadow broodmares and their foals.

Daily Racing Form from cover to cover daily. She digested an endless stream of material in such periodicals as *The Blood Horse, The Thoroughbred Record, Turf & Sport Digest,* and *The Horseman's Journal.* She worked hard to acquire a total familiarity with the basic vocabulary and slang of the track, the nuances of handicapping, the intricacies of bloodlines and breeding, conformation, feeding, the ailments of horses, and the causes of unsoundness. In short, she had undertaken to absorb more knowledge about racing in a couple of years than most people do in a lifetime.

Penny realized she had a lot to learn. While never an outsider to Meadow's operations, she wasn't really schooled in the mechanics of managing a breeding and racing concern. "I was close to my Dad as a daughter to a father," she recalled, "but he was a man who had his own ideas. He didn't want a lot of help or advice. . . . There wasn't any place to really help him or take an active role. People ask, 'Weren't you always in on it?' Well, yes, from a distance. . . . Oh, I was on the board, but all I did was go to the meetings and learn what had already happened and say 'Aye.' "

However, her background helped equip her for the challenge.

Christopher Chenery's love of horses had been passed on to his youngest child. Growing up in Pelham Manor, New York, Penny rode constantly—in shows, in the hunting field, anywhere—just for pleasure. A special treat was trailing along with her father to the Meadow and to the race track to see his race horses. On those trips, her fascination with the wonderful creatures became a permanent part of her.

After serving with the Red Cross in France

Penny Chenery.

and Germany during World War II, she entered the Columbia Graduate School of Business. That training, she observes, was what gave her confidence about running the Meadow and enabled her to tackle awesome balance sheets.

While working toward her master's degree, she met and married Jack Tweedy, a Princeton Law School graduate. They moved to Denver, where Jack began his law practice. In 1971, they moved back to New York. By then, Penny was already long embroiled in the management of Meadow.

She began going to the track in the early

morning hours: "I watched workouts, cooling outs, tryouts, standouts, and throwouts—and asked stupid questions."

She began to make her own mark among racing people. They soon learned that her gentle and very genuine charm (she looks straight into your eyes when she speaks to you, and when she laughs her eyes laugh, too) can quickly shift to that rock-jawed determination that always made a Chenery hard to best in a horse deal.

One difficulty she encountered was that her father's able trainer of more than twenty years, Casey Hayes, still had a tendency to think of her as his boss' little girl, rather than someone with a tremendous responsibility on her shoulders. In fact, Penny found herself beginning to be a bit afraid to ask him "stupid questions." Reluctantly, she concluded that in order to establish her management on a fresh and effective basis, she had to have a trainer of her own choosing.

She turned to Bull Hancock for advice. He recommended Roger Laurin, the talented young conditioner who was the son of the veteran trainer Lucien Laurin.

With Roger's guidance, Meadow cut down overhead and culled out the deadwood among the stock. Meadow's racing string soon began showing a modest profit. Roger was a patient tutor; Penny felt free to ask her "stupid questions," and Roger gave her answers. She credits Roger with teaching her how to really *look* at a horse—that is, recognize good or bad conformation. And that is the *basis* for being a horseman.

In her attempt to keep Meadow economically viable, Penny had other assistance and encouragement. Elizabeth Ham, Christopher Chenery's executive secretary, after whom Secretariat was named; Howard Gentry,

Meadow's farm manager; and Bull Hancock, her father's good friend, had all rallied around.

Elizabeth Ham, Meadow's present financial manager and board member, had accompanied Mr. Chenery in his horse buying over the years, including the providential purchase of the great mare Hildene. An avid horsewoman, she also rode with him and recalls, "You went wild places. He was a bold rider, and he had bold horses." Knowing the workings of the Meadow inside and out, and an old school exponent of doing things in the horse business properly or not at all, she was invaluable to Penny's progress.

Howard Gentry, Meadow's farm manager since 1946, a soft-spoken native Virginian, was a steadfast believer in the kind of limitless patience and proper horsemanship that produce fine horses, and Penny leaned heavily on him for guidance in matters of farm management.

Bull Hancock patiently drilled Penny throughout her learning period on bloodlines, selective breeding, and breeding management. Everywhere Penny went, whether on a business trip or on a fishing trip with her husband Jack, *The American Racing Manual* and *Stallion Register* went along with her. Gradually, she began to absorb the fine points of the thoroughbred business. It was the knowledge obtained by this constant study that was responsible for Penny's sending Somethingroyal to Bold Ruler as one of the mares in the coin toss arrangement. There was a "nick" (a horseman's term for a history of successful breeding) between sons of Nasrullah and daughters of Princequillo. Bold Ruler was Nasrullah's most prestigious son, and Somethingroyal was a stakes-producing daughter of Princequillo. There was a lot of hope riding on the lone foal that was to be the final product of the two-year pact.

The Nasrullah–Princequillo combination was an attempt to combine the best features of two strains. Although Bold Ruler was one of the greatest sires of all time, his progeny tended to have certain drawbacks. There was an accepted but erroneous belief that Bold Ruler's get could rarely be counted on to win at distances much better than a mile, that they tended to do well at the shorter distances run by the two-year-olds, but to disappoint at three when asked to run the longer races. Oddly enough, the records disprove this. Bold Ruler's get considerably exceed the average of American sires in average winning distance. For example, prior to 1972, ten of his sons and daughters won at a mile and a quarter or more. Bold Ruler himself won three out of four races run at a mile and a quarter; in two of them he carried the staggering load of 134 pounds. One unfortunate trait was a tendency to unsoundness. Many of Bold Ruler's offspring had gone lame early. Bold Ruler himself was arthritic and died of cancer in 1971 at the relatively young age of seventeen.

The horses sired by Princequillo were generally a striking contrast. They were tough and durable and could go a long distance. They did not usually display early speed in a race, but as one breeder once impressed on Penny Tweedy, "The Princequillos will run all day, and if the races get long enough and the other horses get tired enough, sooner or later they'll win for you."

But the science of genetics is a far from exact one, and often the most carefully planned matings produce nothing that resembles the better qualities of either parent.

Penny in her learning days.

Seth Hancock in Saratoga.

Roger Laurin.

23

Penny with some Meadow broodmares.

Where Secretariat was foaled.

As witness The Bride, the filly who never won a race, won by Ogden Phipps.

Encouraged by her luck in losing the toss, Penny dared to dream that Somethingroyal's foal might be the winning horse the Meadow needed so badly.

The ten months during which Somethingroyal placidly carried her foal were a difficult time for the Meadow. The economic situation was precarious, and there was even some serious discussion at the board meetings about whether it might be wiser to just sell the Meadow and reinvest the capital in the stock market. Penny's brother, Hollis Chenery, who had limited his role in the farm's affairs to that of occasional economic counsel, advised that Meadow's successful continuance required "a major stakes winner every five years and *some* kind of a stakes winner every other year."

Penny gamely held her ground. Christopher Chenery, she said, would not want the Meadow to be sold, and they owed it to him to give the Meadow a chance to continue. Her argument prevailed, and the stable remained intact.

But in her heart was the sinking realization that the Meadow really needed a miracle of sorts if it were going to survive.

III: Somethingroyal's foal

On a cold, clear Virginia night in March 1970, Howard Gentry was at home, playing pool in the recreation room with his friend Raymond Wood. He had eaten an early supper and was now killing time in anticipation of a long night's work. That afternoon, Somethingroyal had begun to "wax," a sure indication that the birth of her foal could be expected within the next forty-eight hours and might easily occur that very night. Through some quirk of nature, mares almost never foal during daylight hours.

Waxing starts when the mare's udder becomes swollen with milk. A thickish secretion then begins to emerge from the milk canal. Upon contact with the air it dries in waxlike droplets on the mare's teats. When a mare nears her proper foaling time, the groom or night watchman in attendance regularly checks her udder for this sign.

A mare about to foal is separated from her sisters in the main broodmare barn to avoid unsettling the other mothers-to-be by the turning on of lights and the commotion attendant on a birth. In her new quarters, she is kept under constant surveillance.

Somethingroyal had been put in a 24 by 14 foot closed shed with a stall that had originally been built as an open shed for a sickly foal. It had recently been closed in as a spare foaling stall. Gentry had placed the mare in that particular shed because it would be easier for her to maintain her footing on a dirt floor than on the cement floor of the main foaling barn. He had been particularly careful with Somethingroyal; she was an older mare, eighteen years, and he wanted to make sure that everything was as easy for her as possible.

She was being watched by Gentry's watchman of some twenty years, Clarence Richards. He rarely dozes and has yet to miss a mare's time.

Mrs. Gentry was in the kitchen brewing several pots of coffee for the possibly long night ahead. Tired, but knowing that Clarence would phone him from the shed if anything should start to happen, Gentry stayed up shooting pool with Raymond Wood to pass the time. Suddenly the phone rang.

"Mistah Gentry! You comin'? She's startin'!"

Gentry had no sooner thrown on a jacket and filled a thermos with coffee when the phone rang again.

"You comin' Mistah Gentry? You comin'?" Somethingroyal seemed to be in a hurry.

Accompanied by Raymond Wood, Gentry plunged out the door and drove to the little shed. There, at 12:10 A.M., March 30, 1970, he delivered Somethingroyal's third foal by Bold Ruler. He was a big, handsome chestnut colt with three white feet and a star and a stripe on his forehead. He staggered to his feet within twenty minutes and began nursing in about forty-five. Gentry recalls that his first impression was of a "big, strong-made foal with plenty of bone, who, with his breeding, could possibly be one of the best horses Meadow has ever produced."

Some time later, Penny Tweedy, on one of her regular inspection trips to the Meadow, saw Somethingroyal's new foal for the first time. She excitedly made a one word entry in her notebook: "Wow!"

Meadow's miracle had arrived.

TWO

"We have a race horse on our hands."

I: Early Days

There is an old horse trader's saw which advises:

One white foot, run him for his life;
Two white feet, keep him for your wife;
Three white feet, keep him for your man;
Four white feet, sell him if you can;
Four white feet and a stripe on the nose,
Knock him in the head and feed him to
     the crows.

Had the people of the Meadow been influenced by such folksy wisdom, Something-royal's foal might have been among those

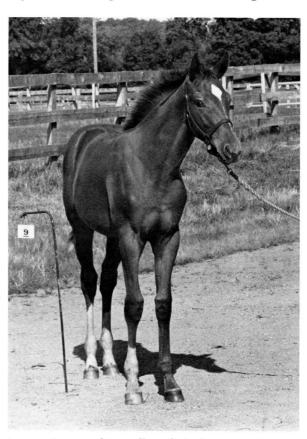

Secretariat was a big, well-made foal.

27

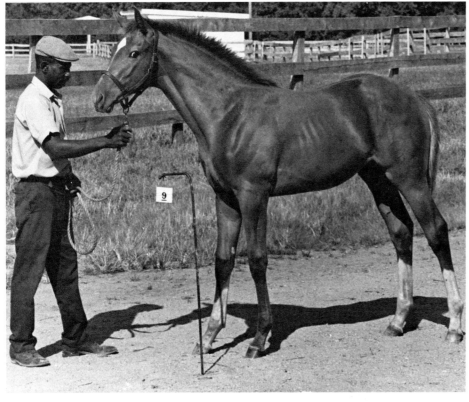

Louis Tillman poses Secretariat for his Jockey Club I.D. portrait.

Romping.

culled that year. He did indeed have a stripe on the nose and three white feet, but these markings were carried by a picture-book colt. He was bigger than most foals, with a wide, deep chest and legs that promised to be clean and straight, with firm, unblemished knees and ankles. As Howard Gentry had observed, he was powerfully made, with "plenty of bone." This meant that he had a solid, well-chiseled frame, not the "mushy" or round, soft-looking joints and skimpy bone areas that spell potential trouble on lesser horses. In physical quality, this colt was a textbook example of what all breeders strive for.

In her farm log, Miss Ham, herself a perfectionist, recorded the sterling qualities of the colt who had been named Secretariat in her honor.

July 28, 1970—Three white stockings— well made colt—might be a little light under the knees*—stands well on pasterns—good straight hind leg—good shoulders—good quarters. You just have to like him.

Somethingroyal had been a beautiful mother to all her foals, and Secretariat was no exception. She was extraordinarily affectionate, always nuzzling and licking her foals. A mare usually does this only when she cleans the newborn foal, but Somethingroyal continued to do it long afterward. This kind of loving care from its mother strongly affects the foal's disposition later on. "She had a wonderful, even temperament, which I believe she passed on to Secretariat," observed Howard Gentry. "His sire, you know, was kind of flighty—goes back to Nasrullah. He could be a rough type of horse."

---

*Miss Ham remembers of that entry that the notation "light under the knees" was an early baby thing that Secretariat lost as he developed.

Meadow's way with its horses could only have enhanced Secretariat's even temperament. The farm is renowned for the gentleness and good disposition of its horses. The staff make a point of handling the horses as much as possible from birth, thus getting them used to people. Every step in a horse's training is taken slowly and carefully, and no horse is ever frightened or forced.

Meadow's care extended to the smallest detail. On many farms, when being led through gates or stall doors foals are allowed to run free alongside their mothers. This invites accidents, since the foal, always wanting to be next to its mother, will try to squeeze through spaces with her that are not big enough for both of them. The result can be a damaging scrape to the hip or injury to shoulders or legs. Meadow puts a halter and lead shank on both mare and foal; thus they can be led separately, preventing unfortunate occurrences.

Secretariat, however, relished his freedom and became a tough customer to handle at the pasture gate. "He was so precocious," said Gentry, "that we were worried that he'd pick up the habit of getting away from men. That could mean a lot of trouble later on. For a time, we put a restraining chain on him to stop him from trying to bolt. But he was so intelligent that he caught on quickly and never developed any bad habits."

"He went on to be a very aggressive type of colt," recalled Gentry, "especially when he got out in the field."

In the field, Secretariat was clearly the dominant foal in the band, displaying a fiercely competitive instinct when they all ran together, playing rougher than the others. Foals love to roughhouse, biting and kicking with such unreserved enthusiasm that someone seeing such a sight for the first time

Turning out at Meadow.

Roughhousing.

29

would be sure that they were mauling each other severely. But although there is an occasional bruise or scrape, the young horses rarely injure each other.

Secretariat was also one of the healthiest horses ever at Meadow, seemingly immune to accident or disease. Meadow's long time veterinarian, a slim capable woman named Olive Britt, mused, "I don't ever remember treating Secretariat for anything to do with sickness the whole time he was here."

Secretariat's only problems in life seemed to be satisfying his bottomless appetite and trying to swish flies away with his stubby foal's tail. He passed an idyllic first summer with his dam in the carefree, lush world of Meadow's rich grass and big shade trees.

The fall brought a rude interruption to this paradise. Elizabeth Ham made another entry on Secretariat's page in her log:

Oct. 5, 1970—WEANED

Meadow had approached the weaning process gradually. In the weeks prior to this event, which would separate mother and son forever, Secretariat was progressively fed more and more grain, until he was happily wolfing down between five and six quarts daily. He showed no aversion to this switch from his mother's milk.

Finally, one afternoon, Somethingroyal and the other mares were taken about a mile down the road and turned out in a paddock, out of sight and out of hearing of their foals. Then Secretariat and the other unsuspecting foals were taken into the barn and put in stalls. This was to prevent them from racing around the field in a panic, frantically looking for their mothers, and risking real injury. They were kept in the stalls until the next morning. Some of them just stood quietly; others literally tried to climb up the walls to get out. Secretariat pawed the ground a bit and whinnied plaintively from time to time. Throughout the night, anguished neighing continued almost without letup. In the morning, the foals were turned out in the field without their dams for the first time. They ran wildly around looking for their mothers, but without the panic of the day before. Some farms like to keep the weaned foals in their stalls for two or three days, but Howard Gentry observed, "We find most of them do better turned out the next day. They're going to run like hell anyhow! Besides, the fresh air keeps down the colds."

Secretariat ran like hell with the rest of them, but had very little difficulty adjusting to his motherless state. Most of his care and affection was now supplied by his groom, Louis Tillman. All of Meadow's foal grooms are like mother hens about their charges, but Louis had always felt that Secretariat was something special. There was a presence about Secretariat, even as a foal, that was obvious to everyone. For a man like Louis Tillman, having charge of a colt like Secretariat goes a long way toward redeeming the years he spends in the long and lonely routine hours of farm work.

Throughout the winter and the following spring, life for Secretariat consisted primarily of just growing. His days alternated between the stable and the big field where he was free to roughhouse with his fellow colts.

Late the next summer, Miss Ham made another entry in her log:

Aug. 3, 1971—Plates on in front
—to training center for breaking.

Now she began a separate page:

SECRETARIAT—TRAINING RECORD
August 3, 1971—Transferred to training center for breaking.

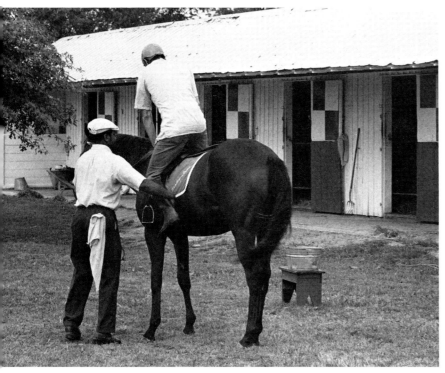

Chuck Ross gives a rider a careful leg up on a yearling.

A set of yearlings galloping on the training track.

Coming in from a gallop.

Grooming after a gallop.

Leaving the barns and fields of his babyhood, Secretariat entered a stable compound located inside the oval of Meadow's training track to begin the tasks he was born for.

Here, Meadow's farm trainer of some twenty-five years, R. M. "Bob" Bailes, took charge of the horse's life. Bailes liked him from the start; this big, handsome colt looked like one of Meadow's finest prospects in years.

"Bob was an unusually patient man with a horse," says Howard Gentry. "He had the most wonderful eye for looking at a horse of any man I ever knew. Some people just have a knack for communicating with a horse—he had it and so does his son, Meredith."

Like the staff of any good training establishment, the people at Meadow invested a good deal of time and patience in the breaking of their horses. Secretariat received a good deal of handling and preliminary familiarization with having a saddle on his back and a proper bit in his mouth. From the beginning, he had a fine, sensitive mouth that responded well to all signals conveyed by the reins. Once he was used to this, he was introduced to the weight of a man. This was done by Meredith, who was given a very slow, quiet leg up until he was able to lay, belly down, across the saddle on Secretariat's back. This is known as "backing a yearling," and if the yearling decides to object, it can be pretty rough on a man's ribs. Secretariat took it calmly. So the next morning, Meredith was again given a leg up, but this time he sat astride the colt. Secretariat's new groom, Charles "Chuck" Ross, making sure that Meredith had a firm seat, led the colt his first few steps with a man on his back. This went so smoothly, that the trio, who had been engaging in these maneuvers in the confines of a stall, immediately advanced to the indoor exercise shed. For the next two weeks, Chuck led Secretariat in circles and figure eights while Meredith taught the colt the meaning of directional signals communicated through the reins to his mouth and through the pressure of Meredith's legs on his sides. Finally, one morning, he was graduated to his first walk and jog guided only by Meredith on his back. Now he was ready to leave the indoor training area and get down to business on the track outside.

By now, the colt had demonstrated enough of his temperament and quality for everyone to agree that a good deal could be expected of him. But there was another facet of his personality that caused a good deal of concern. This was his gargantuan appetite, which went considerably beyond what horsemen call a "good doer." He had begun to put on size and weight at an alarming rate; indeed, when he got on the the training track, he was clumsy and bumbling, and earned the unflattering nickname of "ol' Hopalong."

It began to look as though Meadow had a fat, pretty kid on their hands who wasn't about to shape up into an athlete. But his breeding, his spectaclar good looks, and a certain "something" about him that seemed to be noticed by everyone, made them feel that perhaps it was only a matter of time. Miss Ham recalls, "Our only real worry always was that he was so slow to take any interest in what he was supposed to do." His groom, Chuck Ross, argued that he would be better than Meadow's top horse, Riva Ridge, then making quite a name for himself as a two year old. Meredith countered this with a glum comment: "We've never had a good chestnut." There the matter rested. But while Secretariat was eating and bumbling his way to maturity at Meadow, some major changes had been taking place for Meadow at the race track.

In June 1971, Roger Laurin had been approached by Ogden Phipps to train his coveted racing string. It was an offer few trainers could turn down, for the Phipps stable was one of the most prestigious in the country. But Roger felt he owed the Meadow more than just a thank-you-and-good-bye. So he persuaded his father, Lucien Laurin, who was about to retire, to postpone this move and take over the Meadow stable instead.

The sixty-year-old Lucien had been born in St. Paul, Joliette, Quebec. Like many of the young men from that area, Lucien had put in some time in the lumber camps, but at sixteen he headed for the Montreal racetrack. He began his career "walking hots." In 1929, weighing only 79 pounds, he got his first jockey's license. Riding 1445 races with 161 wins between 1930 and 1942, he describes himself as a "plain mediocre jockey." With his weight going up and the quality of his mounts going down, he decided to become a trainer. He took out his license in 1943, and his first horses were those of a Providence, Rhode Island, cotton mill owner named Ben Lister. As his reputation grew, he moved up from the New England tracks to the glamorous New York racecourses. His first big break came when he was assigned the stable of prominent owner Reginald N. Webster.

The chubby, elfin-faced, sometimes emotional French Canadian has always been liked by his fellow horsemen. A hard worker and chronic worrier, his triumphs were begrudged by few. Much of his success was due to his astuteness with a "condition book" (the booklet provided by a race track that lists races and their conditions for entry: age,

Penny thinks the horse toes in a little.

weight, number of races won, and so forth). He had an uncanny ability to pick the right spots for his horses. He tended to be sparing in his orders to jockeys, though he was adamant about letting a horse run his own race: "I've never believed in fighting horses, trying to change the way they want to run. I lost a lot of races when I was a jock by taking too many orders from people who didn't know enough about their horses." He went on to train some thirty-one stakes winners, including such notables as Quill, Brongerullah, Crafty Skipper, Count Amber, Sorceress, Viscount, Capelet, Thays, National, Repeating, Traffic, Amberoid, and Dike. Quill was voted the leading two-year-old filly of 1958, and Amberoid won the 1966 Belmont Stakes, squashing Kauai King's bid for the Triple Crown.

Rober Laurin had acquired a valuable farewell present to give the Meadow. The shift in trainer from the son to the father came, Penny Tweedy recalls, "just as we were about to hit the jackpot." And hit it they did. A slender two-year-old bay colt by First Landing, Riva Ridge, had emerged as one of the best of his age group. Under Lucien's handling, he won the Saratoga Flash, the Belmont Futurity, the Champagne Stakes, the Laurel Futurity, and the Garden State Stakes. In addition to Riva Ridge, two other Meadow colts, Upper Case and Quill Gordon, were also registering stakes victories. Meadow's fortunes were on the upswing at last.

That fall Lucien accompanied Penny on an inspection trip to the Meadow to look over the yearlings; and he saw Secretariat for the first time. In spite of the big, shining chestnut's awkward circuits of the training track, he could not help but be impressed with him.

Miss Ham's log continued with more entries on her namesake:

> SECRETARIAT'S TRAINING RECORD:
> *Nov. 21*—out of training—to go to Florida with Mr. Laurin
> *Dec. 22, 23*—filling, right hind ankle—ok next day
> *Jan. 10, 1972*—Picked up, hack —canter—
> *Jan. 18 & 19*—rode around farm in van.*
> *Jan. 20, 1972*—Shipped to Florida by van. To Lucien in Florida.

Now officially a two year old, the big red colt had left the rolling hills of Meadow Farm never to return.

---

*At Meadow, rehearsals of new procedures for their horses were common: a colt leaving the farm for the races was always given several rides in a van to familiarize him with travel procedures.

Meadow's vet, Olive Britt, describes a treatment.

An orphan foal with a "nurse mare."

Howard, Penny, and Lucien looking over Meadow's prospects.

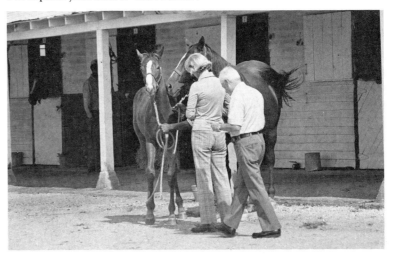

A young one undergoes scrutiny.

Penny and Howard on an inspection tour.

The courtyard at the training barn.

Lucien Laurin, the trainer.

Eddie Sweat, the groom.

II: "We have a racehorse on our hands."

On his arrival at Lucien Laurin's stable at the Hialeah race track in Florida, Secretariat was assigned to Lucien's most trusted groom, Eddie Sweat, whose other charge was Riva Ridge, the Meadow's best horse and a leading Derby prospect.

Eddie Sweat is one of those men whom horsemen describe as having "that touch" with horses. To the two-dollar bettor, horses are the dream of a winning ticket; to the breeders and owners, horses are primarily an investment and, sometimes, a form of amusement; to trainers and jockeys, they are mainly winners or losers. To an Eddie Sweat, they are his life's blood, and his every waking day is concerned with the most intimate details of his horses' lives.

Eddie was born near the end of the Great Depression in Holly Hill in South Carolina's low country. It is a flat, sandy land of marshes and pine woods, good for raising cotton, pulpwood, hogs, and hunting dove and quail. The school bus he rode each morning would pass by Lucien Laurin's training center, Holly Hill Farm. He peered longingly through the bus window at the beautiful animals in the field. As soon as he was able to leave school, he went to Lucien with the notion of becoming a jockey. Lucien gave him his first horse job and even let him do some riding at the farm. But Eddie was still growing. He was a man of tremendous physical strength; when he was eight years old, he had worked after school digging post holes for fences; at fourteen he was able to lift 205 pounds over his head. He struck out for Florida with the idea of becoming a prize fighter. This plan was short-lived, and after working for a while with a construction company, he returned to

36

Holly Hill in 1953. He was now far too big and muscular to ride, so he walked hots and began to learn the fine points of being a good groom. Lucien took him along to New York for the first time in the spring of 1955. In 1956, he was given charge of his first winner, a horse named Lake Erie. Eddie recalls that this "gave me a touch of rubbin' good horses," and good horses he continued to get. Lucien knew he could depend on Eddie totally. For example, during a wildcat strike of backstretch help in 1960, Eddie refused to participate. He singlehandedly cared for seventeen horses until it was all over. Eddie humbly says that the reason he didn't attend the union meetings was that he just didn't have time. With Eddie, his horses always came first.

Now, Eddie regarded the newest token of Lucien's trust with some doubt.

"When I first saw Secretariat, I never thought he'd be no good hoss—too pretty! Too big an' *fat*," recalls Eddie. "That's why

I didn't want to rub him at first. I thought to myself, I'd just stick with Riva Ridge."

It began to look as if Eddie's doubts were well-founded.

"As far as I remember, the best work he had was three eighths in thirty eight*—you know, thas' terrible! Mr. Laurin used to hook him up with a hoss called Gold Bag. Now, Gold Bag, he wasn't much of a hoss, but every time they breezed together, he'd leave Secretariat behind about two lengths."

Lucien concurs with this recollection. "I don't believe he would have stayed sound if I'd given him long fast gallops like the other young horses. He was just too big and heavy. So clumsy! I had a horse of my own, Gold Bag— used to outwork him flatfooted. You'd see a lot of dust and then here'd be ol' Hopalong comin' along behind."

One morning, jockey Ron Turcotte stopped by and looked into the newcomer's stall. Chuckling, he turned his head and called over his shoulder, "Hey, Lucien, who's

---

*A few basics for the reader unfamiliar with racetrack times, distances, and paces:

A furlong is $^1/_8$ of a mile. For Secretariat to have "worked" $^3/_8$ in :38 means he went 3 furlongs in 38 seconds, an average of $12^2/_3$ seconds per furlong. For a "work," this is poor. When you work a horse, you let him go as fast as he can. An average time for a furlong is about 12 seconds. A really good *fast* furlong will be between 11 and 12 seconds—known in the parlance as "11 and some change." A *very* fast furlong is 11 seconds.

A *work* can be at any distance, though the farther a horse goes, the more you have to save him. You don't say that it's a slow work because he doesn't go every furlong of eight in 11 seconds apiece. You can't expect that. You can expect a certain number of furlongs at really top speed, a certain number at an easy speed to give the horse a breather, and you hope he has enough left in him so that his last furlong will be a good fast one. Some other paces are: *Blowout* (called

"Piping Out" in England): This is a sharp fast workout over a short distance. The longest blowout is about a half a mile; usually it's $^1/_4$ or $^3/_8$ of a mile. This is where you get your 11 second furlongs—one or two of them —if the horse is a really good runner.

Breeze: This is between a fast gallop and letting the horse really run. An average of 13 seconds a furlong is about right.

Slow breeze: Usually something called a "two-mile lick," that is, a pace at which the horse would run a mile in two minutes. This is an average of 15 seconds a furlong. Also known as a "fast gallop."

Slow gallop: Roughly equivalent to a canter (which is a horse-show term never used by racetrack people). Secretariat had many slow gallops to build up his stamina and work off his fat. Before a horse gets to gallop, though, trainers like to jog them quite long distances, since this is very beneficial for them. Secretariat did quite a lot of this also.

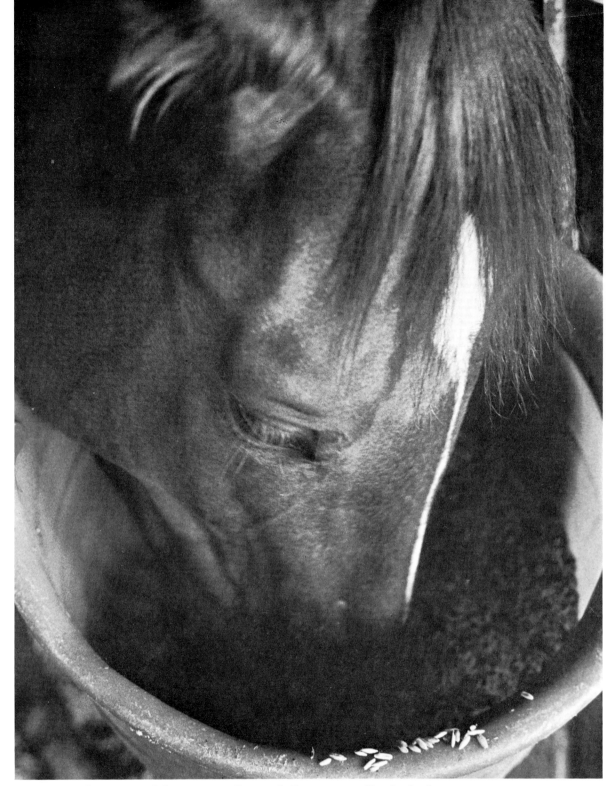

Secretariat, always a good doer, practically eats the bottom out of his feed tub.

the pretty boy here? Kinda *fat,* ain't he?"

Lucien patiently worked the plump red colt down to acceptable training size with steady slow exercise. But although Secretariat, with his even temperament, never acted with the usual two-year-old nervousness on the track, he had become troublesome in other ways. He seemed more intent on exercising his sense of humor than himself. Ron Turcotte remembers, "We used to take the two-year-olds out in sets, and he used to think it was fun to keep bumping into the other horses. You could hear him grunt. It took a lot of time just to teach him to go straight."

Jimmy Gaffney, who exercised Secretariat regularly when he was a two year old, recalls that Secretariat picked up a habit in Florida of trying to throw his riders. He would stop and duck sharply to the left, and the boy would have to hang on for dear life. During one of these playful dumpings, the colt wrenched his back, and for a while his training progress (or rather, lack of progress) came to a halt. The other two-year-olds in the Meadow barn were already out winning races while Secretariat was playing, or nursing a wrenched back, or eating. But everyone had become attached to "ol' Hopalong." According to Ron Turcotte, "Everybody that had

anything to do with him couldn't help loving him. He was such a big clown."

After the colt dumped Paul Feliciano one morning at Belmont, Jimmy Gaffney asked permission to use a special bit on him. With it, he managed to cure Secretariat of his dangerous trick, but the improvement in his manners didn't result in any improvement in his running. Even the faithful Lucien had begun to despair of ever turning him into a real racehorse.

When the Hialeah meeting was over, Lucien's string shipped out for Belmont Park, in Long Island, New York, where Secretariat was led into Barn 5 for the first time. His training was resumed, but even the brisker March air of the northern mornings seemed to have little effect on his sluggishness. He continued to show no speed, still lumbering awkwardly around the track.

Then one June morning, he startled everyone by reeling off 5 furlongs in a blazing :$57^3/_5$ seconds. For the first time, Lucien, clutching his stopwatch in near disbelief, began to think there was really "some hope for the horse." Secretariat's change into a speedster was permanent. He continued to turn in dazzling workouts. Lucien could at last report to Penny Tweedy that "we have a racehorse on our hands."

39

THREE

BEGINNING OF A LEGEND: The Two-Year-Old Campaign

I: Baptism of Fire

Secretariat's older stablemate, Riva Ridge, had been enjoying a spectacular three-year-old season. While the big red colt was still making up his mind whether to run, Riva had won the Kentucky Derby and the Belmont Stakes. He missed taking the Triple Crown by his defeat on a muddy track in the Preakness. It looked as though Meadow at last had the champion it needed so badly, for Riva was virtually sweeping everything before him and was a prime candidate for Horse of the Year honors. But Meadow was not altogether out of its financial doldrums.

When Lucien phoned Penny Tweedy in the latter part of June and told her that Secretariat was ready for his first start, she was pleased. At last, the big, beautiful colt with the fabulous breeding might bring in some money for the Meadow. She said she would miss his first start because she would be away on a trip. When Lucien promptly said, "I'll wait with him," a bell rang in Penny's head. This is not a gesture made lightly by any trainer. "I want you to be here when he runs," continued Lucien. He was saying that this horse was something special. For Penny Tweedy, and for the Meadow, it was welcome news.

Penny Tweedy was in the audience at Aqueduct when Secretariat made his long-awaited debut on the Fourth of July in a $5\frac{1}{2}$-furlong maiden special weights race. But a near-disaster for Secretariat occurred at the start. As the *Daily Racing Form* chart of the race described it, a horse named Quebec (who finished last) "ducked in sharply after the start, causing a jam. . . ." Secretariat, in the rail post position, was slammed inward almost into the rail and out of contention.

*Meadow Farm's Riva Ridge
wins the 1972 Kentucky Derby.*

FACING PAGE:
Roses for Riva.

Riva wins his Belmont.

Upset in the rain: Autobiography takes the Jockey Club Gold Cup from Riva.

Jockey Paul Feliciano later recalled, "If he wasn't so strong, he would have gone right down."

Within a hundred yards or so, the big colt recovered; after running hesitantly a little farther, he really began to run, and in the final quarter of a mile, he made an impressive rush that closed his gap on the leaders by 8 lengths.

Coming from tenth at the top of the stretch, he finished fourth only 1¼ lengths away from the winner, a Calumet colt named Herbull. It was an incredible performance for a beginner who had been nearly knocked down at the start. Lucien and Penny were relieved that he had not been hurt, and thrilled by his powerful move in the final drive. They also observed that after the race he did not act like most other horses who tend to back off their feed after a race; instead, he ate as voraciously as ever. Also, he showed almost none of such usual signs of exertion

Paul Feliciano, Secretariat's first jockey.

from a race as "drawing up" or tightening up of the muscles and abdomen, excessive sweating and labored breathing. He was to act like this throughout his racing career, to the continuing wonderment of a growing number of admirers.

Eleven days later, on July 15, the Aqueduct fans indicated that they, too, had been impressed by Secretariat's powerful stretch run. In his second start, a 6-furlong maiden special weights race, they made him a 6 to 5 favorite. Paul Feliciano was again on board for what was to be the ride of his life. After getting away slowly, the big colt, as Paul remembers, "went past everybody else like they were walking. All I had to do that second time was just hold on." Once he got to the front, the race was all over. Secretariat won by 6 lengths, or, in *Racing Form* language, "with authority."

It was now near the end of July, time for the stables to begin packing up their "traps" (stable equipment) for the annual August migration to that mecca of American racing, Saratoga.

Saratoga Springs is a lovely and haunting old town in the Catskill foothills, with ancient elm trees, broad avenues, and gingerbread Victorian houses. In past decades, it was famous for its spas and mineral waters, and some people still come to Saratoga for these aids. For horsemen, it is a spa of a different sort. The daily routine of early morning workouts and afternoon racing is the same as at other tracks. But the sheer physical pleasure of Saratoga, with its crisp, misty mornings, the farmlike atmosphere of its century-old stable areas, and the incredibly clean mountain air, makes August in Saratoga a working vacation-paradise for horsemen.

Secretariat loses his first race after being bumped badly at the start.

In his second race, Secretariat wins. No bumping this time.

Secretariat arrived at the old Spa in its 110th year of racing. This made it the senior race course in America. Its first meeting had been held on what is now the training track, then known as "Horse Haven." The man responsible for this initial event was Congressman John Morrissey, perhaps the best known figure in sporting circles during Civil War days. Although the meeting lasted but three days and boasted only forty-five thoroughbred entries, it was such a resounding success that subsequently the Saratoga Racing Association was formed. There has been August racing at Saratoga ever since.

Thus, once a year, the beautiful, sleepy old town awakes to the sound of pounding hooves and cheering crowds. Every available room in the old (and new) hotels and every rentable house or room, *anywhere,* that is fit for human habitation has been booked long in advance. Here, in the morning haze and deep shadows of huge shade trees, lurk the ghosts of the legion of horses and people who participated in or enjoyed racing at its finest —the likes of Man O'War, Roamer, Sun Briar, Jim Dandy; of Diamond Jim Brady, Lillian Russell, Tod Sloan. August in Saratoga is a step into the best part of the past and deeply prized by all who experience it.

Here, among the ghosts of racing's history, the big red colt from Meadow was to begin carving his own niche.

Ron Turcotte, Lucien Laurin's first-string jockey, had been recuperating from a fall. About a week after Secretariat's winning race, Lucien called Ron into his office at Belmont and asked him when he could be ready to ride.

"In about a week," said Ron.

"That's good," said Lucien, "because I want to put you on Secretariat on opening day at Saratoga." With a crisp nod of his head, Ron Turcotte became Secretariat's regular rider, and he continued with the colt throughout the horse's career.

Like Lucien Laurin, a French Canadian, Ron was born on a farm near Grand Falls, New Brunswick, in 1941. One of twelve children in a fiercely independent, hard-working family, he learned early the connection between physical labor and food on the table. He also got an early introduction to the lumber camps with his father, and the work soon turned his five foot one inch frame into little more than solid muscle. One winter the snow got too high, and the lumber camps closed. Ron went to Ontario, but there was no work there either. Finally, he went to the race track and started out walking hots for E. P. Taylor's Windfield Farm. On June 21, 1961, he rode his first race, and, in 1963, he was the leading apprentice rider in North America. He moved to the United States in 1969. In the course of his career, his mounts have earned over $14 million, and, at one time or another, he has won most of the important stakes in America. Ron's first association with Lucien Laurin was in 1963 when he worked out Traffic in preparation for the Pimlico–Laurel Futurity. He continued to ride regularly for Lucien until 1967 when Lucien took over the Claiborne Farm string. Claiborne had its own contract rider. Ron didn't ride for Lucien again until 1971 when the latter took over the Meadow Stable. That year, he had ridden Riva Ridge to his wins in the Derby and the Belmont. Now he was about to ride Meadow's promising new candidate.

On opening day at Saratoga, Secretariat was entered against tougher competition in a 6-furlong allowance race for nonwinners

Secretariat wins at Saratoga. Ron Turcotte is aboard for the first time.

of two races. In the paddock, Lucien advised Ron, "Don't rush this colt, let him feel his way, then come on with him."

The crowd had their eye on Secretariat and showed it by making him a 2 to 5 favorite. Out of the gate, the big colt again "sucked back" behind the field in the first furlongs, then made his big rush going around the final turn. At first, it appeared that for a 2 to 5 shot, he would not be able to do it easily enough; but when the field straightened out for the wire, he was clearly not pressed as he coasted to an easy 1 1/2 length win.

For the first time, the crowd observed what was to become a familiar sight: the gleaming chestnut colt with the cocky little Canadian on his back being led into the winner's circle.

Ron's impression after riding the colt in a race for the first time was that "he just floats; you don't feel like you're goin' that fast, but then you look up and you're passin' horses like they were standin' still."

Lucien decided that Secretariat was now ready to compete with stakes horses and entered him in the 6-furlong Sanford Stakes on

August 16. The Sanford has been long remembered as the only race in which the great Man O'War was beaten—and by a horse named Upset. This stakes race was a tough place for the colt to begin his career in the big time, for the favorite among his four opponents was a demure looking little speedball named Linda's Chief, who had a string of five wins behind him, and was considered the best two year old around.

The crowd of 18,389 at the Sanford made Linda's Chief the favorite. After the start, Ron let Secretariat hang back, as usual, to gather himself going down the backstretch. "He has a mind of his own, wants to run his own way, and that's all right with me," recalls Ron. The colt remained last for a quarter of a mile and passed only one horse in the second quarter. The race was two-thirds over, and Secretariat had yet to make his move. Going into the turn for the home stretch, he came up against a wall of horses. He shifted gears and, with that tremendous rush of his, swooped right through his competition, scattering them out of the way like so many tenpins. He streaked the last quarter in :23 4/5 seconds to a 5-length

First stakes victory— the Sanford.

Secretariat takes the Hopeful.

victory. The time was 1:10, the fastest 6 fur-longs at the Saratoga meeting.

Al Scotti, the able trainer of Linda's Chief, was stunned. "I didn't think any horse alive could have beaten my horse that day. He had made the pace and had a good lead at the head of the stretch. Secretariat was jammed up behind horses, but Ronnie found a hole, and he just busted through on the inside. It was unbelievable! He ran away from me like I wasn't even there."

Al Scotti was not the only person around the track who had begun to realize that Meadow's beautiful bombshell was as good as he looked. And, as for his looks, only a blind man could fail to notice that spectacular appearance. Though only two years old, he already stood 16 hands, $^3/_4$ inch high. (A hand is four inches, and the horses's total height is measured from the point of the withers, or small ridge at the base of the top of the neck, in a straight line to the ground. Thus Secretariat was $64^3/_4''$ high, or, $5'$ $4^3/_4''$ at the withers.) There are various generalities about "types" of horses, but Secretariat was classic in every aspect. He had a clean, broad

head with lovely bright eyes, which to horsemen signifies intelligence and good sense. Ron Turcotte observed as an indication of his intelligence that "his ears are back a lot, not because he's mad, but because he's aware of his rider." His neck already had the arch known as a "stallion crest," and his back was short and strong. He had a powerful, well-sloped shoulder, a deep chest and girth, and he was blessed with his maternal grand-sire Princequillo's balance and straight hind legs. As the sage turf writer Charlie Hatton put it, "Trying to fault Secretariat's confor-mation is like dreaming of dry rain."

But there were those who tried anyway. One writer announced a general consensus that Secretariat was slightly "goose rumped." This is a horseman's term for an undesirable downward slope of the top of a horse's quarters (from the top of the loin down to the base of the tail). This comment might have been evoked from some less experi-enced students of conformation by Secretar-iat's manner of walking. He walked "wide" in front, Bold Ruler fashion, and rather "short" behind, a Princequillo characteristic.

49

Secretariat at two years was as big as a three year old.

Observed from behind, he seemed almost to waddle. The "short" steps he took with his hind legs also resulted in his hind end being tucked up under him, making it look more slanted that it was. The truth of the matter was that he already had a hind quarter on him that put one in mind of a Sherman tank, a characteristic which was often unwillingly viewed by many horses and jockeys.

After Secretariat's victory in the Sanford, turf writers prodded Lucien to comment on whether he thought he now had the top two year old. Lucien looked over to where the horse, standing in the shade of a huge old elm, was being sponged down with a refreshing bath of hot water and a pine disinfectant. He mused, "Don't count out Linda's Chief, and I'll tell you why. For a while, a good big horse can beat a good little horse, but sometimes the big ones go tracksore. Holding that big colt of mine together is my main concern." Lucien was living up to his reputation as a worrier. But he could have saved himself this particular worry, for Secretariat showed no inclination to come apart. It seemed as if there had never been a sounder horse. One small problem—a slight skin rash along the neck where the reins touched him —was no deterrent to his turning in a blistering final work before his next race, the $86,550 Hopeful Stakes, his richest test to date. Burning up a half mile in :46$^2/_5$, he moved trainer Al Scotti to scratch Linda's Chief, his main rival. On the same track that morning, Linda's Chief had gone the half mile in :49$^1/_5$.

But an incident two days before the Hopeful could have severely damaged the big red colt. Like most horses, Secretariat had a strong dislike for automobiles. That morning,

Jimmy Gaffney, his regular exercise rider when he was a two year old, was returning to the barns with him from a gallop on the track. There was a moving car in the stable area, and, to top it all off, a passing horse van that backfired. That was more than enough for Secretariat. "The horse spooked, threw me, and then dragged me halfway the length of a barn," recalls Jimmy. "I wouldn't let go of the reins. I kept thinking how valuable he is, so I held on. He finally did pull loose, but a groom from another stable caught him right away. He didn't hurt himself, thank God."

On the day of the 6$^1/_2$-furlong Hopeful, the odds board closed with Secretariat a 3 to 10 favorite over the eight remaining entrants. Once more, when the bell rang and the gates crashed open, the big Meadow colt gave the rest of the field a running start. It had almost become a game, as if he enjoyed stampeding through the crowd. He let them get to the turn, and then, in a move that carried Turcotte and himself around the turn so fast that the other riders must have felt the wake of their passing, he entered the stretch 4 lengths in front. No traffic problems this time: he simply looped around the entire field for a 5-length victory in a time of 1:16$^1/_5$, only $^3/_5$ of a second off the track record. The crowd of 23,094 displayed an ardor for their favorite that was soon to become a familiar phenomenon: they whooped and yelled and whistled and clapped their hands and jumped up and down in a manner that racetrackers had forgotten could happen.

Back at the barn, sponging the big colt down, Eddie Sweat began to suspect that Secretariat might just be as good a horse as Riva Ridge.

51

II: The First Taste of Fame

With the end of August came the end of the Saratoga meeting. The ghosts of racing's greats retreated to their shadows, and Saratoga Springs settled back into its usual quiet. Caravans of horse vans headed downstate for the Belmont Park fall meeting. Among those taking leave from the old Spa was a once fat clown recently turned celebrity.

For the first time, his arrival somewhere drew reporters and photographers to record the occasion. Penny Tweedy, Lucien Laurin, and Ron Turcotte were, of course, used to publicity, but it was a new experience for Secretariat. He took to it overnight, a born ham. The way he sensed the presence of cameras was almost uncanny. At once, he would be "on stage," arching his neck, his eyes flashing, nostrils flared, and ears pricked. The press ate it up; Secretariat was good copy.

One reporter asked Lucien his opinion of the talk that the upcoming 83rd running of the important Belmont Futurity on September 16 was Secretariat's for the taking.

"Ha!" snorted Lucien, "I've been beaten three times this year at one to five odds, and with Riva Ridge. I'm not taking *anything* for granted."

Then, having adequately indicated his worried state, he walked out to watch his big train roar 5 furlongs in 58 seconds. That workout, also keenly observed by others, immediately reduced Secretariat's Futurity opponents from 10 to 6.

After scratching his entry, Master Achiever, trainer Frank "Pancho" Martin remarked of Secretariat: "I've never seen a more perfectly balanced colt, so large and with such a perfect way of going. He could become one of the truly great ones. I took my horse

out. I was afraid he might get in Secretariat's way when he starts that move."

Trainer George Poole, who had also scratched his horse, observed: "He puts me in mind of Native Dancer, who also came on with such explosive finishes. That's how the Dancer won the Futurity of 'Fifty-two."

Two days before the Futurity, Secretariat's regular blacksmith, George Collins, put a brand new pair of running shoes on him for the race. The next day he had to come back and put on yet another pair, for that very morning the colt had broken his new shoes just galloping one turn of the track. He was primed to turn in a stupendous performance.

The Belmont Futurity is a distinguished race with a long history. It was once the richest two-year-old race in the world, and the only American race covered by the world press. Its importance lay in its influence in the planning of breeding programs. The entrants had to be nominated by August of the year they were foaled. Thus, the breeder usually made the nomination rather than, as is usual for other races, the horse's racing owner. Since the race is only 6½-furlongs, the test is for speed rather than stamina. It is the kind of race that in earlier days was extremely important to people like the Hancocks, the Doswells, and the Chenerys. The race is not as significant today because there are now so many high-stakes two-year-old races, but it still draws the best two-year-olds in the country.

The race ordinarily attracts larger than usual crowds, but indications this year were that the big drawing card was Secretariat. The eyes of both the general public and the racing world were now focused on the shining red horse who liked to turn a stretch run into a stampede.

On the Thursday before the Futurity, there

was a tragic distraction. Bull Hancock, the man who had played such a major role in the production of classic horses in America, died of cancer at the age of sixty-two. The man whose advice to his old friend's daughter about bloodlines had helped to bring about the match that had resulted in the birth of Secretariat would not be there to see him compete in this historic race.

It was a somewhat solemn Penny and Lucien who watched Eddie Sweat lead their colt into Belmont's shady saddling area. A well-wisher patted Lucien on the back with the comment, "You've got tons the best horse." With his usual before-race expression of near suffering, Lucien confessed to anxieties. "They've just beaten two favorites out there, and those jocks are all going to be looking for Secretariat."

The crowd, especially its younger members, had begun to show signs of Secretariat-worship. A pretty girl with the standard long straight hair and blue jeans turned to her escort and gasped, "He's so beautiful! Please, if we can't bet on him, please, let's not bet against him!"

Bull Hancock and noted racing owner Liz Tippett.

As the horses approached the starting gate, the board went off, showing Secretariat the 1 to 5 favorite. This reduced a bet on him to a gesture of moral support rather than a possibility of monetary gain.

Secretariat didn't need anything that day. Again, as if following a standard script, he did not start his move until midway in the turn from home. When he did, it was all over but the shouting, and there was plenty of that as he sped across the finish line $1^3/_4$ lengths in front.

His victory was a fitting memorial to Bull Hancock, the man who strove to do "the usual unusally well," and to his lifelong dedication to trying to breed the perfect classic horse.

As Secretariat and Ron Turcotte approached the winner's circle, something occurred that was not usual for the often stoic New York racing crowds. A woman standing down among the grandstand crowd near the rail said, "Let's give him a hand," and began clapping. Starting as a ripple, the applause spread like a prairie fire high into the stands.

As Meadow's tally of stakes wins continued to pile up, the back stretch people began referring to Barn 5 as the "Murderers' Row of the Chenery Stable." Having two stars like Secretariat and Riva Ridge next door to each other in the same barn led to inevitable attempts to compare them. These tended to turn up more differences than similarities, except for the fact that they both won races.

Ron Turcotte, who rode them both, observed, "They're entirely different types of movers. Secretariat hits the ground a little harder in his action. Riva Ridge just seems to skip along."

From Eddie Sweat's perspective, Secretariat was a big clown. When he was putting bandages on Riva Ridge's legs, the bay colt

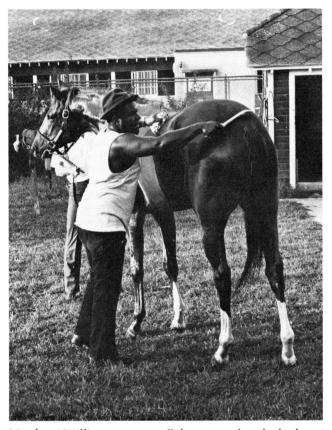

Mordecai Williams scrapes off the water after the bath.

Galloping in the early days.

just stood politely. But the big, rough Secretariat always wanted to play. "He'd be all over you," remarked Eddie, "tryin' to bite and kick. He didn't mean nothin' by it, but you got to watch out for him just the same."

The New York Racing Association's veterinarian, Dr. Manuel Gilman measured both horses' heights at an identical 16 hands, $^3/_4$ inch. Secretariat, at two years, already girthed three inches more than the three-year-old Riva Ridge.

Comparisons only seemed to prove that it was impossible even for experts to figure out what a horse was going to do on a racetrack just by looking at him.

III: Ups and Downs for a New Champion

Lucien Laurin began Secretariat's preparation for the October 14 Champagne Stakes with a new factor in mind—distance. This would be a one-mile test, and already the inevitable question had been raised. Could the son of Bold Ruler handle the length of this trip? Lucien seemed unperturbed.

When a horse is campaigning, it is important to keep him racing. Although there was a month-long gap between Secretariat's last race and the Champagne, the confident trainer pointed out that he had not missed a day's training. On October 4, the colt went

Jimmy Gaffney on the two-year-old Secretariat.

55

through his main primer, a fast mile work, and his time of 1:37 indicated that he could be tough at a distance.

One thing that did stir a ripple of worry around Meadow Stable was Secretariat's come-from-behind grandstand style.

"They could catch him back there some day and he wouldn't get up in time," fretted Lucien.

Penny Tweedy agreed that this was possible, but she felt that this was "the chance he must take each time he runs—but there are a lot of horses to run around in the Champagne."

The answers to everybody's questions about whether Secretariat could go a distance came on the day of the 101st running of the $146,000 Champagne. Possibly encouraged by the hope that Secretariat could not last the trip, eleven trainers sent out their best two-year-olds to challenge Meadow's juggernaut.

A 7 to 10 favorite, Secretariat proceeded to give his backers something to remember. Last to leave the gate as usual, he trailed the leaders by a worrisome 15 lengths. Ron Turcotte began to show some concern about the situation by pumping his arms and legs to urge on the colt. Still, Secretariat hung back. As Ron had said, the horse had his own idea about when he would begin to run. As they entered the turn for home, and Secretariat was still nowhere, the situation looked hopeless. Surely no horse could possibly come from so far behind, so late in the race, and manage to pass so many of the best colts in America. It looked like Lucien's fears about Secretariat's come-from-behind grandstand style were justified.

Suddenly, there was an explosion. A copper-colored streak zoomed around the outside of the entire field and down to the finish line as if the other horses had stopped for

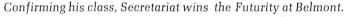

Confirming his class, Secretariat wins the Futurity at Belmont.

lunch. The crowd went wild. No one had ever seen anything like this. But there was a shock. On the tote board, the lights of the first two result numbers began to blink, and the sinister word "Inquiry" appeared.

In the winners' circle, time seemed to stand still. Then the decision. Jockey John L. Rotz on Greentree Stable's second-placed Stop The Music had done just that for Secretariat. The Steward's ruling was that in his spectacular final rush, Secretariat had brushed the runner-up around the vicinity of the $^3/_{16}$ pole. It was a technically correct, but most unpopular verdict. Even the owner of the declared winner, Jock Whitney, indicated to Penny that he would have much preferred to win in a different manner. Secretariat's superiority had been embarrassingly obvious. Considering how fast he was going, his "brush" probably did more to propel Stop The Music forward than to slow him down.

Penny Tweedy's reaction to the stewards' decision.

Secretariat wins the Champagne Stakes, only to be disqualified.

Covered with mud, Secretariat heads for the winner's circle after the Laurel Futurity.

But there was no champagne for Meadow that day.

There were no sour grapes at Barn 5 either, and Secretariat wasted no time crying in his oats. While revenge was not a factor in Meadow's preparation of the colt for the 50th running of the $133,800 Laurel Futurity, revenge was what they got.

On October 28, 12,846 fans braved a heavy rain to watch Secretariat meet his rival on a sloppy track. Again, he left the gate a heavy favorite. Hanging back fifth in a six-horse field, he once again began his rush in the middle of the turn for home. Again, he charged to the lead on the outside. He reached the wire still opening an 8-length lead over Stop The Music. Even in the rain and the slop, his time was only $^1/_5$ of a second off the record.

As Penny Tweedy led him down the lane into the winner's circle, Secretariat decided to rest his head on her shoulder, muddying her dress and arm. "He has a mind of his own," she said to the reporters, "and I was not about to argue with him." With this victory, the two-year-old championship was unquestionably Secretariat's.

On that same rainy day at another sloppy track, yet another championship was to have been decided. A race between Riva Ridge and his chief rival, Paul Mellon's Key to the Mint, would settle the question of which of them was to be three-year-old champion and Horse of the Year. A victory for either in that day's $113,700 Jockey Club Gold Cup at Aqueduct would clinch both titles. But a talented outsider trained by Frank "Pancho" Martin proceeded to confuse the issue. Sigmund Sommer's Autobiography won by 15 lengths, Key to the Mint was second, and Riva Ridge, whose most serious defeat, the Preakness,

had also been on a sloppy track, finished a heart-rending third. Eddie Sweat, who had remained in New York, faithful to his first Derby winner, sadly led his big horse home in damp defeat.

Meadow decided to run Secretariat one more time as a two year old, since he was still eligible to earn the biggest pot of all, the $179,199 prize of the Garden State Stakes in Cherry Hill, New Jersey. As the colt went into training at the New Jersey track for the race on November 18, some people had begun to say that perhaps Secretariat would be named Horse of the Year.

Lucien Laurin had little time for these rumors, since he was busily shuttling between his string at Belmont and Secretariat at Garden State. Secretariat trained beautifully on the track's fine surface. On November 9, the colt burned up the track in a 7-furlong workout of 1:25 $^4/_5$, easing out the mile in 1:40. Lucien announced he had decided to couple a stablemate, Edwin Whittaker's Angle Light, in an entry with Secretariat. Riding Angle Light would be Ron Turcotte's younger brother, Rudy.

The entry of Secretariat and Angle Light went to the post the odds-on favorite. The race was another carbon copy of Secretariat's usual method. Passing the leaders on the turn, he drew away to a $3^1/_2$-length victory, with Angle Light finishing second. There were a few moments of tension in the winner's circle when the rider of Knightly Dawn claimed foul, but the claim was disallowed and Secretariat was posted the official winner.

The crowd, as usual, roared their approval. Lucien's face crinkled in that jovial expression which reminds some people of Santa Claus, especially with Lucien's white hair. "They really love him," he said to Penny. "They look for that big move and when it begins they roar. That run of his is like something they do in the movies."

Secretariat's racing was all over for the year, and Lucien shipped him to Hialeah for a letdown from the hard campaign. Life became relatively peaceful among the palm trees and gentle breezes of the Florida track.

One sunny day, a turf writer walked into Lucien's Hialeah stable office.

"Lucien," he said, "I got some good news and some bad news."

"Better give me the bad first," replied Lucien, "I can chase it with the good."

"Riva Ridge lost out on Horse of the Year and Best Three-Year-Old honors."

Lucien's face fell.

"But Secretariat's been named Horse of the Year."

The little trainer was ecstatic. "That's fantastic! I've been training for thirty years, and this is the greatest thing that's ever happened to me. Can you imagine? The first two year old voted Horse of the Year!*

Ron Turcotte was similarly enthusiastic. "It's just beautiful, just beautiful. You know, he still acts like a big kid, but he gets more serious everytime out. He's a man's horse, a big, heavy-headed colt. And he's not timid—I've read where some people say he is afraid of getting bumped around because of what

---

*Secretariat was the first two year old voted Horse of the Year since the inauguration of combined voting by the Thoroughbred Racing Association (TRA), the *Daily Racing Form,* and the Turf Writers of America, 1971.

Previously, the three organizations had awarded Horse of the Year Honors separately. The TRA *had* by itself awarded Horse of the Year honors to two two-year-olds—Moccasin (a filly) in 1965 and Native Dancer in 1952.

happened in his first start, and that's why he gets away slow. But that business of coming out and then pulling himself up is just part of his childishness. He just wants time to settle into his stride. Once he starts running, though, there's no horse who can beat him right now."

For the Meadow, it had been a banner year. The stable had earned $1,171,207, mostly because of Secretariat and Riva. Secretariat led with earnings of $456,404 (nine starts, seven wins, one second, and one fourth). Riva was second with $395,632 (twelve starts, five wins, one second, one third, five unplaced). All this in a year that saw the stock market plunge to its lowest level since the Depression. Penny's steadfast insistence that the Meadow be allowed to prove itself had reaped ample rewards, and the farm was now out of financial difficulties.

The Garden State Stakes. Lucien puts on the blinkers.

Secretariat (1A) on the outside.

Settling down after the break.

Past the stands first time Secretariat trails.

Secretariat hangs back.

Into the backstretch Secretariat gets into gear.

Secretariat begins his big move.

Down to the wire—no contest.

FOUR

Horse of the Year, 1972

On January 3, 1973, Christopher T. Chenery, the founder and architect of the great Meadow Stable, the bold, energetic man who loved to ride the wild places, died at the age of eighty-six. Tragically, his health had declined so badly that he never knew of the spectacular triumphs of the big red colt of whose breeding he had been the guiding genius. Like his old friend, Bull Hancock, he left the racing world a priceless legacy in the bloodlines of the horses he had bred.

Penny Tweedy was able to pay a final tribute to her father and to Bull Hancock on the evening of January 27 in Los Angeles, California, where racing's equivalent of the movies' Oscar ceremonies were held. More than 1100 members of the thoroughbred racing world were in the Century Plaza Hotel's ballroom for the annual Eclipse Awards dinner, sponsored by the Thoroughbred Racing Association, the *Daily Racing Form,* and the National Turf Writers' Association.

Lucien Laurin was given the award as Trainer of the Year, but the night really belonged to two men who were not there— Christopher T. Chenery and A. B. "Bull" Hancock.

Four Eclipse awards to the Meadow were accepted by Penny Tweedy: Leading Owner, Leading Breeder, the Juvenile Championship, and, of course, Horse of the Year. She spoke in a soft, emotion-filled voice:

"I want to pay tribute both to Dad and the late Bull Hancock. Dad set the standards, and they were high ones. Bull Hancock, another remarkable man, helped me try and meet those standards after Dad became ill. They were both wonderful men."

Bull Hancock, described as the "world's most distinguished breeder," was honored with a posthumous award accepted by his sons Seth and Arthur Boyd, III.

65

Lucien receives the 1972 Eclipse Award for Trainer of the Year from the 1971 winner, Charlie Whittingham.

Penny and her sister Margaret accept Secretariat's 1972 Eclipse awards from Buddy Fogelson.

Seth later remarked: "Two things Dad stressed in his breeding program were nicks and breeding away from unsoundness. When he found a nick that was successful, such as the Nasrullah–Princequillo cross, he preferred to stay with it as much as possible. He was a great teacher, a great man, and, most important to Arthur and me, a great father. We feel we can honor him best by carrying on his work. We won't let him down."

After the acclamation of the Eclipse awards came the return to a sad, hard reality for Penny Tweedy and her father's beloved Meadow Stable. There was the awesome task of settling estate and tax problems. Miss Ham, the executrix of the estate, was already hard at work. But it became painfully evident that unless Penny could quickly raise a large amount of money, it would be necessary to sell Christopher Chenery's priceless broodmare band, racing stock, and, possibly, part of the farm itself.

The immediate and obvious solution was to syndicate Secretariat for stud. This is a normal procedure when a horse has proven himself on the race course and has thus become a good breeding prospect. Of course, syndicating a stallion is horse dealing at its highest level. The horse's owner is eager for the highest possible price, while the prospective syndicate manager has to arrive at a share price that will satisfy the owner without driving off the buyers.

Seth Hancock had been at Christopher Chenery's funeral in Virginia. It was there that Penny, mindful of the alliance of Meadow and Claiborne throughout the years, first indicated that she might call on Seth for help. Later, at Hialeah, where the Meadow racing string was running for the winter, Penny told Seth that she had had some offers for the syndication of Secretariat.

Seth replied that Claiborne would be more than happy to handle any possible syndication. Penny nodded. No more was said then. But late in February, Penny suddenly flew to Lexington and met Seth at a local restaurant for lunch.

"Y' all ready to talk about a little business?" she opened.

"Yes, Ma'am," he replied, and began taking notes on a paper napkin as fast as Penny talked.

Their agreement settled, Seth returned to Claiborne and began making the telephone calls that were to put together the deal of his life.

When his father died, Seth Hancock was twenty-three years, one month, and twenty-three days old. His brother Arthur was twenty-nine. Like Penny Tweedy, the two brothers had been faced with the staggering task of satisfying estate taxes, and in the Claiborne tradition, they turned to the sales ring. In November 1972, in a tent on the Belmont Park back stretch, twenty Claiborne yearlings and horses of racing age were auctioned off for $2,580,000, an average of $73,714 a head. In that sale was a beautiful dark brown horse named Sham, who was purchased by trainer Frank "Pancho" Martin for owner Sigmund Sommer.

The brothers Hancock, their immediate money problems abated, started out by sharing supervision of the farm. Arthur was in charge of yearlings, weanlings, and all the sales operations. Seth took over the twenty-five stallions and their bookings, along with

Penny and Lucien at the Hancock dispersal sale at Belmont.

the broodmare band. Their father's will had also appointed a committee of three advisors to help guide operations. The intention was to preserve as closely as possible Bull's manner of doing things.

But on the very day before the Eclipse Awards, Arthur announced that he was withdrawing from Claiborne's management. He wanted to devote his attention to nearby Stone Farm, which he had already operated for almost three years under lease from the Claiborne Corporation. He had established his own place, his own way, and wanted to concentrate on his own ideas.

Seth was left alone to prove to a skeptical horse world that, at twenty-three, he could successfully direct the huge Claiborne operation.

The syndication of Secretariat gave Seth an unparalleled opportunity to prove himself. For two days and two nights, his life centered about the ring of a telephone. It had been his task to convince at least twenty-eight breeders all over the world that one share of Secretariat was worth the asking price of $190,000. One share entitled the buyer to breed one mare a year to the horse for the rest of his life (usually about twenty years). Now he was waiting for replies.

One by one, the acceptance calls began to come in. On February 26, it was officially announced that Secretariat had been syndicated for $6,080,000. This surpassed even Bull Hancock's record $5,440,000 syndication of the English Triple Crown Winner, Nijinsky. The Syndication was based on thirty-two shares at $190,000 each. Of the thirty-two shares, four were retained by the Meadow. Twenty-eight were sold to breeders in the United States, England, Ireland,

The sale that saved Clairborne for the Hancock brothers.

68

France, and Japan. In addition, Claiborne received four shares as its commission for putting the deal together and absorbing the expenses of Secretariat's maintenance and breeding. Another share went to the deserving Lucien Laurin.

Secretariat had again come through for the Meadow—and had given the youthful Seth Hancock a fabulous beginning as the master of Claiborne.

In Florida, Secretariat was in training for his three-year-old campaign. At the outset of his stay in Hialeah, a small splint had shown up on one foreleg. The injury, which was probably due to an accidental blow, was pinfired. This is a process in which a needle-like hot iron pierces the affected area in order to produce strengthening scar tissue. After that, the colt was gradually stepped up to a full training schedule again.

However, because of delays over the settling of Christopher Chenery's estate, Secretariat's racing program was interrupted. Although his handy workouts led turf writers to conjecture about the possibility of his being pointed for the $100,000 Flamingo Stakes, Lucien felt that because of the delays, it would be better to start the colt's three-year-old racing year in New York. On March 9, Secretariat left Florida, somewhat heavier and a full inch taller.

The colt was already being mentioned as a possible Triple Crown winner. No horse had been able to make this sweep in twenty-five years—the Kentucky Derby, the Preakness, and the Belmont Stakes. Could this stupendous red colt be as spectacular as a three year old as he had been as a two year old? Could he possibly be that good? His admirers speculated—and dreamed.

FIVE

Road to Churchill Downs

To the residents around Belmont Park, the coming of spring is heralded by the appearance of loaded horse vans rolling through the stable gate off Hempstead Avenue. With New York racing dates expanded to include part of February, "spring" may seem a little premature to the locals. But to the horsemen who race their strings at the New York tracks, the return to Belmont *is* their spring—and the real beginning of the year's campaign, as they arrive from winter quarters in Maryland, Virginia, the Carolinas, and Florida.

For Secretariat, the return to Belmont after an inactive winter in Florida began the most important and demanding year of his life. After his spectacular two-year-old season, resulting in Horse of the Year honors and his $6,080,000 syndication, every eye in the racing world was on him. As a three year old, even more was expected of him. He had his detractors, who said that like some two-year-old stars, this son of Bold Ruler might not be able to handle the more arduous trials of the three-year-old season, and would simply fade into obscurity. However, most observers were already casting him as the probable winner of America's classic three-year-old races: The Kentucky Derby, the Preakness, and the Belmont Stakes—the fabled Triple Crown. No horse had been able to accomplish this in the last twenty-five years. The Meadow people believed in their big horse, but they were also well aware of the grueling campaign that lay ahead.

To win the Triple Crown, a horse must maintain peak condition for at least six weeks—from the time of the Derby on the first Saturday in May to the Belmont on the first Saturday in June. He must be able to travel well, from Kentucky's Churchill Downs to Maryland's Pimlico to New York's

71

Returning from the track on a rainy morning.

Belmont Park. He must be able to handle different kinds of tracks and different kinds of racing conditions.

In the Kentucky Derby, the three-year-olds are running the mile and a quarter distance for the very first time. They must endure a long straining run to the first turn. The Derby is usually a crowded cavalry charge, in which a come-from-behind horse can often win.

The Preakness distance of a mile and three-sixteenths is run on a track whose sharp turns make position extremely important; a horse on the outside can lose a good deal of ground on the turns, and, thereby, even the race. The greatest advantage goes to a horse who can race to an early lead and hold it.

The Belmont is sheer, vast distance. Horsemen consider this mile and a half test the hardest of all. Because Belmont Park has so large a track, a mile and a half oval instead of the usual mile, its turns are gentle, and position is not as crucial. The whole question is whether the horse can handle the distance; the homestretch here is the longest dirt straightaway in the world. The Belmont is an awesome race.

It is truly a classic horse, in every sense of the word, who is able to take the Triple Crown.

In addition, of course, there were the races leading up to the Derby in which the best three-year-olds in the country—all potential Derby contenders—were entered. It was a long, hard road to the Triple Crown and for Secretariat, the campaign was to begin on the New York racing circuit.

The reappearance of Meadow Farm's big red colt in Barn 5 brought out his growing press corps. Reporters and photographers struggled to adapt themselves to the horseman's daily routine of spending cold early morning hours in dimly-lit shed rows and enduring the wind knifing across the open spaces of the race track. The majority of them sensed that this horse was already on his way to becoming a racing legend. Extra sweaters and lost sleep seemed a small price for being there every step of the way.

As Secretariat began his training, eager photographers would catch him at various hours of the morning, in various weathers, running freely and easily, with that great lunging stride that had captured the imagination of the American public. On misty mornings, he would suddenly sweep out of the fog, a ghost horse on his way to everywhere. When it was sunny, he could be seen all the way around the giant oval, his red chestnut coat catching the sun. Lucien Laurin, stopwatch in hand, watched from the railside; he had carefully arranged Secretariat's training schedule to bring him up to his best form for the Bay Shore Handicap on March 17. For horses taking the New York route, this is the first of the races considered mileposts on the road to Churchill Downs.

Secretariat's work routine was complicated by the burgeoning army of his camp followers, who flocked around daily with cameras, microphones, and tape recorders. The public seemed to want to know everything about Secretariat, and the communications media was ready to oblige. Penny and Lucien were relatively hardened publicity veterans by now, but even they were beginning to find it difficult to cope. Although Pinkerton guards had sealed off the Meadow Stable area, horses, and crew from all unauthorized personnel, trying to carry out normal stable routine under such conditions was a strain on everyone. Despite some inevitable temper flares and turnover in staff, Lucien's foreman

On the walking ring before going to the track.

Secretariat and entourage on the way to the track for a workout.

73

and crew did manage to get the string of thirty-five thoroughbreds through their routines.

Lucien's fears that Secretariat might be distracted from performing well or made unduly nervous by the attention of the press proved groundless. The colt continued to train flawlessly and to eat, with that relentless appetite, everything he could get. He always knew when he was on stage and thoroughly enjoyed all the fuss, posing at the softest click of a shutter.

The big colt's work day began at 5:30 A.M. Greeted by nickering and the pawing and stamping of steel-shod feet, a skeleton crew dispensed the morning ration of oats from steel measures. This meal was polished off in fast form by the racing-fit thoroughbreds. Secretariat, as usual, practically ate the bottom out of the tub.

Next came stall-cleaning time. Large burlap squares, usually four to six feed sacks sewn together, were laid out in front of the stalls. The dirty straw was thrown out onto them, the corners of the burlap gathered, then the load hefted onto the grooms' backs and carried to the manure pit. Trucks later took the sacks to greenhouses or mushroom growers in Pennsylvania.

The exercise boys arrived about 6:00 A.M. Hanging outside the tack room was a clipboard with the morning's training schedule. While the riders gathered the tack for their assigned mounts, the grooms went to work with bristle brushes, rubber curry combs, and rub rags, and made their horses shine in the faint morning light.

Eddie Sweat groomed Secretariat. The big colt, always restless and full of energy, was a handful, shifting around and cheerfully trying to bite and kick, but the powerful Eddie handled him like a baby. During the grooming, Eddie ran his strong hands gently over the six-million-dollar legs, carefully checking for signs of any heat, swelling, or other indications of trouble. "I don't care if I'm rubbin' a claimer," said Eddie, "I checks 'em all every mornin' to see if they got any heat or anything."

Then Secretariat was tacked up and his feet cleaned of any debris with a steel hoof pick. Eddie remarked of those feet, "You know, he has one of the beautifullest set of feets of any horse I ever rubbed. He's got nice everything, you know. Big and round. Some hosses got like cracks or chips, you know, but his are *smooth;* just smooth all over. But, you know, *he's* perfection all over."

Then Secretariat was led out for a turn around the outside walking ring in order to stretch his muscles and let the tack settle. After that, Jimmy Gaffney, his regular exercise boy, went to him and got a leg up. Jimmy settled into the saddle gently; it is important to be careful of a horse's back and kidneys when first mounting for the day. He stood up in his stirrups for a few steps, adjusted them for proper length, and tightened the girth a notch to insure against saddle slippage. He allowed Secretariat to make a few more turns around the ring, allowing him to play a little and get the kinks out while Lucien and his foreman, Henry Hoeffner, had a chance to inspect him and the others. Then, with Lucien, they all departed for the track for the morning workout. The press, as usual, swarmed around, taking pictures and asking questions.

Most thoroughbreds are so high strung that any sudden noise or strange crowd of people is enough to make them too nervous to do anything right. But Secretariat coursed through his work routine with apparently only one thing in mind—shaking out the powerful muscles aching to be used—running.

His long slow gallops were alternated with short, fast blowouts, and longer slow breezes. These, with an occasional long, fast work, would bring him up to his peak condition. Secretariat needed more than the usual amount of drilling just to keep him in shape.

"Secretariat loves to work," commented Lucien as the colt proceeded to dazzle trackside spectators once again. He moved around the track so effortlessly that veteran racetrackers gasped when they looked at their stopwatches. "Most people make a great mistake when they have a really good horse," the soft-spoken Canadian explained in his Quebecquois accent. "They pamper him. You have to treat a good horse as hard as you would any other horse, it's better for him." There could be no doubt that Secretariat thrived on his conditioning; he eagerly ran as hard and as far as Lucien would let him.

Eddie Sweat was constantly amazed at Secretariat's workouts. "You know, when you take Red out an' work him, say three-quarters of a mile, he looks like he can't outrun a pony. One day he worked a mile in one thirty four an' pulled up a mile and an eighth in forty seven an' change. I didn't believe it. I thought maybe he'd gone in thirty six or thirty seven at the most an' gallop out in maybe forty nine or somethin', 'cause the way he was movin' I was just countin' the poles—sort of tryin' to figure it that way. I guess I just misjudged. He was movin' *so* easy an' it was a sloppy track."

On his return from the track, the steaming Secretariat would be met by Eddie Sweat with a bucket of hot water and "body brace"

disinfectant; he would then be given the refreshing bath that aids in the "cooling out" process. During his bath, Secretariat was never still, wringing and switching his tail and doing a lot of happy mock biting and kicking. "He's a clown," said Eddie of his charge, "a big clown." After his bath, a light-weight "cooler" (a wool sheet) was put over him, and an exercise boy hot walked him around the walking ring, letting him stop every several turns for a few swallows of water from a bucket on a stand. (Each horse has his own bucket for hygienic reasons.)

When Secretariat finally was "watered off" (stopped drinking) and his coat was dry and cool, Eddie led him off to the side for his final daily grooming, or "doing up." The last item in this process was picking the colt's feet again, removing sand or other foreign matter that may have accumulated during his workout. After this, his hooves were painted with a dressing to prevent dryness and cracking.

Then, for a few hours, the stable was quiet. It is a peaceful time, probably the most pleasant time around a stable. Random chores such as washing saddle cloths and bandages, neatening up medicine boxes, and scrubbing out tubs and buckets are done in a relaxed atmosphere of talk about horses, racing, ball games, etc. There is a good deal of joking and teasing. Later in the afternoon, the grooms return to neaten up the stalls, water the horses, and prepare the evening feed.

But, when one or more of its horses happen to be in a race, the afternoon can be a bustling time around the stable. Usually the groom and a pony boy take the horse to the paddock and bring him back after the race. Then at least two men administer the cooling

Opening gun, 1973: winning the Bay Shore at Aqueduct.

Secretariat defeating Champagne Charlie in the Gotham.

out bath to make the process faster and get the horse out on the walking ring as soon as possible. When a horse has exerted himself to the maximum, he needs this intense care to safeguard his health and condition. A horse not correctly attended to may get chills, internal cramps, founder, or even contract pneumonia. It is the critically important knowledge of how to care for a horse at times like these and the sense of responsibility to do so properly that make a man such as Eddie Sweat so valuable to a trainer.

These days, the Meadow people seldom enjoyed a relaxed moment. Lucien, Penny, and Ron were constantly trying to figure out new ways of politely avoiding the daily overdose of press coverage. The small building that served as Lucien's office and sometime living quarters became the little group's principal refuge. It became a ritual that, at a certain point in the morning, Lucien would

pull Penny away from the press, sit her down at a table inside, and cook eggs and Canadian bacon for her. Ron Turcotte, with a jockey's occupational attention to weight, would sip only coffee.

Secretariat continued to work with his usual calm. On the Wednesday before the Bay Shore, he stupefied observers by roaring three-eighths of a mile in a freakish :32³/₅. He was pronounced "better than ever" (certainly an understatement) by the confident but always cautious Lucien.

The day of the Bay Shore broke raw and cloudy. The Meadow Stable area buzzed with excitement. Today, their big horse would begin his campaign for the Triple Crown. In the morning, Eddie and Jimmy saddled up Secretariat and took him out to the walking ring; there, Ron Turcotte mounted up and then galloped the colt for a mile and a quarter.

76

Hollis Chenery and Margaret Carmichael join Penny in the winner's circle.

"He almost pulled my arms out to keep him from busting off," said the jockey with a grin when he rode back in. The big gun was about to explode.

Secretariat entered the paddock to the cheers of fans who would not let the grim weather stop them from welcoming him back to the Big Apple. They sent him off at the ridiculously short odds of 1 to 5.

Breaking slowly from the gate, as usual, Secretariat was well behind as the field reached the head of the stretch. As he was about to begin his habitual late run, there was suddenly nowhere to go: he was surrounded and neatly blocked by all the other horses. There was a gasp from the more knowledgeable observers in the crowd. It was a short race, only 7 furlongs, and it appeared to be over right there. But the big red colt was determined to win. In a marvelous display of courage and raw strength, he pro-

ceeded to bull his way through the traffic jam, racing clear of the pack to win his 1973 debut by a healthy $4\frac{1}{2}$ lengths. It was an extraordinary performance. His freewheeling running style, somewhat like that of a football broken-field runner, elicited the admiration of even the most disbelieving of his critics. His time of $1:23\frac{1}{5}$ for the 7 furlongs was excellent for the wet, heavy track.

Jubilation reigned in the Meadow barn, where the customary afternoon tranquillity had given over to the hustle and bustle attendant on Secretariat's debut. A joyous Eddie Sweat and an assistant administered Secretariat's triumphant cooling out bath. "You' on your way, Red," chortled Eddie, as the colt mischievously kicked out at his happy attendants.

Some of Secretariat's critics tried to dismiss his performance by claiming that he had not won against any top contenders. His defenders countered with such track homilies as, "It ain't what you do; it's the way ya do it," and "He didn't beat nothin', but it was the way he won that impressed."

Secretariat proceeded to "impress" again in the $55,800 Gotham mile at Aqueduct on April 7. In this race, he departed from his usual pattern of running behind during the early part. Perhaps the memory of his crowding in the Bay Shore was still with him. He surged to the front immediately and stayed there. The good stakes colt, Champagne Charlie, went to him, making a game bid to challenge. For a while, it looked like a horse race; then Secretariat just shifted into high gear and opened his lead. He sailed across the finish line by a comfortable 3 lengths and equaled the track record of 1:33^2/$_5$ set in 1968 by Plucky Pen.

So far, so good. The Meadow people were heady with success. The shining red horse appeared to be sweeping everything before him. Lucien began plotting out the big colt's training schedule for his final and stiffest test before the trip to Kentucky, the one and an eighth mile Wood Memorial at Aqueduct on April 21.

But through the air of happy confidence at the Meadow barn at Belmont, there wafted just a touch of tension. On the other side of the backstretch, another horse was beginning to be noticed, and his confident trainer was being quoted by the racing writers. The horse was the beautiful brown colt, Sham—a sensation in California, with impressive wins in the Santa Catalina and the Santa Anita Derby. (Ironically, he had been purchased the previous fall in the Hancock dispersal sale.) His trainer was the fiery Cuban, Frank "Pancho" Martin. Asked how he felt about running against Secretariat, Pancho replied, "When

Frank "Pancho" Martin, Sham's trainer.

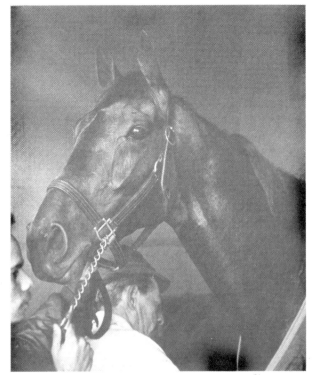

Sham, out to challenge a legend.

you get a good horse like Sham, you don't avoid anybody." The racetrack world, always on the lookout for a challenger, began to make side bets.

Sham looked every inch a casting director's dream for the role of an ominous challenger. Big, a dark seal brown that was almost black, graced with a beautifully muscled and streamlined conformation, he looked fast when he was just standing still. His linear frame was a contrast in type to the broad, powerful Secretariat, who, as turf writer Charlie Hatton put it, "has muscles in his eyebrows."

Frank Martin was a contrast, too, to the slight, white-haired French–Canadian Laurin. He had been nicknamed Pancho after the famous Mexican bandit leader, Pancho Villa. With a deep, growling voice and strong, jutting features surmounting a fighter's frame, Martin tended to impress someone meeting him for the first time as a pretty formidable character. His men, almost all of them Spanish-speaking, were fiercely loyal to him, and he was reputed to run a tight ship. But belying his gruff appearance was his unfailing courtesy and accessibility to strangers, something that most trainers, usually a standoffish breed, often deny outsiders (especially the press) who intrude on their working time. And sometimes Pancho's tough front would drop as he gave a favorite horse a rub on the nose or a pat on the neck.

You could tell Pancho was proud of Sham. He smiled a lot and didn't growl around him. He watched every move the horse made, delighting in the sight of him. If Sham or anyone around him made a move that might somehow jeopardize the colt's condition, he tensed immediately. But these were the reactions to be expected from a man

Sham blowing out for the Wood Memorial.

Secretariat goes into the gate for the Wood Memorial.

who had the potential to upset a legend in his hands.

Amidst all the attention paid the impending match between the two champions was a racing news item which hinted that, by running Sham in a three-horse entry against Secretariat, Martin was looking for an advantage. Lucien Laurin was quoted as saying, "The only way they can beat Secretariat is to steal it." To a veteran racetracker, "steal" is track slang for winning by opening a long, early lead with a false pace. A two-horse or three-horse entry could thus sacrifice one or more horses in the entry, leaving one runner still fresh to come up and take command.

Perhaps Martin did not understand the slang meaning of that word, for he took it as an aspersion on his honesty. He angrily scratched all his horses except Sham. Lucien calmly held to his plan, which was to run Secretariat with another Laurin-trained horse, Angle Light, owned by Edwin Whittaker. This was the beginning of what was to be a notable tempest in a teapot.

During Secretariat's final workout Ron checked him to a slower pace because there was a riderless horse on the track, a potential danger that no horseman could ignore. A loose horse is like a moving car without a driver, unpredictable.

The $114,900 Wood Memorial was the first meeting between Sham and Secretariat. That day, Penny Tweedy had as her guests ten bankers from Chase Manhattan Bank and their wives. The bank was a coexecutor of the Chenery estate, and the bankers were out for one of their educational visits to the track.

At the very beginning of the race, Angle Light "stole" an early lead. Although the pace was slow, Secretariat followed his usual pattern of hanging behind. As the field stormed around the final turn, the crowd waited expectantly for the big colt's late grandstand rush. It never came. Secretariat never seemed to get in gear. In a shocking upset, his stablemate, Angle Light, stayed on the lead and won, with Sham a close second. Secretariat trailed in third by a huge gap of 4 lengths.

Up in her box, Penny Tweedy sat immobilized by the disaster. Down in the winner's circle to accept the trophy as the trainer of Angle Light, Lucien Laurin looked as if he had been struck. Pancho Martin, on the other hand, was jubilant. Even though Sham had not won, he had proven himself by defeating the great Secretariat. Secretariat was not invincible, and the Kentucky Derby was now a wide open race.

The colt's defeat was a personal blow to yet another man in the crowd. Seth Hancock had come to see Secretariat run for the first time since he had engineered the fabulous syndication. Now, in less than two minutes, his six-million-dollar design was imperiled, and his judgment and his place as his father's successor as master of Claiborne Farm were still very much on trial.

A pall hung over Meadow stable, and its inhabitants went about their tasks looking stunned. Their dismay was the more intense because there seemed to be no good reason for Secretariat's defeat. In jockey Ron Turcotte's words, he "just didn't have it." Ron himself began to wonder if his having had to check Secretariat to a slower pace in his final workout might have contributed to the colt's defeat. Then, too, the morning after the Wood, a boil or abcess had been found in Secretariat's mouth right where the pressure of the bit would have hit it. Since the colt loved to lean into the bit when he began to really run, perhaps the sore caused his poor performance. But Lucien never offered this as an alibi—and perhaps this was *not* the reason.

Only Secretariat seemed unperturbed by his defeat. He came out of the race in excellent condition, as usual, and resumed training superbly, turning in one blistering workout after another. Watching his tarnished idol sweep easily around the track, Lucien remarked to a bystander, "He's better than he ever was." On the basis of his workouts, no one could deny that. But a distinct shift had occurred in the atmosphere at Meadow. While their faith in Secretariat's ability was not shaken by one defeat, the people of Meadow Stable were living with the grim realization that in racing you can take nothing for granted. Secretariat's detractors were already speculating that the colt had proven himself to be a moody son of a moody sire and had inherited an inconsistent ability to go a distance. Around Barn 5, there were no such doubts, just the sobering thought that the best horse in the Wood Memorial had been beaten. The Kentucky Derby was less than two weeks away. They could no longer assume it would be an easy win for Secretariat—or, for that matter, that he would win at all.

Wood Memorial.

First time around in the Wood Memorial.

Angle Light wins. Sham is a close second; Secretariat a dismal third.

Secretariat after losing the Wood Memorial—still news.

A morning at Belmont.

85

TOP LEFT:
Secretariat is given a few turns on the ring before going to the truck.

TOP RIGHT:
Galloping in the early morning mists at Belmont Park.

RIGHT:
Jimmy Gaffney holds Secretariat for his bath.

FACING PAGE:
Steaming hot from his workout, Secretariat enjoys a bath.

After his bath, Secretariat is hotwalked.

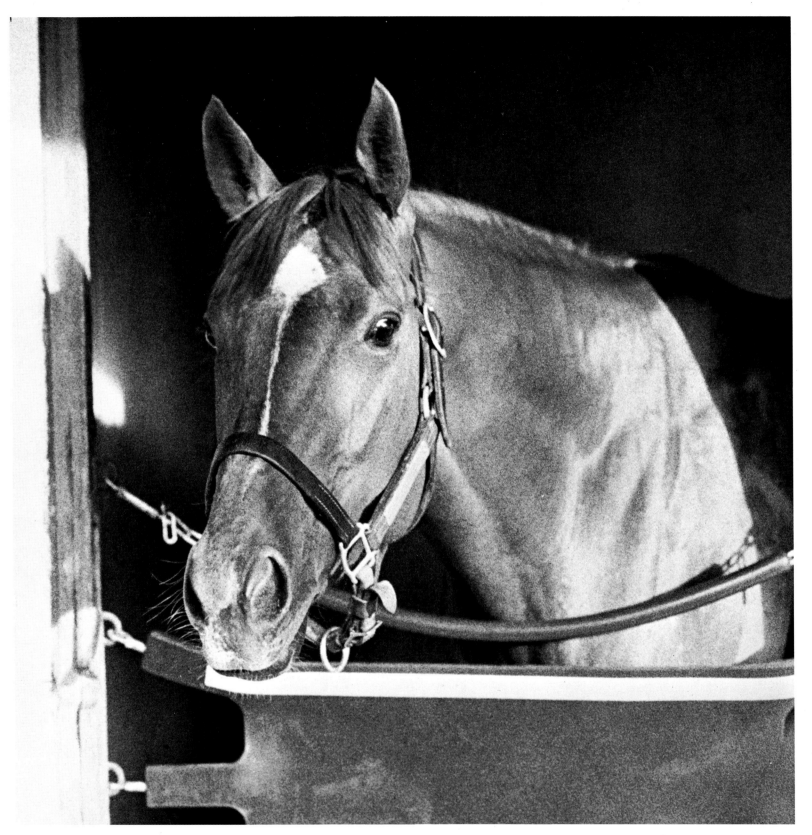

Secretariat.

SIX
Triple Crown

I: The Kentucky Derby

For most Americans, the Kentucky Derby *is* horseracing, embodying all the excitement, tradition, and heartbreak that are a part of this ancient sport. Every horseman dreams of a Derby winner, and no one is immune to the magic of the Kentucky Derby, even the cynics.

One way to experience the deceptive magic that transforms Churchill Downs during Kentucky Derby week is to go there for the first time with the attitude that the Derby is one of those overblown, over-publicized events. It requires being there from the time the first Derby entrant arrives on the grounds until the winner is led off the track.

If you accompany that first horse through the steel mesh and barbed wire surrounding the backstretch area, your cynicism will appear to be dismally justified. The stable area looks as though it had been built as an afterthought. The barns are constructed of a conglomeration of cement blocks, corrugated tin, red and green asbestos shingling (the kind you see on the sides of many small southern farmhouses), and wood that seems nailed on by carpenters using a dubious rule of thumb for their measurements. The stables are arranged in staggered rows with pitted dirt roads and manure pits in between. A paved road skirts around the outer rim of this area. Alongside it are patches of grassy areas where at various times of day horsemen give their horses a chance to graze a little. An occasional tree squeezes itself in among all this and serves to give some feeling of country to it all. "It's the bush leagues!" you exclaim to yourself. Then you look around again and say, "Well, maybe not, but it is kind of seedy." You do notice, however, that

Churchill Downs in the morning—the stable area.

Under the stands.

everything is utilitarian and workmanlike. You can train horses here, you guess, but that's about it.

Then you drive onto the road that leads through a tunnel under the track's backstretch and, surfacing in the infield, you cruise through toward the old grandstand. In the infield are the first signs of the Derby: empty stands with weathered signs proclaiming the availability of Mint Juleps and Derby souvenirs. You continue through another tunnel under the stretch, and, when you emerge, you suddenly find yourself someplace straight out of an old tintype.

When you leave your car and walk into the area under that ancient grandstand, you immediately wish like hell there were more stands like it. If this first approach is made early in the morning when the grandstand is empty, you can almost sense the presence of ghosts rushing forward to escort you through their particular domain. The present structure, with all its gingerbread architecture of decorative mouldings, curly cornices, carved eaves, and the famous twin spires, was built in 1895 after the Derby had outgrown the original stands. Adding to the

rambling charm of it all is a hodge-podge of elaborate additions which make it seem as if the place just grew in whatever direction felt right at the time. A fresh coat of white and green paint is over everything. But it's still the same old wood and the same old stands. You go up dark creaky old stairs to a series of wonderful, stuffy old restaurants with white walls and dark floors. Here you can get, among other things, Kentucky burgoo, a kind of highly seasoned soupy beef stew. I like to think the dish was created by someone with an overdose of Kentucky bourbon who spilled a box of red pepper (and some bourbon) into a beef ragout. (In 1932, a horse named Burgoo King won the Derby.)

Back outside, you see that the grandstand seating and box areas are also all a tangle of ancient white wood with green trim and dark wood floors. It all has a wonderful kind of musty old attic quality about it. It's as if every year someone opens up an old trunk, and out comes the Derby! Underneath the stands, where the crowds promenade between races, the floor is not the usual sterile modern-age concrete and cement but red brick. Over the years, the bricks have settled on different

The saddling paddock.

Here dwell the ghosts of racing's past greats.

levels, and the walking surface is wavy and uneven. Ladies in high heels must proceed with care. The bricks have been laid flat in a regular building pattern, and, in the early morning, freshly swept by the maintenance staff, they shine with that smooth, rubbed down sheen that only years of wear can bring.

The brick walkways lead you out through an elaborate small park of tulip beds, real red and yellow tulips in an almost gaudy profusion. In that park, you look up to see on the surrounding walls, in gold letters, the names of all the past Derby winners and the dates of their victories. There is room left only for a few more years, you think to yourself, and then they'll have to build another addition.

Beyond the tulip park is the screened-in paddock. It was not constructed for charm but for saddling horses and keeping out the crowd. A tanbark walking ring runs in front of the line of saddling stalls. In the center of that ring is Churchill Downs' only compromise with artificiality, an island of plastic grass where the owners can stand and watch their horses.

Back out on the racetrack, you look up at the spires again. Your first cynical impres-

sions are beginning to fall apart. There is *something* about this place.

Derby entrants began to fill up the Churchill Downs barns. On April 23, the Monday after the disastrous Wood Memorial, Secretariat and his stablemate Angle Light, accompanied by Eddie Sweat and exercise rider Charlie Davis, flew to Louisville. Already there was a thick cloud of rumor and conjecture about the possible reasons for Secretariat's sudden descent into the ranks of ordinary horses.

A Las Vegas oddsmaker and columnist known as Jimmy "The Greek" Snyder, who specialized in baseball, football, basketball, and election results, suddenly became an authority on Secretariat. He wrote that "insiders" had told him the horse had a bad knee, that Laurin's men were frantically "working on with ice packs."

Lucien, who arrived at Churchill Downs the next day, vehemently denied this. He offered to pay Snyder's expenses to Kentucky and to have the horse examined and x-rayed by his choice of vets, and sportingly bet him $1,000 that the horse was sound. Jimmy the Greek sat that one out.

93

The Churchill Downs stands.

The old theory that Bold Rulers were unable to go the distance came back into favor. And a rumor spread that the horse hadn't been worked properly. And another that he was a sulker. And on and on. All of this, of course, made good copy for the Derby press corps. With their eager attention, the cloud of rumors got thicker.

That year, the Derby press corps was like something out of the Keystone cops. (This is said with all due respect to the veteran turf writers and photographers who were forced to join this unruly mob for the week.) The Derby is famous for drawing horses that don't belong in the Derby, and every now and then that kind of a horse wins it. This makes a good story and is one reason why the race draws a great deal of press from all over the world. Secretariat's Derby drew even more press, and many of these people knew little about horses. They would gather in the early morning at a little cement block building in the stable area commandeered by the duty press officer of the day. He dispensed coffee, donuts, and the latest Derby information releases, and tried to at least give a start in the right direction to those members of the press who came out early in the morning to see the horses. Derby veterans know that most of the Derby horses are from out of town, and most of them are their trainer's only horse there. These trainers, therefore, see no reason to get that one horse out before 7:30 or 8:00 A.M. In that respect, Derby week is something of a vacation for them. Most of the stories written about a Derby horse galloping out of the early morning mist are hogwash because almost none of them are ever out that early. But many zealous first timers were there at the crack of dawn looking for local color, most of which, unfortunately, seemed to be

94

concentrated in their bloodshot eyes. The veteran Derby press would roll by at a sensible hour and drop in to get some coffee at the little press house. There they would invariably find four or five of these poor greenhorns shot with fatigue, having been out looking for Derby horses since 6:00 A.M.

Some of these inexperienced members of the Derby press corps tried to get as close to their subjects as possible. This can be extremely dangerous, both for the horse and everyone around him, for racehorses tend to be extremely nervous. Too closely badgered by the noise and crowding of strangers, they are liable to bolt, throw their riders, and run blindly out of control through the stable area injuring themselves and other horses. And, of course, anyone crowding a fit thoroughbred risks being kicked, hard.

The security at the Derby was massive, but the horde of press that week had horsemen on edge. The security police's frantic attempts to keep disruptions to a minimum had some innocent victims.

Penny Tweedy had flown down to see Secretariat work out on the Wednesday after his arrival. As the horse was walking out to the track, accompanied by his usual parade of press and onlookers, Lucien decided to drive Penny to the grandstand to watch him work. When they attempted to take the horseman's route through the underground tunnels, they were halted by an over-zealous security guard. By the time they got to the railside, Secretariat was already pulling up. Lucien and Penny had missed the colt's first workout on the Derby grounds.

Then, of course, there was the inflated feud between Lucien Laurin and Pancho Martin that followed them to Kentucky. By now, it had become a real nuisance to Laurin.

Lucien's two horses were stabled at one end of Barn 42, where most of the top out-of-town entrants were housed. At the opposite end, on the reverse side of the shed, was Pancho Martin with Sham. The stage was set, all that was needed was for the press to kindle the fire.

Each morning the same scene would be reenacted. You had Martin hanging around one end of the barn, Laurin at the other, usually about the same time. As soon as one of them showed up, the press corps would pounce on him en masse, pencils at the ready for that day's first historic words from the trainer of Secretariat or the trainer of Sham. Martin would usually just stand there nonchalantly, chew on his cigar, and toss off something less than complimentary about Laurin. The newest jewel of copy was instantly noted on little pads. Then one senior reporter would say, "Thank you, Mr. Martin," closing the interview in the manner of a presidential news conference. Then they would all scurry down to the other end of the barn. Lucien would just shake his head and say, "He's great, I don't know what this is all about, I've got no gripe against Mr. Martin." One of his few digressions from this attitude was when the press told him Martin had offered a $5,000 bet, horse for horse, and Lucien snapped, "I don't want to talk about it."

But the press would dig and coax until they elicited some small tidbit that hinted of Secretariat's superiority over Sham. Then they would rush back to Martin with a report that wasn't a hint but something to the effect that Lucien had said *his* horse could run all over *your* horse, etc. They'd get another satisfying explosion out of Martin, and then race back to Lucien and say, "Do you know what *he* said about *you*?" And so on, back and forth.

Interspersed with all this nonsense was their coverage of the Derby horses. Someone would holler, "There goes Royal and Regal to work out," and the entire corps would zoom off, giving Barn 42 some temporary respite.

The press used to find it difficult to spot the Derby entrants among the army of horses on the track during the morning. Then several years ago, Raymond Johnson, the big, likeable publicity director, veteran of many a Derby, devised a solution. Each Derby horse would be issued a number cloth, a different color each year, to wear under his saddle during the morning workouts. When the press saw number cloth (for Secretariat's Derby, it was yellow with black numbers), they could refer to the corresponding number on their information sheet for the name of the horse, the owner, and the trainer.

But racetrack people are notorious practical jokers. Pranksters quickly acquired their own number cloths, picked out some mule of a horse in their barn, and saddled him up with a number. Then they would ride out to the track, and immediately half the press would be traveling after them. They would get away with this until somebody came along who knew his horses a little better than the rest of them. "For crying out loud," he would sputter, beginning to laugh, "that's not so-and-so, *he*'s down *there*!"

A serene Secretariat, with Eddie Sweat.

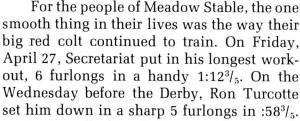

Secretariat (left) and Sham galloping at Churchill Downs.

For the people of Meadow Stable, the one smooth thing in their lives was the way their big red colt continued to train. On Friday, April 27, Secretariat put in his longest workout, 6 furlongs in a handy 1:12³/₅. On the Wednesday before the Derby, Ron Turcotte set him down in a sharp 5 furlongs in :58³/₅.

During all this, Penny and Lucien not only had to field question after question from the press, but also from various members of the syndication group. Their minds were on all the rumors, and they were anxious to know just what the situation was with their investment.

Jockey Ron Turcotte felt every nickel of that six-million-dollar investment. He still partially blamed himself for the colt's Wood defeat. The perceptive Penny Tweedy realized this and would often have dinner with Ron, attempting to feed him more reassurance than food. To get Lucien, and herself, away from all the pressure, she would sug-

gest a drive to nearby Lexington to look over studs for future Meadow breeding.

The rumor mill kept grinding right up until the eleventh hour. The day before the Derby, Angle Light came back from a work, bleeding slightly from his nostrils. Often this is a sign of severe distress; sometimes it is just unaccountable and not serious at all. In Angle Light's case, it was not serious. The rumors started immediately.

"One of Lucien's horses bled!" turned into "Secretariat bled this morning!" which turned into "Lucien is going to scratch Secretariat!" which ended up as "Secretariat's scratched!" Lucien exclaimed to one group of reporters that if he hadn't just come from the barn, he'd have been scared to death.

That same day, an important ritual took place in the musty old horsemen's office under the grandstand. This was the 10:00 A.M. drawing of post positions. As early as 8:00 A.M. people began crowding in to be sure

Drawing post positions for the Kentucky Derby.

of a good vantage point. At ten sharp, a leather covered bottle was brought out. Little ivory balls with numbers, one for each horse entered, were dropped into the bottle. A shake of the bottle, and a ball was withdrawn. If the number were, say, 4, that would be the post position of the first horse on the list of entrants. The procedure was repeated for each horse on the list. At the Derby, about three positions out from the rail is considered choice because the field is usually so large no one wants to be right in on the fence. It's too easy to get boxed in. Secretariat drew number 10, far on the outside, not exactly soothing to Lucien Laurin's nerves.

With the hectic Derby week nearly over, the old Derby magic began to pervade the area. Even the stables no longer looked shabby; they had acquired an aura of greatness that began to settle in every corner. This funny old racetrack in the middle of the Louisville outskirts starts getting to you, and you are never quite the same again.

It was, finally, Derby Day. Louisville clocks were an hour earlier than in New York, and at 4 A.M., Secretariat, whose stomach was running on daylight saving time, was looking for Eddie. He and Angle Light nickered eagerly when Eddie emerged from the tackroom where he had his cot set up. Eddie took the steel measure, scooped out two quarts of oats for each horse, and returned to his cot. Sleep was scarce because he was doing double duty: his daily routine with the two horses and night-guarding them.

"Down here we don't have a night watchman so I have to be it. I sleep a half hour or so, then I jump up an' look around. Down here I want the job done right, so I'd just as soon do it myself. Not that I don't trust 'em, but it's my horses, and if anything went wrong, it'd be my responsibility."

After the two horses finished their breakfast, Eddie cleaned their stalls, groomed them, and waited for Lucien. When the little trainer had made his way past the intensified security lines, Eddie led Secretariat out for inspection. Lucien ran his hand over every inch of those golden haired and gold plated legs.

"Okay, Eddie, give him a few turns."

Eddie then turned Secretariat over to George "Charlie" Davis to handwalk him. Charlie, who was also from South Carolina, and who had come to the track from Lucien's farm, was now Secretariat's regular exercise rider. Secretariat was full of energy. As Charlie led him down the shed row, it became clear that the horse, not the man, was doing the leading. After Secretariat had gone a few turns around the walking ring, dragging Charlie at a half-run, Eddie hooked a restraining bit to the horse's halter so he could be controlled.

At 10:00 A.M., the blacksmith swung by to check the two colts' shoes. After he had finished, Eddie gave them a half-quart of oats apiece for lunch.

"Now they'll know sump'in's up," muttered Eddie, referring to the fact that the ritual reduction of feed before a race, in order to preclude stomach cramps during it, is a sure sign to a horse that he is about to run.

If Secretariat was keyed up, he didn't show it. As soon as he finished his skimpy noon feed, he did his next favorite thing to eating, he lay down in his stall and slept for about three hours before his Kentucky Derby.

Across the race track, it was a far less sleepy scene. The stands and the infield were

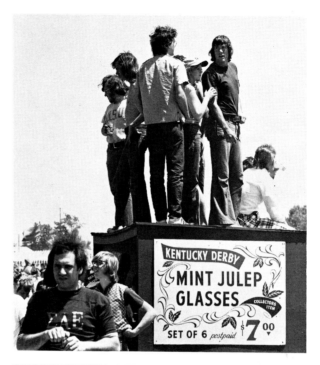

The infield crowd at the Derby.

99

rapidly filling with what would be an uproarious record crowd of 134,476 people.

The infield began to resemble racing's answer to the Woodstock rock festival. Beer flowed in rivers to a mass of happy, half-naked, and in a few cases, totally naked, occupants. A national guardsman and a local policeman, part of the contingent on hand to contain this crowd in their specified areas (what the crowd did in those areas, short of murder, seemed to be of no concern), looked at each other in amazement. "Lordy, did you see that girl just run by? Hell, she didn't have a damn thing on but a pair of shorts!" said the guardsman.

"I didn't see a damn thing," replied the policeman.

In the stands, hawkers were everywhere, dispensing the sweet, bourbon concoctions that pass for mint juleps on Derby Day, which people buy mostly to get the souvenir glasses. It was obvious that the real thing was flowing from some place. One wondered how the crowd was going to survive through the eight races before the Derby, but they always do, and they did again.

Lucien and Penny picked at their lunches. The tension was now almost unbearable, and it seemed an interminable wait until the ninth race. Ron Turcotte worked his way through the crowd to the jock's room, signing autographs, and trying to avoid spilled mint juleps and good luck slaps on the back. About an hour before the Derby, Lucien made one more trip to the backstretch. Satisfied that there was nothing further for him to do there, he left it up to Eddie and Charlie.

"How's he doin', Lucien?" someone asked.

"I don't think he'll disgrace himself," answered Lucien solemnly. "As God is my

judge, I think he will redeem himself today."

The long awaited time had arrived. One by one, the Derby hopefuls appeared on the track and were led past the crowd to the saddling area underneath the stand. You could feel a tangible change come over the people in the grandstand. This was the Derby.

Among Secretariat's twelve rivals heading for the paddock was his childhood work partner, Gold Bag, who used to kick dirt back in the face of the fat colt who always trailed him.

The bugler sounded the traditional call to the post, and a cheer went up. Saddled, their jocks up, the Derby horses reappeared out of the tunnel from the paddock. Secretariat looked like something straight out of a fairy tale, every inch a horseman's—or, for that matter, anyone's—dream. The band struck up *that* song—"My Old Kentucky Home"—and the whole place became totally still. It is at that moment that the full impact of Derby Day is felt. The Derby is not just *a* horse race. It *is* racing. By now, the most cynical disbeliever finds himself choked up, the last shreds of any resistance to Derby magic crumbled away like sandcastle walls at high tide.

The band ended their song, and the horses continued on their way to the post in a tense silence. The starters began to load them into the starting gate. The pre-race tension was not to be relieved that quickly, however. There was trouble in the gate. Elmendorf Farm's Twice a Prince reared and fell backward, throwing jockey Angel Santiago and delaying the start a full five minutes.

Ron Turcotte noted later, "I was glad to have that number ten spot then. We weren't in the gate yet, so the delay didn't hurt us.

But it sure didn't help the horses who had to stand in there all that time."

The incident hurt Sham the most. An extra assistant starter was shifted to calm Twice a Prince, and Sham, left with no assistant, banged his head against the gate as the doors crashed open. Then he stumbled, brushing his quarter against the gate.

Secretariat got a clean start and dropped back to tail the field. As expected, the speedy Shecky Greene took the lead and made the pace on the lightening fast track. By then, Sham had steadied himself and jockey Laffit Pincay sent him up to run with the leaders.

"Oh, God Almighty," muttered Lucien Laurin to himself as the field passed the stands for the first time with Secretariat trailing. "Don't tell me it's gonna be another race like the Wood!"

But going into the first turn, Secretariat began to move up between horses. After picking up two spots, he proceeded to take the rest of the field on the outside. Walter Blum, who was on Royal and Regal, remembers that point in the race very well. "My horse was running good at that time. We were moving from fourth to third when I felt this big whoosh of air go by and that was all there was to it. He was fantastic!"

Midway, going down the backside, Shecky Greene was holding on to his lead but being challenged by the brave Sham. Coming up fast behind them was Secretariat. Going to the quarter pole, Ron reached back and used his stick on Secretariat, "just enough to let him know I was serious," and they quickly passed the faltering Shecky Greene.

Veteran jockey Larry Adams, aboard Shecky Greene, attests that Secretariat could be a terrifying sight as he swooped down on his competition. "I glanced back and saw him coming and thought, if I get in his way, I'll get killed! He looked like the Red Ball Express!"

Sham raced into the turn holding his lead. At the eighth pole, Secretariat, looping wide around the turn, ranged up alongside Sham. Here was the duel the racing world had waited for since the Wood Memorial. But it wasn't to be. Ron Turcotte merely tapped Secretariat three final times as he felt his momentum check briefly after their wide swing around the turn. At the feel of the stick, the big red machine shifted to a speed no other horse had ever possessed in that final Derby quarter of a mile. He rocketed over the finish line in a new Derby record time of $1:59^2/_5$, smashing the previous record set by Northern Dancer in 1964 by three-fifths of a second. Sham, in second place, also broke the previous record by about one-fifth of a second.

Poor, game Sham. On any other day, against any other horse, he would have been a clear winner. But Secretariat's last incredible burst of speed had sent him that last quarter in twenty-three seconds. He had also accomplished something unheard of in a race of that distance: he had gone the route in successively faster quarters. John Finney, a brilliant observer of horsemen and president of the famed horse auctioneering concern, the Fasig–Tipton Company, calculated those quarters as—$:25^1/_5$; $:24$; $:23^4/_5$; $:23^2/_5$; and $:23$.

It was all over but the usual melee in the Derby winner's circle.

As Secretariat headed back for the barn with Eddie and Charlie, Penny said proudly, "Well, there's *one* Bold Ruler who can go the distance." There also seemed to be considerable doubt cast on Jimmy the Greek's source of medical information on a race horse's legs.

The winning team from Meadow was then ushered into the Director's room, where champagne and mint juleps flowed, with Governors and Senators and other VIPs playing second fiddle to a horse that day.

There was champagne flowing back at Barn 42, too. Up at Secretariat's end, a local merchant had pulled up a pickup truck with a tub of champagne and Charlie Davis took on the role of acting host. Eddie refused to join in, except to pose with a glass of champagne for a picture with Secretariat. He sipped a brief toast, then poured the rest in a bucket. He didn't have time, he had a lot of responsibility.

At the other end of the shed there was something flowing, too, but it was not champagne. It was blood. Sham had knocked two teeth completely loose when his head banged the starting gate, and Martin's crew were busy cauterizing the wound.

But Pancho Martin was not making any alibis that day.

"I cannot tell if it bothered him. I know if I lost a tooth it would bother me. He ran his race, and I make no excuses. We need no excuses. I beat him once and he beat me once. When he beats me three out of four, I'll call him great." His jockey, Laffit Pincay, still a little stunned by the destruction of that last quarter, wondered if he hadn't gone to the front too soon. But it was all moot now.

Two hours after the race, station wagons were provided for the VIP's and their party was shifted to the stable. When the champagne had stopped flowing and Secretariat was cooled out and settled in his stall, Eddie began mixing his supper.

As Eddie recalls it, "I gave him six quarts of oats, a quart of sweet feed, two quarts of bran, and cut him up some carrots."

Lucien Laurin came by for one last check and saw the feed Eddie was setting in.

"He won't finish that in three days!"

Ordinarily a horse coming off a hard race such as Secretariat had that day would back off his feed considerably. But it took Secretariat approximately an hour and a half to finish his meal. At 10 P.M., the stable was all quiet except for a steady munching sound from Secretariat's stall. At 10:45 P.M., Eddie went to check on him again. Secretariat was lying down in the deep straw, fast asleep.

The morning after the Derby, Secretariat was so full of energy that Eddie and Charlie found it impossible to hand walk him like the other horses who had raced the day before. Charlie had to saddle him and ride him around the shed to give him his exercise. A number of the more attentive turf writers noticed this energy powerhouse. It was then that Secretariat's "super horse" image began to emerge.

II: The Preakness

At 9:30 A.M., on the Monday after the Derby, a fresh, eager Secretariat was led up an airplane ramp by Eddie, and the two flew to the next way station on the Triple Crown road: Pimlico racetrack outside Baltimore, Maryland.

Once again, they were stabled at the end of a VIP barn, with their chief rival Sham at the opposite end. Sham was recovering quickly from his Derby battering, and his loss of teeth was not affecting his eating. Pancho Martin pointed out, "Fortunately, horses chew their food with their rear teeth, and the two he lost were up front. He can't pick grass

Going to the post for the Preakness.

right now, but outside of that he's fine and regaining his energies.''

The two weeks before the Preakness were days of relative quiet and business-like preparation. Here there were no hordes of sensation seekers or press corps determined to keep alive a controversy with the other end of the stable, just the normal pre-Preakness press coverage.

Two days after their arrival, Secretariat and Sham had their first gallops on the Pimlico track, which was muddy from all-night rains. While Secretariat was cooling out, Lucien stood back and observed, ''Look at him! He just keeps getting bigger. He's so thick that Ron may have to have a special saddle made just to ride him. You know, the saddle started to slip some in the Derby, even though I took care to make sure it didn't.''

Several days later, Ron Turcotte did have a new girth made up for his Preakness mount. Secretariat had girthed an enormous seventy-five and one-half inches prior to his run in the Gotham that spring, but he had increased two full sizes by the Preakness. Ron found that the forty-nine inch girth (extra long by most standards) buckled so low on the colt's sides that the buckles were rubbing his ankles. In order to get the buckles back up under the protective leather flap of the saddle, he had to have a special fifty-three inch girth made up.

During the Preakness training period, the pressure was off enough to give the experts time to do some research. They had theorized that, with his incredible bursts of sudden speed and his ability to go long distances in record time with little apparent effort, Secretariat might have one of the longest strides in racing history.

Six days before the Preakness, Secretariat worked five eighths in a fast :57$^2/_5$, and the

104

Derby Day.

Secretariat enjoys some blue grass.

105

Secretariat appears on the track.

The challenger Sham.

Secretariat trails the field the first time past the stands.

Secretariat wins the Derby in a new record time of 1:59⅖.

Across the finish line.

Lucien tightens the extra-large girth on Secretariat.

Secretariat begins his sensational looping rush.

Secretariat leaves Sham behind in the stretch.

Over the finish line to win the second jewel in the Triple Crown.

The presentation of the Preakness trophies.

distances between his hoof prints were measured. The longest stride was twenty-four feet, eleven inches. This was something of a letdown at first. It seemed almost mediocre compared to the great Native Dancer's stride of twenty-nine feet. Some time later, NYRA's Dr. Manuel Gilman called attention to an interesting aspect of Secretariat's way of doing things. According to a NYRA press release:

> The big red colt . . . employs two different strides with equal facility, one long and the other short—and the *SHORT* one was measured at the Maryland track.
>
> While little scientific study has been done on the stride of the horse, . . . we know that stride is related to conformation, and the length of the horse between front and hind legs usually determines the length of his stride.
>
> The distance-running type of horse is generally long in the body and so takes long strides, at least in theory. Sprinters, on the other hand, are generally more heavily muscled and short-coupled and take shorter strides.
>
> Secretariat is a most unusual horse. He's very heavily muscled and looks like a sprinter for that reason, but he also has the body length of the long striding horse. He's an all-purpose horse, a sprinter and stayer— and he uses the typical stride of each at different points in a race. All horses probably alter their stride in this way, but none to the successful extent that Secretariat does, and the way he accelerates is fantastic.
>
> At the time they measured his stride at Pimlico, he was obviously sprinting—and so they were measuring his *shorter* stride. How much longer his long stride is I couldn't even begin to guess.*

In the winner's circle.

---

* NYRA press release.

Ron Turcotte, himself a student of conformation and horses' action, supported the theory:

> From riding Secretariat so many times, . . . I'd say he changes the length of his stride like no other horse I've ever seen. When he's relaxed and going easy on his own, he stretches out and covers an awful lot of ground. When he digs in and goes all out for speed—that's when he shortens his stride.
>
> Actually, it's more the quickness of a horse's stride than its length that's important, and Secretariat's is the fastest, especially when he accelerates to overtake a lot of horses.*

Elizabeth Ham had noticed that Secretariat had a habit of reaching out with his front leg for a little extra distance before he brought it down. It was almost a second motion, as though he were straightening out his foot and pointing his toe. Turcotte agreed with this observation, saying that when he was riding Secretariat, he could feel him give what felt like an extra little kick with every stride.

Trainer Lucien Laurin said of the whole thing, "I judge horses by results, not by stride."**

Training for the Preakness continued smoothly and calmly. Exercise rider Charlie Davis became more ecstatic every time he worked the big horse out.

"It's like ridin' on air," he explained in his soft Carolina low-country dialect. "So smooth it's like ridin' in a Rolls-Royce. You don' feel the bumps. You know, sorta like an airplane. Jus' put 'im on the runway—when you wants to take off, you jus' move your han's on him and he takes off—whoosh!"

---

*NYRA press release.
**NYRA press release.

And, by Saturday, May 19, the big red jet was definitely warmed up for a takeoff.

What draws the Preakness crowd to Pimlico that Saturday each year is not any quaint atmosphere, because although it's a fine racing strip, it has little charm. What people come to see is whether the winner of that year's Derby can take the second leg of the Triple Crown. With the bonus of that year's Derby winner being Secretariat, they came in droves: a record 61,657 that not only filled up the stands but every foot of the infield as well. That day, Baltimore experienced the most massive traffic jam in its history.

For Penny and Jack Tweedy, the afternoon didn't begin well. To relieve the tension, they had decided to stop for a long lunch. They turned into a place about two blocks from the track and had settled down to Maryland crab cakes when there was a commotion in the parking lot. The attendant had parked their car in such a way as to cause it and three others some $5,000 in damage. So the Tweedys finished their lunch and walked to the track. There they found that Meadow had no credentials at the gate, and they ended up having to pay to see their big horse run.

It was time for the Preakness. During the saddling in the paddock, Secretariat, full of energy, kept lashing out one hind leg after the other while Lucien tightened his oversized girths.

Pancho Martin and Laffit Pincay had worked out a new plan this time. No sending Sham to the front. They would let him lay behind the leader until he tired, and then send him forward.

The band played the Preakness song, "Maryland, My Maryland," as the horses paraded to the post. That day, there were no unfortunate incidents in the starting gate,

Elizabeth Ham shares her victory champagne with the Preakness winner.

and starter Eddie Blind sent the six horses on their way with no fuss. At the outset, the pace was slow. Ron had eased Secretariat behind the field at the break, as usual. But as they passed the stands and approached the first turn, there was a sudden change in Secretariat's scenario.

Ron explained later, "The pace was slow for the first quarter (twenty-five seconds) so I decided to go around horses." This was a somewhat understated description of what actually happened.

Secretariat lunged into a drive which carried him past two horses *entering* the turn, and then, in a spectacular, soaring sweep around the entire field *on* the turn, he rocketed ahead into the backstretch. Pincay, realizing what had just happened, quickly swung Sham out from behind the horses in pursuit.

"Once he got to the front entering the backstretch," continued Ron, "he drew out on his own. I just let him go as he pleased."

Pincay saw his strategy coming apart. He was laying second, but that speedball up front wasn't tiring. He watched for Turcotte to hit his horse, a sure sign that the incredible pace was telling on him, but it never happened.

Going into the last turn, Pincay was frantic, and resorted to the whip all the way around the turn. It was just no use. The massive quarters in front of him only seemed to gather momentum. The race ended with a 2¹/₂ length gap between the two rivals, the same as in the Derby.

Secretariat eased up around the turn, hardly blowing after that tremendous effort. His enormous lung capacity had always been one of his greatest running assets. In the Preakness, at least one jockey remembered that particular aspect of his rush to the front. Starter Eddie Blind recounts a moment in the race related to him by jockey George Cusimano, who rode Ecole Etage that day.

"I was riding along, and I had plenty of horse; my horse was running *easy.* Now I seen this shadow out here goin' into the backside, and I knew it wasn't my horse's shadow. So I got after my horse a little bit. But that shadow kept right on comin'. Then I got to hearing this noise beside me—them big nostrils goin'—and I knew what it was. When he came by, it felt like a freight train passing—blew the number right off my sleeve."

"I've handled six of the eight Triple Crown winners," said Eddie Blind, "and I'd have to say Secretariat's one of the greatest. He was the biggest bull I ever saw. He was a man and he knew it, and it took a man to handle him."

Chick Lang, the General Manager of Pim-

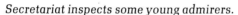

Secretariat inspects some young admirers.

lico, was moved to say of Secretariat, "It is as if God decided to create the perfect horse!"

But in the middle of all the jubilation over this victory in the second leg of the Triple Crown, there was one disappointment. A malfunction in the track's electronic timing device had prevented an accurate record of the time. (It was later surmised that some of the infield crowd that had broken through the security guardlines and rushed to the rail had broken the electronic beam.) The *Daily Racing Form* clockers and other clockers in the press stand all agreed within one-fifth of a second that Secretariat had set a new Preakness record. But E. T. McClean, Jr., the official track clocker whose time must be used in the event of a timer breakdown, disagreed. His official time of 1:55 was a full second off the record of 1:54 set by Canonero II in 1971. Thus, Secretariat was deprived of what could have been his second Triple Crown record. Two days later, the officials revised the time to 1:54²/₅. This was still not enough for a new record.

At Secretariat's end of the barn that day, champagne was again flowing. This time it was in a bit more reserved manner, for Penny was hostess that day. The Meadow people drank to the Derby, to the Preakness, and to the Belmont-to-come. Their hopes and their confidence were high.

At the other end of the barn there was a scene of some serious stock-taking.

Talking to no one in general, Sham's trainer, Pancho Martin, looked up from the ground suddenly and said, "The hell with the Belmont. I don't want any more part of my horse looking at that big behind. Maybe we go to the Jersey Derby."

But Sham was to continue his rivalry with Secretariat one more time.

III: The Belmont

It was raining the morning after the Preakness. Eddie came out of the tack room at 4:30 A.M. to feed Secretariat, and, as usual, the big red horse was waiting eagerly for him. His right eye was swollen, probably from a clod of dirt thrown early in the race, and Eddie daubed it with ointment.

"Red, you really got it to do now," he said, and was answered with a toss of the big head in the feed tub.

That day they shipped out for Belmont Park and the final leg on the grand slam.

What respite the Meadow crew enjoyed in Pimlico was over now—in spades. Eddie and his big horse returned to what looked like a fortress at Barn 5. There were guards everywhere, and, also, or so it seemed, half the people in New York. Press passes had suddenly sprouted like early summer crab grass, and everything that could make itself fit the description of a publication or a network, from CBS down to underground scandal sheets run off on a mimeograph machine, had their staffs, their girlfriends, their cousins, and so on out to shadow every move made by Secretariat, Penny Tweedy, Lucien Laurin, Ron Turcotte, and now—in new celebrity status—Eddie Sweat and Charlie Davis. Both Eddie and Charlie became quite deft with questions and, with tongue in cheek, gave the delighted reporters some beautifully embellished, if not quite accurate copy. It wasn't Keystone Cops like it had been at Churchill Downs; it was mayhem. This new, expanded Secretariat press corps was like an invasion of ants. They would have been harmless except for the fact that so many of them, in their ignorance of race track procedure, made it difficult, and sometimes dangerous, for horsemen to get their work done. They could be found running, shouting, ducking out from behind trees, and scaring nervous thoroughbreds out of their wits. Some horsemen, a bit unfairly, but understandably, began to resent the Meadow group for this incursion into their domain.

Penny and Lucien worked hard to cope with it all. Penny made a real effort, and, in many cases succeeded, to get to know her press. She remarked of the regulars from the long campaign, "What used to be a blur of faces at a press conference after a big win is now an assemblage of people I know and like."

But things got worse. Racetrackers are a gregarious lot and like to visit their friends in the neighboring barn during breaks should the fancy strike them. Lucien's crew found themselves almost prisoners in this heavily guarded compound. To visit or be visited was now an exercise in dealing with red tape.

But everyone stuck, because bigger than any of the inconveniences was being part of the excitement surrounding Secretariat's bid for the Triple Crown. Not only people in racing, but the entire country, dreamed of this eventuality. Red was now a national hero. Within the same week, *Time, Newsweek,* and *Sports Illustrated* all carried Secretariat's picture on their covers. He was now being called a "super horse" without any reservation whatsoever.

A conquest of the Triple Crown hadn't been accomplished for twenty-five years. In ninety-one years, only eight horses had managed to win it at all. The last winner, Citation, in 1948, had been one of a crop of 2860 registered thoroughbred foals in his year. Racing had grown considerably since then, and so had the odds. Tenfold. Secretariat had

to compete for racing honors against 25,003 fellow thoroughbreds of the same age.

The Belmont would be the toughest race of the three. The one and a half mile distance provides a long run to the first turn for position, long gradual turns that make crowding a rarity, then a long and killing stretch run home. The test, an honest one, is for distance. Once again, the question mark in Secretariat's "sure thing" status was whether he could do that freewheeling thing of his for such a long trip without coming apart from sheer exhaustion.

As the Belmont drew nearer, Eddie Sweat began to show some signs of strain. Late one afternoon, when even Barn 5 was quiet, Eddie admitted to a friend, "Sometimes I get pretty nervous bein' so responsible for him all the time. That's an awful lot to a lot of people standin' in that stall."

Eddie sat on an overturned bucket, absentmindedly playing with a twelve-toed kitten called Scooter. Scooter was Barn 5's "Derby cat," one of a litter born the day before Secretariat left for Kentucky. Scooter was as a kitten, as Secretariat had been as a colt, the "tough guy" of the litter and a local character to the Laurin crew.

"You know," mused Eddie, "If I live to be a hundred, I'll never see another horse like Secretariat. All my life I dreamed of rubbin' a great hoss, an' now that I've done it, I don't think I ever want to do it again. He's just too good to be true. You know what I mean—you got some good hosses you can figure gonna win a good race a lot of the time—but him— he jus' goes out an' does it *all* th' time. It's like he's not real."

On Friday, June 1, Secretariat appeared on the track for his final long sharpener for the Belmont. It was a formidable performance.

Scooter, the Derby kitten.

Eddie Sweat ministers to his Big Horse.

He broke down the backside and began splintering fractions like bits of glass: three eights in :35$^2/_5$; five eighths in :59; and the final three-quarters of a mile in 1:11$^3/_5$. It seemed to all those who watched, horseman and greenhorn alike, that all he had to do was keep breathing and the Belmont was his.

Pancho Martin and Sigmund Sommer, however, had decided against throwing in the towel. Sham would run in the Belmont.

The pressures began to wear everyone down. Lucien, normally so gracious and accommodating to the press at all times, became increasingly tense and abrupt. Penny had learned to make a mad dash from her car into the sanctuary of the stable enclosure fast enough to avoid being enveloped by microphones and cameras. But the time did pass.

On the night before the Belmont, the Meadow Stable contingent was the center of a great deal of attention at the lavish Belmont Ball.

A less fashionable gathering, but equally fervent in their feelings about the upcoming event, was the army of young people who were camped out along the parkway outside the racetrack to ensure themselves of a good vantage spot the next day. They had traveled and hitchhiked from all over the country to see a new folk hero called Secretariat.

Eddie Sweat had a nightmare on that Friday night. The horses were running. Secretariat had opened a huge lead and was swinging into the final turn. Then—a gasp of horror from the crowd—Secretariat was down! Horses passed him. He regained his feet with Ron Turcotte still aboard. They

Eddie gets the nuzzle from Secretariat as Riva Ridge watches.

made a game chase of it, but it was too late. Sham had won the Belmont.

Eddie woke in a cold sweat and muttered, "I got to turn that dream around!" His wife Linda tried to get him back to sleep, but Eddie remained sleepless, unable to shake the effect of that dream.

The next morning, he began the usual race day regimen, arriving at the track at 4 A.M. The morning passed, and the hours dragged, and Eddie Sweat agonized.

Penny Tweedy was up at six. She fidgeted through the morning, and then joined her husband Jack, enduring her nervousness through a luncheon with New York Governor and Mrs. Rockefeller and Senator and Mrs. Jacob Javits.

When the entrance gates opened, the faithful streamed through by the thousands. Each race seemed to take too long. To everyone connected with Secretariat, it felt as if the time for the eighth race would never arrive.

Elizabeth Ham appeared, wearing the same hat, the same dress, and the wristband she had been issued at the Kentucky Derby.

This had also been her costume for the Preakness. Although she is not a superstitious woman, she was not above a little insurance. Penny Tweedy's young cousin, Alan Chenery, and two old friends of the Tweedys, the Timberlakes, had done the same thing.

Penny had some insurance, too—a pendant that had been her mother's, a gold horse's head.

Penny and Jack Tweedy moved down to Box A-17, joining her brother Hollis Chenery and his wife, her sister Margaret Carmichael, and Mr. and Mrs. Robert McNamara.

On his jacket, Jack Tweedy wore a large button proclaiming: "Breed more Secretariats."

The button had come from friends in Virginia, and Penny said she had pinned one on Governor Rockefeller, too.

Penny had now been spotted by the crowd. They cheered and held up homemade "Good Luck Secretariat" signs. One bearded young man scaled the wall in front of the box section in order to shake Penny's hand, but had to satisfy himself with Jack Tweedy's instead.

Back at Barn 5, the announcement was finally made.

"Bring your horses to the paddock for the eighth race."

Charlie climbed aboard the lead pony, Billy Silver, and Eddie, after taking one last wipe with a rub rag across the gleaming copper flank, led Secretariat out for the most important day of his life—all their lives.

People followed him like the pied piper, droves of them, of all ages and descriptions. Everybody felt it. He wasn't a horse. He was magic. The magic was about to happen again. And they wanted to soak up every drop of it.

As Secretariat entered the paddock, the applause was deafening. People had planted themselves along the rail as early as 8 A.M., just to get a good look at him.

It was a miracle that Lucien was able to get Secretariat saddled. The little Canadian was one raw nerve.

It was a clear, beautiful day, and a beautiful setting. Five horses for the Belmont being carefully saddled in the shaded paddock with an ancient and carefully preserved big pine overlooking the whole scene.

The faint voice of the paddock judge called out, "Riders up!" The moment had come.

Ron Turcotte got a leg up and looked down at Eddie.

"What's the matter, Sweat?"

"A little nervous, I guess."

"Me, too, but it's all in the game, isn't it." Eddie nodded. His face was grave.

Charlie, on the lead pony, Billy Silver, came up to Secretariat. Then they moved out of the paddock together. In the tunnel under the stands, the noise of the crowd was almost terrifying. Some of the other horses began to lunge and sidestep nervously.

Sham led the parade out onto the track, followed by Secretariat. The band struck up the Belmont song, "Sidewalks of New York." The "now generation," most of whom had spent the night by the parkway, was out in force. This horse was something they could believe in. Something honest and real—and oh, wasn't he beautiful.

The starting gate was drawn into position directly in front of the stands. One by one, the five horses were loaded into the stalls by starter George Cassidy's expert crew of assistants. Then the doors were slammed shut. A start would come at any second.

Secretariat was on the inside, then Pvt. Smiles, My Gallant, Twice a Prince, and Sham on the outside. All of them stood well. George Cassidy, satisfied, tightened his forefinger on the button and released the electric circuit that held the doors closed.

The bell rang as the doors crashed open with an awful sound. In this, his life's most demanding test, Secretariat wasted no time. He left the gate on the lead and stayed there. Pincay quickly sent Sham up to challenge. The rangy, dark horse struggled to overtake the driving, heaving chestnut quarters before him. Up the awesome straightaway to the first turn he chased. On the turn, Pincay could finally see those red quarters by his boot, then Turcotte's blue and white form. Stride for stride, head and head, the two horses strained, totally enveloped in the sound of their own breathing and the din of their hooves. The race was now clearly a private duel. Then it happened—Sham began to draw past Secretariat.

The dark, beautiful head, then the lean neck, glistening with effort—and, at last, half his body. Now Secretariat must chase him. The two horses had reeled off fractions far too fast for a race this long: the first quarter in :23$^3/_5$, the next in only :22$^3/_5$—a half mile in :46$^1/_5$. Horsemen in the crowd gasped. It was suicide! No one could maintain a pace like this in the Belmont! They would kill each other off. But Sham and Pincay drove on. They had drunk the bitter cup of defeat twice because of this red devil thing beside them, and the memory of it drove both man and horse.

Then, suddenly, it was over as quickly as it had begun. The gallant Sham had given all he had, and it was not enough.

Secretariat stormed to the front at the

Secretariat's well-wishers for the Belmont Stakes.

Into the starting gate for the Belmont.

same killing pace. Another quarter in :23³/₅, the next in :24²/₅, finishing the mile in an amazing 1:34¹/₅. And still he went on. Now he was 7 lengths in front. Sham held on in second place, his drive putting him 20 lengths in front of the rest of the field. Secretariat continued to increase his lead. It couldn't last.

But it did. And it went on. "Oh Gawd," thought Eddie Sweat, "It's just like my dream! Stay on your feet, Red, stay up!"

Secretariat reached the mile and a quarter point in 1:59 (two-fifths of a second faster than his time for the same distance in the Derby). He and Ron Turcotte were no longer racing other horses, for the others were now only a measure of the extent of his victory. They were racing the clock. Ron turned his head, not to look for other horses, but to check the time on the infield tote board. No easing of the pace now; he was determined that no one would take this record from Secretariat. And Ron felt only willing response under him. Oh, how this horse loved to run!

Above, Lucien Laurin turned to Penny Tweedy, grinning a tight smile. "The only way he can lose now is to fall down."

All by themselves, leading by one-sixteenth of a mile, horse and rider sailed the last quarter in :25 flat, hitting the wire for a 31 length victory. Their time of 2:24 shattered Gallant Man's previous record by an unbelievable two and three-fifths seconds. In the race of his life, Secretariat had delivered the performance of his life. Columnist Charlie Hatton observed, "You couldn't find the other horses with two pairs of binoculars."

To say that there was pandemonium in the Belmont stands would be a limp description. Actually, the management would have been well advised to bring in a good team of engineers the next day to check for damage to the foundations.

Hollis Chenery went out to greet Meadow's champion, and then led him to the winner's circle. This had now become a miniature battleground, with over a hundred photographers trying to get some sort of vantage point in a ridiculously small area meant to accommodate less than a quarter of their number. Somehow, Secretariat and his ecstatic company, Penny, Ron, Lucien, the beaming Miss Ham, Hollis Chenery, and Margaret Carmichael survived the crush and, at some risk, moved in for the presentation. At one point, Governor Rockefeller was pushed aside by a man with a TV camera and told to wait his turn. It was joyous mayhem.

To one side, virtually unnoticed, stood a very happy young man—Seth Hancock.

After the official ceremonies, some T-shirted youngsters in the crowd yelled, "Hey Miz Tweedy, could some of us little people have you now?"

"You sure can," she said and went over, happily pumping hands and signing the flood of programs and pictures shoved at her as fast as she could handle them.

A good many horsemen and officials were to observe that her friendly and spontaneous manner was one of the best things that had ever happened to racing. Where so many "big" owners remain aloof from the crowds who come to see their horses run, Penny went to them willingly, sometimes turning her back on the assembled hierarchy to do so.

The one tragic figure that day was the gallant Sham. Thoroughbreds are brave and willing creatures; they can and do become demoralized by defeat. In any other year but Secretariat's, Sham would have swept everything before him. To be put away again in

The starting gate crashes open.

The run for the Belmont begins in earnest. Secretariat plunges forward.

123

such a duel with Secretariat may have been the final straw for him as a racehorse. However, several days after the race, a hairline fracture of a cannon bone was found, and Sham was retired to stud.

Secretariat, with his winning of the Triple Crown, and the way in which he had won it, had now virtually become a legend in his time. Howard Gentry, who had brought Secretariat into the world, reflected on that day: "Sometimes I look at the proud way he carries himself, and I think he's just living up to what he thinks he is."

But it was left to Mr. Holly Hughes, the senior horse trainer of America, to put the cap on it all. Hughes also saw Man O'War run, and saddled the winner of the 1916 Kentucky Derby, George Smith, before Man O'War was even born. When asked, he said he didn't like to compare the two great red horses and would only say they were the two best horses ever. But, after the Belmont, he did say, of Secretariat, "Why, he's the greatest horse that has been yet developed in this century. . . . Yes, he's the Horse of the Century."

Secretariat takes command.

Sham (1A) rushes to challenge.

Secretariat begins to open up what will be an incredible 31-length winning margin.

Secretariat's fans go wild as he races the clock in the final 100 yards.

Ron and Secretariat have it all to themselves.

At the finish, Turcotte checks the teletimer. Secretariat shatters the old record by an incredible 2⅗ seconds!

The first horse to win the Triple Crown in a quarter of a century.

Early morning at the Saratoga track.

On the track for an early morning gallop.

To the paddock for the Whitney.

They're off for the Whitney. (1)

Settling into stride. (2)

Onion bids for early command. (3)

They pass the stands for the first time. (4)

Past the stands. (5)

To the first turn. (6)

Onion takes command. (7)

Secretariat tries to rally. (8)

Onion beats the champion.

Secretariat's first work on the grass.

135

SEVEN

HORSE OF THE CENTURY:
Triumphs and Disasters

I: The Champion

After his first good night's sleep in weeks, Lucien Laurin announced that Secretariat would be given a rest and then pointed for the Jim Dandy at Saratoga, a month away. He thus laid to rest rumors that the colt would be retired on his Belmont win. He added that the million-dollar winnings mark was one of the next goals for the big red colt. Secretariat was to be handwalked for a few days, then given daily "light" exercise for the next month.

That was *his* plan.

Secretariat was so full of himself that when Charlie Davis, Mordecai Williams, or anyone else, tried to handwalk him, he dragged them around on the end of the lead shank until they swore they needed longer sleeves in their shirts. It was going to be difficult to cope with giving him a "vacation."

Eddie Sweat had now taken to calling Secretariat not "Red" or "Big Boy," his usual names for the colt, but "Big Red." The use of the name spread, and, coupled with "Big Red's" billing as "Super Horse" and "Horse of the Century," began to stir up a controversy fired by the defenders of the original, immortal Big Red—Man O'War.

Thousands of words were written and, probably, thousands more spoken across tables by partisans on both sides.

There were some superficial similarities: both were flaming chestnuts with a white star and stripe on the forehead. Both were sound and physically outstanding; their differences could be reduced to the fine points of conformation studies.

But their temperaments were entirely opposite. Secretariat was always calm about

Man O'War.

Secretariat.

everything he did (with the exception of being an eager glutton for exercise and food). Man O'War was highly volatile, and sometimes it required four men to get him saddled for a race. He was usually led to the post by a man on foot and had a habit of raising pure hell at the start.

Secretariat had considerably more competition in his age group. He was one of a crop of approximately 25,000 thoroughbred foals. Man O'War, born in 1919, was one of a post-World War I crop of only 1680 foals.

Secretariat still had to be tested against older horses. Man O'War ran against an older horse only once—in his match race with the first Triple Crown winner, Sir Barton.

Comparing times did not prove anything because track surfaces, levels of pace, the quality of competition, nutrition, racing shoes, etc., were all different. There were too many variables for any valid comparison of the two horses to be possible.

Jonny Nerud, the trainer of Gallant Man, whose 1957 Belmont record Secretariat had broken, put the whole controversy in perspective: "Man O'War is a myth. I suspect he always will be. He's like Babe Ruth. No matter how many home runs Hank Aaron hits, he'll never replace Babe Ruth in the fan's estimation. It's the same with Jack Dempsey in boxing and Barney Oldfield in auto racing. They're myths."

"Actually," he concluded, "you can't compare generations."

Secretariat was a hero to *this* generation: the young people who idolized him and couldn't care less about comparing him to any other horse, present *or* past.

Secretariat's fame had become almost overwhelming for the Meadow Stable people. In one instance, it was sad: Scooter, the tough little "Derby" kitten with the six-toed feet, disappeared, probably taken by someone who thought he was the big horse's mascot. It began to look as though life around the Laurin stable would never be normal again. There wasn't too much complaint about this anymore, however. The Meadow people had long since become inured to their inconveniences, and, besides, what better fate could a true racetracker hope for than to belong to a barn that had the best horse in the country —and maybe the world?

But there was one individual in Barn 5 to whom all the attention paid to Secretariat had become unbearable—Riva Ridge. So much so that the gentle, sociable horse who loved people had turned into a recluse.

"He knows what it's like to be the center of attention," remarked Lucien worriedly. "But now he sees Secretariat getting all of it, and he doesn't like it. Look at him, he's got his head stuck back in that corner, mad at the world." A concerned Penny Tweedy added, "Riva's depression really bothers me because he's always been my pet."

Lucien and Penny decided that the best remedy for their first Derby horse was a victory and all the hurrah from the crowd that went with it. To fill this prescription, they chose the $50,000 added Massachusetts Handicap, to be run at Suffolk Downs on Sunday, June 17.

After being worked a handy three-quarter mile in 1:12^2/$_5$, Riva was shipped to New England. He got some of his applause when Eddie led him to the paddock, and seemed to nod his head in happy response. Then he went out and won his race handily, equaling Whirlaway's 1942 record of 1:48^1/$_5$. He easily defeated an old rival—Bee Bee Bee, who had deprived him of the Preakness and his Triple Crown in 1972. In the winner's circle, there was more applause, and Riva Ridge returned to his barn at Belmont a happy horse.

In the meantime, Secretariat continued to gallop through his "rest" routine, nearly pulling out Charlie's arms before regular morning audiences of fans who came to see their big horse over breakfast.

"You never could back off him much," observed Lucien. "He'd try to tear the barn down. This horse is a brute! Then, too, he's liable to put on too much weight."

Ron Turcotte agreed. "He always took a fantastic amount of work. Needed at least a fast five eighths or so a day before a race."

It was becoming increasingly difficult to hold the big horse back; he wanted to run.

The problem of trying to give Secretariat a vacation was solved on June 19 by an invitation to run him in a match race at Arlington Park, near Chicago, against two old rivals: Linda's Chief and Our Native. The offer was accepted, and Secretariat was allowed to step up his schedule, to the relief of everyone who had been trying to slow down the eager powerhouse.

While Secretariat was being prepared for his trip to Arlington, the controversy over his Preakness time came up again. On a CBS television Sports Special, CBS presented a visual argument for Secretariat's claim to Canonero II's record. Using a split screen, they showed the running of the 1971 Preakness on one half, and the 1973 running on

139

the other. With the two races synchronized, so that both horses left the starting gate at the same instant, the film gave an apparent victory of about 3 lengths to Secretariat. However, one factor that had to be taken into consideration was the actual physical placement of the starting gate, which could vary from two to fifteen feet. Since the actual timing of the race begins when the first horse breaks an electronic beam at the $3/16$ pole, roughly fifteen to twenty feet from the gate, the gate placement could make a slight time difference. CBS synchronized the start as exactly as possible by showing the gate lined up in both instances with a manhole cover by the rail, thus reducing any variation in gate placement to inches. However, the substantial margin of Secretariat's victory indicated that even the placement wouldn't have affected the outcome.

After viewing the CBS program, Penny Tweedy dispatched a telegram to the chairman of the Maryland Racing Commission, J. Newton Brewer, asking for a review of Secretariat's official Preakness time. Her reason for this was not just the question of the Preakness record. If it could be established that Secretariat had set a new record in the Preakness, which many people believed he did, then he would have officially made a clean sweep of *all* the Triple Crown records.

The Commission granted a hearing and also agreed to review the videotape as supporting evidence. However, they decided to adhere to their ruling that in cases of failure of the electronic timing equipment, the official clocker's time had to be taken as final. The official time would remain in effect. Meadow Stable accepted this judgment and pressed the case no further.

Around Barn 5 there was no looking back. The Arlington race had been expanded from its original match race status and now included a few more would-be victims. But

Charlie Davis on lead pony, Billy Silver, leading Secretariat to the track.

Big Red jogging before his prep workout for the Arlington match race.

Lucien Laurin cautioned, "There is no such thing as a cinch around a racetrack." And, accordingly, he stepped up his big horse's training. This was welcome relief to Ron Turcotte, whose arms had also been aching from restraining Secretariat. Big Red had now taken to trying to buck off his riders to free himself to run as fast as he wanted.

Lucien now obliged the big colt and gave him a sharp work. The happy Secretariat breezed a 5 furlongs in :58⁴/₅ and galloped up the three-quarters in 1:12⁴/₅.

Lucien commented, "The Preakness and Belmont were his top forms, and the natural turn of events would be for him to come back a little after the Belmont. But him—it doesn't look like he's ready to slow up yet!"

Once again Secretariat and Eddie were airborne, landing in a Midwest, U.S.A., that had suddenly gone racehorse crazy. The Arlington management marveled at the crowds one horse could draw just by going out for a slow gallop. Veteran horsemen pushed for a spot on the rail as eagerly as the starry-eyed kids just discovering racing.

On Saturday, June 30, an overflow crowd of more than 40,000 came to see him do more than just gallop. Secretariat reacted with his usual calm to all the excitement. Three rivals had been offered up by their sporting owners: Arthur J. Appleton's My Gallant, Mrs. M. J. Pritchard's Our Native, and Phillip Teinowitz's Blue Chip Dan. As the four horses were walking out from the paddock on their way to the track, Secretariat's lead pony, Billy Silver, slipped on the cement walkway and threw Charlie Davis. Immediately, there was a good deal of commotion among the other horses, but Secretariat just stood quietly until everything was back in order.

On the track, his attitude was similar. Breaking slowly from the gate, Secretariat rolled almost nonchalantly around the outside of his three rivals on the Clubhouse turn

Secretariat, all by himself, easily winning the Arlington race.

Riva Ridge becomes a millionaire with his win in the Brooklyn Handicap.

and coasted to a 9 length walkover. It didn't matter to the crowd how easy his win had been. They roared their approval of this super horse, now $125,000 richer.

The big red colt returned from Chicago with his lust to run satisfied for the time being.

The other famous resident of Barn 5 was also busy. On July 4, Riva Ridge produced an Independence Day bang in the Brooklyn Handicap at Aqueduct by shattering the world record for one and three-sixteenth miles with a time of 1:52$^2/_5$. He earned $67,200 for his win, which made him Meadow's first, and racing's twelfth millionaire. Seth Hancock, with Penny Tweedy's go-ahead, wasted no time in putting together another syndication. On July 23, it was announced that Riva Ridge had been syndicated for stud for $5,120,000.

The annual Saratoga meeting was about to begin and, early in the morning, Sunday, July 22, the world's most valuable shipment of horses were vanned from Belmont's Barn 5 to Saratoga Springs. The trip was completed without mishap except for a thirty minute stop for repairs to the van. At 10:30 A.M., the cavalcade rolled onto Union Avenue, and the old ghosts of racing that haunt Saratoga in August retreated temporarily to their elms from the hubbub. Hordes of people were on hand for the arrival of the two horses, but, of the several stable area gates that the Meadow horses could have entered, the main crowd had picked the wrong one. It was the first wrong choice of the Saratoga meeting.

The Laurin stable on the backside of Saratoga's main track was again an armed camp. A cordon of security guards held back press and public who swarmed around the unloading area. It was the usual hullabaloo, and the Meadow Stable crew found themselves more isolated than ever.

As the ghosts of racing recovered and ventured back out upon the awakening old town, they found more signs that this was not a normal race year. The very streets had become a shrine to Secretariat. Blue and white checkered flags, the colors and design of the Meadow racing silks, flew from lamp posts. Souvenir stands were selling everything from Secretariat T-shirts to statues to charm bracelets to . . . manure. The latter was a short-lived enterprise that opened up shop just after the horse's arrival. On a little stand set up by a sulphur spring water fountain, there was displayed a neat row of small brown paper bags, and a sign boasting: "Secretariat manure—$3 a bag." Saratoga had become a Secretariat happening. The town, whose permanent population of 17,300 usually doubles in August, was preparing to accommodate people in layers.

The target of all this attention spent his first few days in Saratoga doing what all horses from downstate New York must do— getting adjusted to the thinner, semi-mountain air. Horsemen and horses alike undergo varying degrees of respiratory, blood, and metabolism changes. This is difficult for some of them, and often a horse's racing form will alter radically here.

Secretariat seemed to feel little effect, although Eddie noticed he was eating fourteen quarts of oats a day rather than the sixteen he usually wolfed down at Belmont. He had never eaten much hay, and that didn't change. To avoid having to adjust to Saratoga's highly mineralized water, both he and Riva Ridge were drinking bottled spring water shipped in from elsewhere.

Secretariat began his Saratoga training routine by being "ponied"—that is, exercised without a rider, led by a man on a lead pony, in this case, Charlie Davis on Billy Silver. Then the big colt was worked up to long slow gallops. It had been decided to point him for the Whitney Stakes on August 4, where he would face older horses for the first time.

For a three year old to compete against older stakes horses is something of an event. For one thing, there is a tremendous maturity gap between a three year old and a four year old. In human terms, it is analogous to competition between a fifteen year old and a twenty year old. The older horse has reached his full growth, but the younger one is still growing. Since the races for older horses tend to be longer, the three year old is also running against a four-year-old's stamina. Even the weight allowance doesn't make up for the difference. However, a four year old competing against five- and six-year-olds doesn't have the same problem, for, to continue the analogy, a twenty year old man competing with a twenty-five year old is a pretty even match. For a three year old to take on older horses and beat them is quite an accomplishment.

While the big horse was preparing for his confrontation with older horses, something unique was happening in American racing. On July 26, it was jointly announced by the NYRA and the Philip Morris Corporation that Meadow Stable had agreed to a match race between Secretariat and Riva Ridge. The race would be inaugurated as the Marlboro Cup and run at Belmont on September 15. The brainchild of John T. "Jack" Landry, vice president for marketing for Philip Morris, himself a race horse owner, the proposed match race immediately touched off a storm of controversy. An accepted practice in

Europe, commercial sponsorship of races was new to the American scene; to many conservatives, this kind of corporate participation had to be proven constructive before they would give it their blessing.

While the Marlboro Cup promised to have redeeming features for the future of racing, an avalanche of other commercial schemes attempted to exploit Secretariat's popularity with something less than justifiable taste. Penny Tweedy was finding it impossible to cope with the volume of requests for commercial releases. On the advice of the NYRA, she designated a theatrical and literary agency in New York City to handle these matters. For the most part, this solved the problem. But comic difficulties did arise from the agency's difficulties in adjusting to the fact they were representing a horse rather than a two-legged star. For example, how does one sue for breach of privacy on behalf of a race horse?

Penny also had to cope with another, more welcome flood of correspondence: Secretariat's ever increasing fan mail—as many as two-hundred letters a day. She had to hire a second secretary just to handle answers and requests for pictures of Secretariat, Penny, Lucien, Ron, Eddie, etc. Penny considered it her obligation to answer as many of the letters and fulfill as many of the requests as possible, and she was tireless in her attention to Secretariat's young fans. They would appear at the track in the chilly early morning hours to see their hero gallop, accompanied by parents, or on special tours (for example, crippled children). She would often join them, answering their eager questions and signing pictures, programs, parimutuel tickets, casts, any surface she could write on. To her, and she knew, to his fans, Secretariat had become much more than a race horse. He was a symbol of something true and wonderful. Something people could believe in. (One U.S. Congressman was reported to have stood up in the House and stated that Secretariat would be a welcome addition to the White House staff because people knew they could trust him.)

At Saratoga, the races began on schedule on June 30. On the third day of the meet, Meadow suffered a setback. Riva Ridge, running in an allowance race to prep him for later stakes, ran second to a 56 to 11 shot named Wichita Oil. Suddenly, there was a dent in the invincibility of Meadow's Murderers' Row, and a first spot of tarnish on the brand new Marlboro Cup.

II: The Whitney at Saratoga

Saratoga was having one of its wet Augusts. The soul-soaking quality of an extended period of Catskill rains can more than match any monsoon season. On the Friday a week prior to the Whitney Stakes, Lucien sent Ron and Secretariat into the soggy morning mist to give the big horse his trial work for the race. Mud seemed to have no effect on Secretariat's ability to destroy stopwatches. With Ron and the exercise saddle adding up to about 130 pounds (he was assigned 119 for the Whitney), Secretariat sloshed through a mile of Saratoga mud in a sizzling 1:34^4/$_5$. The stopwatch read: :11^1/$_5$; :22^4/$_5$; :33^3/$_5$; :45^2/$_5$; :57^2/$_5$; 1:09^1/$_5$; and 1:21^3/$_5$; he had galloped out the mile and an eighth in 1:47^4/$_5$. As an added attraction for the morning audience, he had melted two track records along the way: the mile and the mile and an eighth.

Therefore, it was little wonder that Lucien, who walked out on the track with his son Roger on the day before the Whitney and found it shin deep in sloppy mud, expressed his lack of concern about the awful going.

"Really, the condition of the track makes no difference to him. You know, the track wasn't any better than this last week when he worked so fast. He moves up ten lengths in the mud, no kidding!"

Another trainer who checked the going that morning hoped for something a little different as he watched the army of NYRA track specialists with their battery of heavy equipment treating the track to aid the emerging sun and light wind in drying it out.

Trainer Allen Jerkens, whose homebred charge Onion, owned by Jack Dreyfus' Hobeau Farm, had won by 8 lengths three days before on a fast track, breaking the $6\frac{1}{2}$ furlong record, remarked, "If we don't get any more rain, they'll have the track lightning fast by tomorrow. And I want to hear my horse's feet rattle."

The four-year-old Onion, who was a speed merchant with an impressive record, promised a fast pace. He was just one of the seasoned older veterans that Secretariat was to face in his first venture beyond his age class. In addition, there were the sometimes brilliant stakes winner West Coast Scout and the hard driving Rule by Reason. This did not shape up as a casual outing for Big Red.

But while horsemen looked forward to a real contest, the rising tide of Secretariat followers which now engulfed the old Spa and streamed to the gates of the historic racetrack had come with something else in mind: to see Big Red do his thing again. Horses and riders going to and from the main track area for their early morning works had to make their way through a steady stream of pedestrians. Carrying camp stools, beach chairs, and Racing Forms, the faithful got into place in the queues at the admission gates. There they settled down for the long wait which would insure a vantage point for the horse's appearance. (Three days before, a record early morning turnout of 5000 fans had watched the big horse put in a final half mile blowout, restrained to a slow :$48\frac{1}{5}$ by Ron, as ordered by Lucien.)

That afternoon, for security reasons, the saddling area for the Whitney had been moved from the traditional tree-shaded paddock to the infield in full view of the stands. All eyes were on Secretariat. To experienced horsemen, he looked as though he had lost a little weight. Brilliant sunlight drenched the scene causing the big horse's muscles to jut out in bas-relief. He looked like a living, burnished copper sculpture. It was beautiful weather, a perfect day to see Secretariat. And the conditions were just what trainer Allen Jerkens had prayed for.

The Chenery family was there in force for the saddling, and Howard Gentry was up from Virginia on a horseman's holiday. After Ron had mounted and as Eddie started to lead Secretariat into position for the post parade, Elizabeth Ham reached out to give her very special namesake horse one final pat on the neck. Her solemn expression seemed to say, "Run your best, for something new is being asked of you today."

A record Saratoga crowd of over 30,000 sent him to the start with a 1 to 10 odds vote of their confidence.

As the field of five were settled, one by one, into the gate by starter George Cassidy's assistants, Secretariat displayed an unusual eagerness to get it all over with. He lunged

145

forward in the gate, banging his head against the bars. When the bell finally rang and the gates crashed open, he broke head and head with his field. Then, as Secretariat dropped back in what looked like his old style, jockey Jacinto Vasquez sent Onion to the front. Rounding the first turn and entering the backstretch, Ron and Secretariat seemed to be looking for a spot to leave the traffic jam that had formed behind Onion. Down the backstretch, Vasquez held Onion well out from the deeper footing on the rail. Behind him, Secretariat raced in close quarters with West Coast Scout. In order to challenge the equally weighted (119 pounds) Onion, Ron had to make a choice: swing to the outside on better going and lose valuable ground by going around the wide-racing Onion, or drop down to the heavier going on the rail and take him on the shorter inside route. With the memory of Secretariat's sensational workout in similar heavy going, Ron chose the inside and drove Secretariat up to challenge.

But although the two horses came out of the final turn and entered the stretch in a head and head duel, Secretariat never gave Ron the powerful thrust into the bit that indicates his shift into high gear. Instead, he seemed to labor, and Onion began to draw ahead of him. Ron recalled, "Usually when you wanted to step on the gas with him, you'd just pick his head up, pull him together, and ask him to run. He's very willing, very generous. You switch holds on him and he'll lay right into the bit and start rolling. That day, I kept changing holds and nothing happened. He didn't respond. Also, he really moves from a stick. That didn't work either." The crowd fell almost silent in shock as they watched their mud-caked idol struggle to

gain the advantage. It was no use: Vasquez slowly but steadily increased Onion's lead to win by a length.

The silence prevailed as the horses returned to be unsaddled. The polite upstate crowd refrained from the catcalls or boos that often greet such an upset at Aqueduct or Belmont. But they did honor Onion with some well-earned applause. As the dispirited and mud-splattered Ron Turcotte made his way to the scales, a scene of unrestrained joy unfolded in the winner's circle. Both trainer Allen Jerkens, and his son, Allen Jerkens, Jr., unashamedly wept with happiness and near disbelief.

"This was the day of the horse's life!" exclaimed Allen.

A breeze flurried in the ancient elms as the ghosts gave one another knowing looks. Saratoga's reputation as "the graveyard of champions," was justified again. Secretariat joined illustrious company in his defeat. Racing's two most noted upsets had occurred at Saratoga: Man O'War's defeat by Upset in the 1919 Sanford, and Jim Dandy's 100 to 1 triumph over Gallant Fox in the 1930 Travers.

It was definitely *not* the day of his life for Philip Morris executive Jack Landry. He had, in 1:49$^1/_5$, seen a second puff of something other than cigarette smoke cloud his dream for the Marlboro Cup match race. The going was getting a little muddy in Marlboro Country.

However, the faithful were not to be so easily disillusioned. When the downcast Ron Turcotte emerged from the jockey's room enclosure, he found the equally glum Lucien putting on his best, kindly face and struggling to oblige an onslaught of autograph seekers. Heroes do not die easily.

As the sun set, the blue and white checkered flags still flew from the lamp posts in Saratoga.

That night a friend telephoned Elmer Henbeck, Jr. at Hobeau Farm in Florida to tell him that a horse that he had raised defeated Secretariat.

"Thanks," he replied, "and I'm glad you called today."

"Why?"

"I'll probably get fired in the morning," answered Henbeck.

"Why?" asked the puzzled caller.

"It was I who gelded him!"

It seemed everybody had a theory why Secretariat had been defeated in the Whitney.

One camp said Turcotte had been suckered to the deep going on the inside. Another said that Secretariat had been openly interfered with by his opposition while trying to get to Onion. When he did get to Onion, jockey Jacinto Vasquez, now twice a victor over Big Red, rode a canny race by going to the front, slowing down the pace, and holding his lead. But Vasquez maintained, "I was just lucky to ride against him and win twice when he didn't fire up. The best horses have days like that." When the word came out of the Laurin stable several days after the Whitney that Secretariat had a virus infection and fever, the critics even suggested that the horse had been run with knowledge of his illness. It was an incredible insult to a man like Lucien Laurin, but he stoically endured the storm, suppressing what must have been an overwhelming Gallic instinct to reply with a lance or two of his own.

Ron Turcotte, the target for a large share of the critical barbs, was probably more qualified than anyone to discuss the actual race.

"You had to look at the films with a clear mind. Look at it like you hadn't seen the race.

Okay, we came out of the gate, horses bumped a little. But nothing much. Barely touched. Now we came on to the first turn, Belmonte's horse, West Coast Scout, really veered out and now I came to the inside of him. But all the way, he never got close to me until just before the point of the turn, and even at that time he never brushed me; I always had room. West Coast Scout was in front of me, and I had room inside of me all the time. I was quite a ways off the fence, and people that claim to know so much about racing should be able to judge the distance off the fence a horse is. When you look at the turn from the stands, the more boot and saddle cloth you see, the farther the rider is from the fence. When you get close to the fence, the boots get buried from sight. In the movie in the pan shot, you can see that my boot is way above the fence, which means I was away from the fence.

"What people don't realize is that he never bothered me. As a matter of fact, I came out to get off the rail around the turn—I never really got down to the rail till about one-sixteenth of a mile before the next turn. I didn't go around horses because I didn't feel I could. My horse wasn't running like he should. He should have picked it up around the first turn. He wasn't picking it up. He was just grinding it. I went to the inside because I had all the room in the world. A lot of people say that Onion came in on me. Well, if you look at the film, you could possibly get that impression. But if you look at it close, head on, you will see he never did come in much till he was like a half length in front of me.

"And about the going on the fence. He wasn't laboring at all. The only thing is that Secretariat wasn't himself, and that's the answer to that race. If he was himself, I'd have gone to the front with him early. But when I felt I didn't have the horse I should have under me, I just took the shortest way. The rail was good. I came back and won on the rail in a race later that day. No, the horse just wasn't himself.

"As to his being sick, none of us knew that then. We checked his temperature the morning of the race, and it was okay. But, you know, even with humans, there are times sickness won't show up until you are placed under heavy strain. He didn't act right going to the post, and he was far from himself during the running. In view of the virus showing up soon after that, it must have been coming on him."

For many days, Secretariat continued to run a fever and fall off in condition. An anxious Eddie Sweat watched the colt's appetite dwindle. Gradually, hope was abandoned that he would be well in time to run in the great Saratoga classic, the Travers. The presence of the heavy security around Barn 24 only seemed to seal in the dispirited air that prevailed under its shed. Every morning, Elizabeth Ham went to stalls 10 and 11 and stood a steady vigil as Eddie worked tirelessly with his two big horses. She had seen storms come and go for many a year with Meadow. Storms were meant to be weathered, and she gave one the feeling that if sheer will power could disperse clouds, hers would do it for Meadow Stable.

Penny Tweedy was faced with a decision. Saratoga in August and tradition are synonymous. For years, Christopher Chenery had entertained leading horsemen and their guests at an annual party in the rambling house on North Broadway. It was a wide, classically prim Victorian avenue where a house-to-house list of residents reads like the owners of the post parade for a great classic stakes race. The Meadow party was itself a tradition, with its tables of matchless, aged Kentucky and Virginian hams, crisp tiny biscuits, roast turkeys, old bourbon—and all the other historic horse country delights now seldom encountered. Penny Tweedy decided to continue her father's tradition and give the party. A horse race was a horse race, and a losing one not to be brooded over. That the horse was sick was tragic, but Saratoga in August was a place to savor, not to despair.

Her invitations included a number of press people whom she had come to know as friends. They knew the invitation for what it was: the offer of good food, good drink, and good conversation. It was not a working occasion. Unfortunately, some eager journalists felt that any gathering in excess of one in Penny Tweedy's presence constituted a bona fide public happening. But while Meadow could be a gracious host, it could also be firm in the defence of its hour of privacy—especially in the case of one group of crashers from a society periodical. No one seemed to notice, for the conviviality of the gathering drew the shade on all but tradition for one evening in Saratoga.

Racing continued, but it continued without Secretariat. Lucien let it be known that Secretariat was definitely no-go for the Travers. The crowds had seen Big Red race at the Spa for the last time.

Toward the end of the meeting, Lucien ventured out with Secretariat in an effort to get him started back slowly. The colt broke out in such a sweat galloping that he was returned to hand walking until he was shipped to Belmont.

During the meeting, Onion's trainer, Allen Jerkens, paid $65,000 to buy a horse

Secretariat loosens up for the Arlington.

he'd had his eye on for Hobeau Farm for about a year. This was the four-year-old King Ranch colt Prove Out, who had ankles that always needed work and a reputation for lugging in (pulling or veering toward the inside rail) during his races. It wasn't the sort of event that drew much attention, especially in Saratoga, where horses traditionally change hands for fortunes. It was a significant buy, nonetheless.

As the meeting closed in Saratoga, horsemen packed up their traps and took their reluctant last looks at the beautiful old town for another year. One by one, the vans began to roll out of the stable areas. Once again, the ghosts of racing's past retreated to the shadows with a rustling of the leaves of the ancient elms.

III: The Marlboro, The Woodward, and the Man O'War

Would Secretariat be well soon enough to run in the Marlboro Cup? The new race for which he had been the inspiration had changed its conditions. The allure of a match race between him and Riva Ridge had been dampened by their defeats in Saratoga. It was now an invitational handicap, open to the best horses in the country.

Lucien struggled to bring Secretariat back up to form for the race. A worried Jack Landry fretted every inch of the way with him. He had put a lot on the line for this dream race, and many people whose initial reactions had been hostile, now expressed a grudging respect for the company which had stood fast in the face of the worst kind of uncertainties peculiar to this sport.

Three days before the race, Wednesday, September 12, Secretariat made everyone breathe easier. On this sunny Belmont morning, looking very much his old gleaming red self, he displayed his regained vigor in a lightening 5 furlongs in :57, a fifth of a second faster than Riva Ridge had drilled the same distance the day before. The Meadow people began to smile again.

Lucien and Ron agreed that the colt was as fit as he could be in the time they had had, but both of them wished for yet another week to hone him to an even finer edge. However, Secretariat was, without any question, back up to form in one area. Eddie happily knifed carrots into small pieces to add to the growing feed tub contents which were being consumed to the last oat by the newly healthy glutton, who was only $17,911 short of being a millionaire.

While Lucien had walked a tightrope between taking care of Secretariat's health and drilling him hard enough to bring him up to peak condition, Allen Jerkens had gotten another race into Onion. However, Onion made a poor showing, finishing seventh in the Governor Stakes at Belmont a week before the Marlboro. Jerkens finished out Onion's preparation for the rematch with a final short breeze on the day before the race.

It rained all night before the Marlboro. This did not favor either Riva Ridge or the speedy California stakes horse, the great Cougar II, trained by ace trainer Charley Whittingham for Mary F. Jones. At seven, Cougar II was the oldest of the seven entrants. The Chilean bred horse, racing his last season before retirement, had become a familiar sight in the winner's circle with his trainer, the head-shaved ex-marine, honored as the top trainer of 1971. His horse would carry 126 pounds to Riva's 127 and Secretariat's 124. Whittingham stiffened his challenge by coupling Cougar II in an entry with five-year-old Kennedy Road, 1971 Horse of the Year in his native Canada.

Elliot Burch, the soft-spoken, perceptive trainer for Paul Mellon, entered the lists with Rokeby Farm's formidable Key to the Mint, who had edged out Riva Ridge for the 1972 three-year-old honors. Key to the Mint had a decided liking for off tracks at Belmont.

The only other three year old was the Travers winner, Mrs. Patricia Blass's Annihilate 'Em, another off-track specialist trained by Doug Davis. And then, of course, there was *that* horse—Onion.

It was an awesome collection of thoroughbreds that filed out of Belmont's paddock for the first Marlboro Cup. Collectively, they were worth incalculable millions: they had accounted for more than $6 million in winnings, 64 stakes victories, 5 Eclipse Awards (not counting the awards claimed by owners, trainers, and jockeys involved in the race), the Triple Crown, and a foreign championship.

The afternoon had remained partly cloudy, but the track had dried out well from its soaking the night before—as the fast times for the preliminary races indicated. The horses who did poorly on muddy tracks had nothing to worry about. Considering the outstanding cast assembled for the Marlboro, the crowd of 48,000 was a light turnout. But the cream of the racing world was very much in attendance. There was barely breathing room in the privileged confines of the shady paddocks. Penny Tweedy and the Meadow entourage slowly made their way to the area.

Big Red handles the grass course superbly as he surges to the lead in the Man O'War stakes.

On his way to a five-length victory and a new course record.

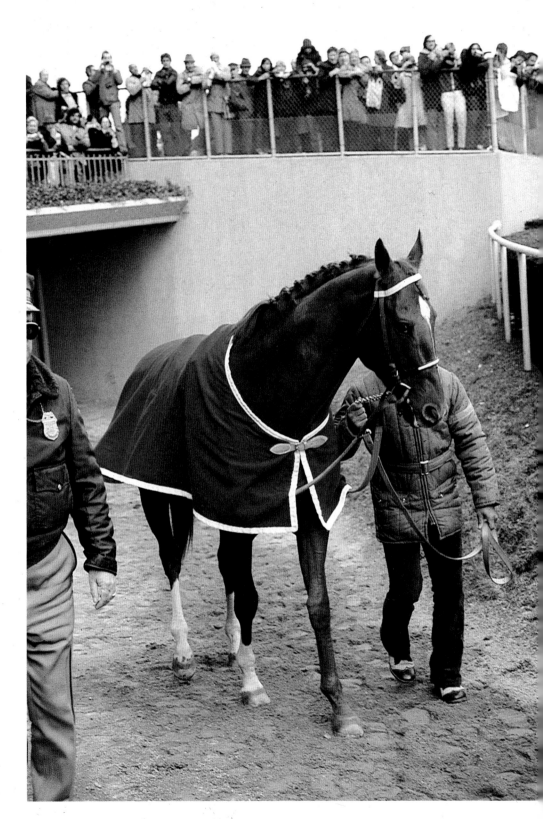

Eddie Sweat leads Secretariat out for his final farewell at Aqueduct.

Secretariat Day. The last gathering of the old team: Lucien, Penny, Eddie, Secretariat, and Ron.

Eddie and Big Red board the plane to Kentucky.

Secretariat's arrival was no secret to horse-loving Kentuckians.

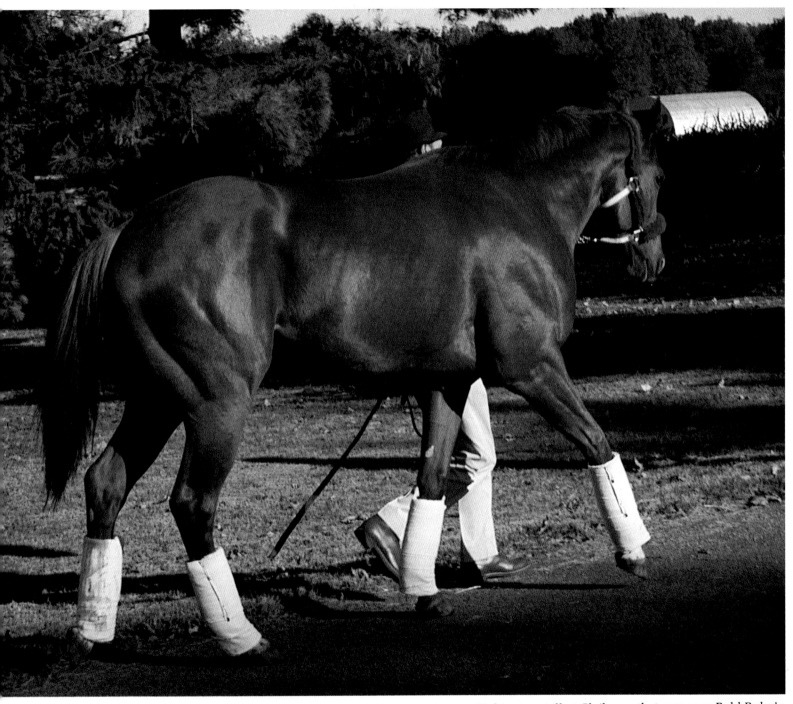

To his new stall at Claiborne that was once Bold Ruler's.

Slowly, because Penny, a slight figure dressed in off-white, was tirelessly and cheerfully signing the endless programs pushed at her by hands straining over and through the fence.

With Ron Turcotte riding Secretariat, Riva Ridge had the services of jockey Eddie Maple for the first time. Tension showed visibly as Lucien briefed his two riders. There wasn't much to tell Ron Turcotte about riding his big red horse. Both Ron and Lucien knew that the ride had to be a cautious one until Secretariat indicated the extent of his recovery. However, Lucien did confide to Ron that Riva was the horse he had to beat. Eddie Maple went to the post knowing that he and Riva were to go all out for the win. Riva and Secretariat were a Meadow team, but there would be no favors for each other. For tense owners and trainers, mother hen grooms, and anxious two-dollar bettors, the long march to the starting gate on Belmont's distant backside seemed interminable. Across that vast infield expanse of greenery and ponds with lazily swimming swans, the horses and colors became almost indistinguishable.

At the gate, George Cassidy's crew of assistants set the ritual into motion like a well-oiled machine. In went Key to the Mint, then Cougar II, Onion, Annihilate 'Em, Kennedy Road, Riva Ridge, and finally, on the far outside—Secretariat.

George Cassidy, cooly poised on the starter's stand, chose the precise moment and let the gates crash open.

Out they came in a wave of color and power. Onion and Kennedy Road rushed to the lead with Riva Ridge right on top of them. Annihilate 'Em and Key to the Mint fell in behind as Secretariat and Cougar II dropped back. Ron, feeling his big horse laying into the bit and acting himself, let him settle into his stride. Down the backside and into the turn, Onion led with Riva Ridge a close second. Then Ron "chirped" to Big Red and the big train gathered steam. Moving around horses, they rolled out of the turn and into the stretch. There, at the head of the long Belmont straightaway, the Marlboro Cup reverted to what its creators had originally intended—a match race between Riva Ridge and Secretariat. Knowing that his horse was totally back to his old form, Ron really set him down at the quarter pole. Eddie Maple was pumping on the game, hard driving Riva Ridge as Secretariat streamed by on the outside. For a few seconds, as the two stablemates were head and head, both riders noticed that the red colt's stride reached past Riva's by about three feet. Then Secretariat drew away to a $3^1/_2$ length lead at the wire in a one-two sweep for Meadow that set a new world record of $1:45^2/_5$ for a mile and an eighth. Onion was 14 lengths behind in fourth position. The Whitney in Saratoga had indeed been the day of his life.

On the way to the winner's circle, Ron detoured Secretariat from the direct route and jogged him the length of the grandstand for a round of applause rarely given by a New York racing crowd.

A beaming Jack Landry met them in the winner's circle for the presentation. A red and white blanket of carnations was draped over Secretariat, and the silver Marlboro Cup presented to the Meadow people.

With this victory, worth $150,000, Secretariat had become the 13th equine millionaire, then ranking eighth on the all-time money-winning list with $1,132,089.

Back at Barn 5, Charlie Davis led Secretariat out to graze for a while after his cooling out. A small crowd of horsemen and their families stood around watching him in admiration.

When Riva Ridge also came out to graze, Elizabeth Ham called out, "Riva, you're beautiful. We love you, too." Penny's sister, Margaret Carmichael, and her brother, Hollis Chenery, also joined in the fuss over Riva. No one was going to let him feel left out that day.

The next day, reassured by the dazzling Marlboro victory that their big red horse was totally back to form, Penny and Lucien announced that he would begin training on the grass. Turf racing was the one area where he still had to prove himself. It was an important one, not only because of the rich grass classics open to him and his offspring in America, but also because European races are all run on grass. Since a number of Secretariat's syndicate owners were either European or interested in European racing, it was desirable that he perform well on this surface.

Not all horses, even top stakes horses, can make the switch from dirt to grass racing surfaces (or vice-versa) and retain their top form. With many horses, their entire way of going, even the pattern of their stride, is altered by the switch. Some improve, some can't handle the change at all. Still others maintain their ability equally well on any surface.

On Monday, Penny announced that Secretariat would be pointed for the $100,000 Man O'War grass classic on October 8. Secretariat galloped during that week; on Friday, Lucien sent him out for his first drill on the Belmont grass. He was accompanied by Riva Ridge, who was also being considered as a possible entrant for the Man O'War, and who was to work separately that morning. Quite

Secretariat and Riva Ridge finish one-two in the Marlboro Cup at Beln

an audience of horsemen had gathered, curious to see how Big Red would handle his new environment.

After a long jog back to the head of the stretch, Ron reversed Secretariat and began to gallop, accompanied by Charlie Davis on Billy Silver. Because of soft going along the rail, the "dogs" (a series of small plastic cones or barriers) had been set up to keep horses about ten feet from the rail. This meant a longer trip around the turns. As they approached the half mile pole, Ron began to ease Secretariat off, and they passed the pole running. Stopwatches clicked. The first quarter, which included the turn, fell away in :25; then, in the final straightaway quarter, the great horse really began to move. As he approached the wire, viewers could see that he was moving with classic grass horse "daisy cutter" action—running with his feet close to the ground and none of the high leg action that slows down some horses on the grass. The stopwatches clicked again. The last quarter had been polished off in :23$^3/_5$, leaving no doubt that for Secretariat grass was for running. (Riva, who had worked the same distance, had gone a full second slower, and did not appear to like the going.)

Dismounting after the return to the stable, Ron exclaimed, "Secretariat loved it!" He remarked later, "His action was beautiful. It never changed, which is an indication he can handle any going. I could ride this horse over broken bottles or a plowed field if we had to! He adapts to anything. After a sixteenth of a mile, he knew exactly what it was." Secretariat's impressive performance on the grass gave Penny and Lucien some leeway in planning their two big horses' racing schedules for the final weeks before the agreed-upon retirement date in November.

First time past the stands in the 1⅝-mile Woodward.

Secretariat (1A) behind Prove Out (5).

Lucien announced, "Our schedule will depend largely on the weather. We will have both entered for the mile and a half Woodward on the main track here on September 29. If it's fast that day, I'll scratch Secretariat and start Riva Ridge. If it rains and the track turns sloppy, I'll run Secretariat. That will also be our plan for the Man O'War and the Jockey Club Gold Cup at Aqueduct. I want that to be known now so the public will understand and the other horsemen can make their plans, too. I don't want anyone to claim we scratched either horse at the last minute and they weren't informed."

Penny then added, "We will not run them together again. We want both to have maximum opportunity before they retire on November 15, and, as Lucien indicated, the weather will control our plans."

Lucien now had to gear Secretariat's training schedule to ready him for a race against the best grass horses in the country, while at the same time peparing him for the eventuality of substituting for the mud-shy

Riva Ridge in the long Woodward if the going came up soft. The drills on the grass continued.

The formidable Allen Jerkens was also busy readying a horse for the Woodward. This was the Hobeau Farm's Saratoga purchase, Prove Out. While observing Lucien Laurin's training schedule for Secretariat like a hawk, the patient, methodical Jerkens stepped up Prove Out's preparation for the Woodward's long haul with a grinding routine: Wednesday—gallop three miles. Thursday—gallop three miles. Friday—walk. Saturday, race day—open, fast gallop for a mile and a quarter.

Allen Jerkens is a big, solemn man consumed by his life as a horseman. It is not only his work but his recreation (he is an ardent polo player). He is regarded by fellow horsemen as a man who specializes in horses other people couldn't make run. As one trainer put it, "Allen is a helluva dangerous man to sell a bad horse to!"

As the day of the Woodward approached,

160

Secretariat begins his rush.   *Up to challenge, to no avail.*

the weather reports got more doubtful. Lucien reluctantly prepared for the possibility that Riva would have to be scratched. No one at Meadow liked the prospect, for they would have preferred to save Secretariat for an all out turf effort in the Man O'War. But, as Penny sighed realistically, "The Woodward is too big a stake just to hand over without a try."

On Saturday morning, it began to rain. Secretariat would definitely have to carry the Meadow silks in the Woodward. Toting 119 pounds, he would face one other three year old, Amen II, also carrying 119, and three older horses carrying heavier weights. Cougar II shaped up to be the main competition, although he was not one to favor mud. The Rokeby Stable's fine mare, Summer Guest, and the Hobeau Farm horse Prove Out were considered by the experts as simply rounding out the field.

By early afternoon, the Belmont track was slop. A crowd of 32,117 had turned out to see Big Red take on older horses again, this

time over the longest distance he had run since the Belmont.

The instant George Cassidy pressed the starter's button, it became a two-horse race. Just as Allen Jerkens had decreed that Onion go to the front in the Whitney, so today jockey Jorge Velasquez rushed Prove Out into immediate command as the gates opened in front of the stands. Ron Turcotte wasted no time sending Secretariat from the outside post position to chase the leader. Prove Out, who had previously been raced in blinkers and had "weaved" erratically, today ran without the vision-restricting hood. He went straight as an arrow.

Velasquez held his mount to a painfully slow pace as they rounded the turn and entered the backstretch. He recalled, "I was just trying to save my horse. When I saw that big choo-choo train beside me, I thought he'd win easy. I slowed it up only so I could save my horse for the end and maybe get second money."

But Turcotte didn't want any part of that

Prove Out defeats Secretariat by 4½ lengths.

slow pace. He could feel Secretariat starting to laze a little under him, and he moved to shake him up. "Hi-hya, Big Fella, let's go, big fella!" He began pumping with every inch of his muscular frame and managed to get Secretariat to open up a length and a half lead. The crowd roared with delight as they anticipated another of the big red machine's spellbinding performances.

But as they approached the final turn, Ron began to sense that something was wrong. The big horse hadn't really grabbed the bit, and he wasn't increasing the pace. And the fractions showed it—in the Belmont Secretariat had traveled the first three-quarters in 1:09⁴/₅; this day, it took him 1:13²/₅. Ron moved Secretariat out from the rail to some better going, hoping to pick up speed. Still no response. The big horse was tiring!

Behind them Jorge Velasquez' heart skipped a beat. Turcotte had gone to the whip! The big horse must be hanging it up!

Velasquez had kept Prove Out right on the rail, saving every precious inch of ground and ignoring the deeper going. His horse was carrying seven more pounds than Secretariat. As they approached the quarter pole, Velasquez drove Prove Out through on the inside to challenge the laboring Secretariat. Eyeball to eyeball, they matched strides.

It was an all out stretch duel, and its outcome was decided by the crack of Velasquez' whip on the chestnut flanks of Prove Out. The horse responded as if he'd been shot from a cannon, and began to open daylight on Secretariat. Incredibly, the lead grew longer and longer. Now Velasquez settled down to a pumping hand drive on his horse. They had it won! They drew out to cross the wire 4¹/₂ lengths in front of the driving Secretariat, who completed the course a full 2¹/₂ seconds behind his Belmont stakes record.

The hardcore race crowds of metropolitan New York are a cynical bunch with a short sense of loyalty to defeated favorites. Actually, they love an upset, and when Ron Turcotte brought his defeated champion in to unsaddle, they rubbed it in—*hard.*

"How's it feel to be beaten by a *good* horse?"

"SUPER FLOP!"

"Turcotte, you bum, you couldn't ride in a boxcar!"

It was harsh and ignoble treatment of a gallant pair that had provided them with such memorable races.

Prove Out and Jorge Velasquez, on the other hand, enjoyed a riotous greeting as they made their approach to the winner's circle. For Allen Jerkens, it was a moment of total fulfillment. Over and over, he repeated in happy delirium, "I can't believe it. It just doesn't seem real!"

But it was. There was little doubt that the sluggish pace in the early stages had been no help to Secretariat, but whether or not it was crucial to the final outcome was a matter of conjecture.

Once again, Ron Turcotte recounted his impressions of a losing race:

"He ran a great race. He just plain got tired. It's logical. In the time we had between races after he was sick, we really primed him up for the mile and an eighth in the Marlboro. Lucien had been forced to drill him like he was made of steel! Then we switched after the Marlboro and gave him a slow half on the grass and then a mile in one thirty eight. Then we ask him to go a mile and a half. Actually, we were aiming for the Man O'War later on, but instead it came up wet and he had to go the mile and a half in the Wood a week sooner. No, he ran a big race, but I felt him start to weaken as we hit the stretch, he just got tired. Jerkens' horse didn't."

Still another comment came from the man who had engineered two upsets against the great horse: Allen Jerkens. "Secretariat is the best horse I ever saw on his peak performances, which give him an edge over, say, Citation." Then, he cautioned Secretariat's detractors from gloating too much over the Woodward. "Don't forget, except for Prove Out, he was going to win another stake by many lengths."

But the Woodward loss caused trainers to reappraise their chances in the Man O'War stakes. Before, the prospect of facing Secretariat had indicated a small field in the grass classic; now, the defeat of the formidable champion promised the opposite.

The most noteworthy shift in plans came from trainer MacKenzie "Mac" Miller, the tall, good natured Kentuckian who handled Cragwood Stable's Tentam, the little horse whom most experts considered the finest grass runner in the country.

"Tentam can now be regarded as a starter in the Man O'War," Mac told the journalists one morning. "I wanted no part of running my horse against Secretariat, but this seems to be the season for changing plans. Now you can say I've joined the club. Seriously, what occurred to Secretariat on Saturday caused me to adjust my plans, and if all goes well, we'll run Monday. Of course, I am hoping for good footing."

Allen Jerkens, not one to rest on past laurels, was busy readying Hobeau Farm's Triangular for the race. A victory there could produce a triple crown of another sort by taking down Secretariat with three different challengers. Such dreams are what make horse racing such a seductive game.

Lucien Laurin was doing a minimum with his big horse. Secretariat had run a hard mile and a half, so it was hardly necessary to throw any long works into him. Meadow had also joined the plan changers; they would couple Secretariat with Riva Ridge in the Man O'War. As the week wore on, however, this idea was chopped back to the original plan of running Riva Ridge later in the Jockey Club Gold Cup. The weatherman was making ominous predictions again, and the combination of grass and wet going was not in Riva's favor.

Mac Miller had his eye on the weather vane also. "Tentam likes to hear his feet rattle, and if he can't, I should hesitate to start him."

Secretariat rattled his feet loud and clear for all to hear on the Friday before the Man O'War. Going five-eighths of a mile "around the dogs" (about ten feet from the rail) in :56$^4/_5$, he gave spectacular notice that the opposition might just be a little overconfident. His performance delighted Lucien Laurin, and furrowed Mac Miller's good-natured brow. "My colt worked well, and I was fully satisfied," said Mac, "but I also saw Secretariat in his move and it almost floored me. At times he is frightening. I've never seen a colt with more fluid, marvelous action. He's certainly got rhythm in his bones! But then, we'd like to get a shot at consideration for the grass title this season, and we can't very well accomplish this end by staying in the barn, particularly if Secretariat should run one of his big races and win."

Gene Schwartz, the chief clocker at the NYRA tracks, senior of a set of men who rarely miss a horse or a split second in the dim early hours, remarked, "I don't know what happened to Secretariat when he lost three times. But when he's *right,* I don't see how it's possible for him to lose—and he *sure* seems right at the moment."

It is rare that a racehorse, even a great one, can come back after a grueling mile and a half race such as Secretariat had run in the Woodward and five days later work the swiftest 5 furlongs ever clocked on grass. Just such a thought was probably on the mind of every trainer and much of the Columbus Day crowd of 35,878 fans as they watched Secretariat, his giant red frame gleaming in the sun, and six opponents parade to the post for the Man O'War stakes.

The big horse entered the gate completely relaxed and stood quietly. When George Cassidy let them go, Secretariat bounded out evenly with the pack. Then, after a little less than an eighth of a mile, he suddenly seemed to become almost airborne. Here was what the crowd had come to see: this spectacular streak of red erupting from between horses to open up a clear lead. As they picked up the pace, Ron talked to the horse, quietly, confidently, "Easy, easy, big fella. We got a

long way to go." The ears pricked backward as the colt listened to his rider.

They rounded the first turn, opening the lead and saving every inch of ground. As the field entered the backstretch, Jorge Velasquez on Tentam, who had dropped back and saved ground, eased the current grass champion to the outside to pass horses and begin his chase. But Big Red had no time for challengers. Neither Jorge Velasquez nor Allen Jerkens, whose Triangular was already outrun, were going to have another chance at defeating Secretariat that day.

Ron let Big Red settle into his ground-eating stride, and the colt gave and gave. They entered a world all their own in which the only sound was the rhythmic pounding of the great horse's hooves, the bellows of the great lungs, and Ron's quietly steadying voice. "Whoa, big fella, easy now."

Behind them, Jorge Velasquez was tantalized by the easy, almost lazy appearance of the way Secretariat was striding. His own mount, the hard driving, game little Tentam couldn't close ground on the seemingly floating red figure in front of them. As they entered the turn, Velasquez gathered his horse and began a last desperate run at the infuriating apparition. Then he saw Ron Turcotte almost casually begin to move his hands on Secretariat's neck. The flying dirt seemed to double for an instant, smacking into Velasquez' clear plastic goggles. Then there was nothing but the sound of his own horse's labored breathing and the faltering pounding of his hooves.

Stopwatches reeled off testimony to another of Big Red's incredible performances—and to a great feat of training by Lucien Laurin. A mile and a quarter in 2:00, a mile and a half (and victory by 5 lengths) in 2:24$^4/_5$

—a new course record. And then, as an encore, Meadow's champion eased up the mile and five furlongs in 2:37⅘, equaling the world record for that distance on *any* surface.

The crowd greeted him with roaring approval. The Horse of the Century had more than amply vindicated himself.

Mac Miller thought so, too, and he gallantly conceded, "I saw today the greatest horse I've seen in my lifetime—on dirt *or* grass. I must say I don't want to run against him again."

An emotional Lucien Laurin was moved to say that he was glad he had lived long enough to see a horse like Secretariat. And Ron Turcotte added, "He's the greatest, he's so far above any other horse I've ever ridden. . . ."

But amidst the joy in the winner's circle, Lucien and Penny were thinking ahead to Secretariat's retirement date of November 15. The time was so short now, and speculation grew over where Big Red would make his last start.

What new worlds could Secretariat still conquer? Some people wanted to see him matched against the diverse field of horses from different countries scheduled to run in the Washington, D.C., International. Others wanted him to go back against Prove Out in the two-mile Jockey Club Gold Cup at Aqueduct. And then there was the $125,000 Canadian International on the grass in Toronto.

Penny had her mind made up, and she stated her reasons clearly. "Riva Ridge will run his last race in the Jockey Club Gold Cup, and of the races mentioned for Secretariat, I favor the Canadian race. Both our trainer, Lucien Laurin, and our jockey, Ron Turcotte, are Canadians, and this brings a degree of sentiment into the decision. Also, Mr. E. P.

Taylor and the other people in Toronto have done so much for racing up there and in the United States the past few years, I believe it would be nice to reciprocate."

But amidst all these eager plans, a bittersweet resignation had descended on the people of Meadow Stable. They had only too clearly in mind that their Big Horse was to run only one more race. Then the golden days of glory would be over forever.

Elizabeth Ham and Penny lead Secretariat into the winner's circle after the Man O' War.

EIGHT

Last Hurrah

I: The Canadian International

On October 18, there was an official announcement: Secretariat's last start would be in the $125,000 added Canadian International Champion Stakes at Woodbine on Sunday, October 28. Like the other Big Red, Man O'War, Secretariat was to end his racing career in Canada. Turf writers glumly began to sharpen their pencils to write their farewell assessments of The Horse of the Century.

The day the announcement was made, Ron Turcotte was thrown from Awaited Man during the first race at Belmont. The tough little Canadian barely avoided being killed by the slashing hooves around him by rolling under the track rail. Bruised and shaken, he spent the rest of the day in the hospital.

But the next morning, the battered jockey gamely showed up to give Big Red his final drill for the Canadian classic.

"You're a sight," remarked Eddie as Ron stuck his swollen face in Secretariat's doorway.

"I feel worse than I look, too," admitted Ron. But he was able to ride.

Big Red felt fine, and he showed it. Under a strong hold from Ron, he skipped over the Belmont grass in fractions that saw the first quarter in :25$^1/_5$, the half mile in :49, the 6 furlongs in 1:13, and the mile in 1:37$^1/_5$. He eased out a mile and a quarter in 2:02$^3/_5$. The clockers all agreed he looked ready and fit for Canada.

The week before, Lucien had flown to Woodbine to inspect the hillside turf course. He had mentioned to the management that the grass seemed dangerously long, and that he felt the turf strip should be cut and rolled. It was the track's practice to keep the grass a little long to ensure that the course would not be damaged. It turned out that the grass was extra long because of a prolonged wet spell, but Lucien was assured that it would be cut before the race. Satisfied that all would be well for Secretariat's last race, Lucien left for New York.

On Monday, October 22, Eddie Sweat led Secretariat up the ramp onto the chartered plane that would take them to Rexdale, a suburb of Toronto, about five minutes from the Woodbine race course. Big Red's arrival at Toronto's international airport a little before 4 P.M. had generated all the fanfare of a conquering hero's march. An admiring army of photographers, reporters, television crews, and just plain Secretariat lovers had converged on the airport. That evening, he found himself bedded down in Barn 8 at Woodbine, watched over by a team of nine security guards—and protected from any intrusions by the ever-present Eddie.

The next day, a bus packed with schoolchildren passed by on the roadway near the barn. A guide announced through a loudspeaker, "This is an important barn, and there are some very famous people standing here. That little man with the brown coat and the white hair is Lucien Laurin, trainer of Secretariat. And that is Secretariat himself."

In the stable doorway, Eddie Sweat chuckled.

"What're you laughin' at?" asked Lucien with a rueful grin. "Now all those kids are gonna remember me as the little guy with white hair!" But then kids remember Santa Claus, too, and he's a little guy with white hair.

Ron Turcotte and Lucien shuttled back and forth between Toronto and New York, dividing their time between Secretariat's Woodbine preparation and their New York racetrack duties. Most of the big horse's outings were light work, but he displayed a definite liking for the curious, hilly Marshall turf course with its dips and bumps. Ron Turcotte remembers the first breeze: "He was fantastic. You only have to show him something once. He had never been on a downgrade before and balked in the first furlong. He switched leads and bobbled again. It was new to him. Then he settled down and adjusted perfectly. This is the smartest and boldest horse I ever rode. He has never chickened out on anything."

Everything seemed to be going according to plan until the Wednesday before the race. Then a foul claim in the feature race at Aqueduct was made by second placed jockey Braulio Baeza on Sea Sister against Ron Turcotte, who had ridden the apparent winner, Speak Action. The stewards decided the charge was a valid one and handed Ron a five-day riding suspension. Since this penalty was automatically effective at all tracks, he was destined to watch rather than ride Secretariat's last race. And this at the very track where he had ridden his first race! It was one of the most shattering setbacks in his riding career.

Eddie Maple, who had ridden Riva Ridge in the Marlboro, was given the assignment on Secretariat. The day before the Canadian race, Eddie rode Riva Ridge in his last race, the mile and three-quarter Jockey Club Gold Cup. The gentle, bighearted horse who was Meadow's first champion finished an inglorious last. It was a dismal end to an illustrious career, and the jockey flew to Toronto that evening in a disconsolate mood.

Ron Turcotte missed him at the airport.

He returned to his hotel to find that Eddie had already checked in. Ron Turcotte recalls:

> I phoned him and He said he was already in bed.
>
> "Do you work in the morning?" I asked.
>
> "No," he said.
>
> "Well, c'mon over," I said, "because I gotta tell you something."
>
> "I'm tired," he said.
>
> "C'mon," I said, "I know you feel bad. I feel bad the same as you about Riva Ridge, but you got tomorrow to think about now."
>
> Eddie came over and we talked.
>
> "Look, Eddie," I said, "I'm not the trainer, and I can't tell you anything. They'll tell you how they want you to ride. But for God's sake, don't use Big Red for nothing chasing a sprinter. There's no way in the world Kennedy Road's* gonna go one and a half miles off a three-quarter-mile race with less than a month in between. But he's the speed horse, and he's the only one who can do any damage."
>
> "You just get the old boy relaxed. He'll respond anytime, he doesn't know how to quit or to be afraid."**

The day of the Canadian International was a wet, miserable Sunday, so dark that it was hard to see. A heavy mist that was almost rain dampened everything. Despite the eerie gloom, Woodbine had a packed house of 35,117 fans, who had come from all over to see Secretariat run for the last time.

In the paddock, the colorfully uniformed Mounties reminded the Americans that this was Canada. As Eddie Sweat led the big red colt in to be saddled, the cheering began and spread up through the grandstand. But the Meadow people were uneasy. Penny Tweedy remembers, "We were very tense before the race since he was at a strange track and the weather was a big factor. The grass appeared to be slippery and a lot of things were chancy." Someone jokingly suggested that since it was so dark the track really should have night lights. No one laughed. The perennially tense Lucien performed the ritual of saddling and girthing his big horse for the last time. Then it was riders up, and Eddie Maple rode Big Red out to his final test.

Under the European scale of weights employed in Canada, the three-year-old Secretariat was to carry 117 pounds; his rivals, all four years old and over, had to shoulder 126 pounds. This was a nice advantage, but as Eddie Maple observed, "He could carry a house and still get the job done."

It was a dark, sodden post parade, but Secretariat made his own sunshine. The admiring crowd made no secret of their partiality and cheered him all the way to the starting gate.

Breaking on the outside, Secretariat ran evenly past the stands the first time under strong restraint by Eddie Maple. Then down the backside a duel began with Kennedy Road, who, as predicted, was setting the pace. In the darkness, it was hard to see clearly what was going on. Ron Turcotte, whose fists were clenched so tight the knuckles were white, recalls how he saw it:

> . . . when I watched the race, I saw Kennedy Road take the lead and I saw Eddie and Big Red move up.
>
> When he went to Kennedy Road at the

---

* Kennedy Road, 1971 Horse of the Year in Canada, and a keen competitor in the United States, was renowned as a sprinter. He appeared to be Secretariat's main competition in the race.

** From an article by Ron Turcotte in the *Toronto Sun*.

half-mile pole, I felt he should have gone right by. But he didn't.

Something must have gone wrong, I thought, but I couldn't see because they went behind the odds board and, when I did pick them up, Secretariat was in front.

"Did you get bumped at that half-mile pole?" I asked Eddie later.

"Hard," he said, "I had to gather my horse and steady him or I might have been knocked off my feet."

"Did he go whoomp?" I asked.

"I had him steadied because I could see it coming," Eddie said.

Kennedy Road came out and bumped him hard. He must be a hard horse to ride.

Considering that bump—which most of us didn't see—Eddie Maple rode the horse exactly the way I would have.

They were going for a track record, but I knew there was no way because of the wind. The horses had to run into it along the backstretch. Consider that they had to run the backstretch twice and the stretch only $1\frac{1}{2}$ times.

Track conditions?

They were faster yesterday than when we worked out on Thursday morning.

But the wind made the difference.

Eddie shook the stick at him twice, once at the $\frac{1}{4}$ mile pole and again at the $\frac{1}{2}$ mile pole.

With this horse, you only have to shake the stick. Once in a while, mind you, you have to tap him with it just to let him know you'll use it if you have to.*

Eddie Maple said in remembering the race, "I really had to grab for him when the other horse brushed us. That was it—Secretariat just went to the lead by himself. I guess he got mad. I never really urged him until the quarter pole."

*From an article by Ron Turcotte in the *Toronto Sun*.

Big Red crossed the finish line $6\frac{1}{2}$ lengths mad and the grandstand went wild with cheering.

A happy Meadow crew awaited him in the winner's circle, all smiles in the still unrelieved gloom and misty rain. When the presentation had been made and Eddie had blanketed Secretariat and started to lead him from the area, a somber Lucien turned to Penny Tweedy. "That's it," he said.

Penny smiled a little wistfully. "You heard him, boys," she said to the reporters, "That's it. The boss has spoken."

Secretariat's racing days were over.

One final argument was thrown into the Secretariat–Man O'War debate: Secretariat's formidable record against older horses. His victories over them in the Marlboro, the Man O'War, and the Canadian International put his detractors at somewhat of a disadvantage when they compared them with Man O'War's defeat of Sir Barton as their only bullet. It has been written that Sir Barton was so sore that his trainer asked for a guarantee on the purse.

But, argued the Man O'War holdouts, remember that Man O'War had a record of twenty wins out of twenty-one starts, while Secretariat's record was twenty-one starts, sixteen wins, three losses, and one disqualification.

And so the debate will go on—moot, except perhaps to those who dwell in that point in time and space where a match between those two legends might finally be arranged.

II: Farewell at Aqueduct

Rain and fog delayed Big Red's departure from his final battleground. It was late the

Ron Turcotte sits out Red's last race with Eddie Arcaro.

Eddie Sweat leads his Big Horse out for his last race.

Secretariat is all alone as he wins at Woodbine, the last race of his career.

Secretariat wearing his Canadian Maple Leaf victory blanket.

next day before Eddie set Secretariat's feed tub into his own stall at Barn 5.

Secretariat had gone out for his last race, but not his last farewell to the crowds that loved him. Not that anyone wanted to say good-bye to Big Red—in fact, an anguished wave of protests began to be heard about the retirement of racing's brightest star in decades after only two seasons. He had brought a freshness and vitality to racing that it sorely needed. This gleaming red chestnut with the three white feet and the white star and stripe on his forehead had become a hero to millions of people all over the country. It was hard to accept the fact that they would never again see this shining red horse sweep down the stretch in another of his spectacular finishes.

But economic realities left no alternative for Meadow Stable. Secretariat's future contribution to racing would be a long-term one through his priceless bloodlines. Himself the culmination of the years of careful breeding and crossing of strains that Chistopher Chenery and "Bull" Hancock had so assiduously worked at, the "perfect horse" was now about to pass on his bloodlines in the hope of creating yet another "perfect horse."

On Tuesday, November 6, 1973, Secretariat made his final public appearance. It was "Farewell to Secretariat" Day at Aqueduct. Your average New York racegoer can be a

Secretariat at Claiborne.

Lawrence Robinson, stud manager, gives Big Red a bath.   Mares at Claiborne.

Secretariat.

Secretariat showing his best on the grass winning the Man O'War at Belmont Park.

pretty hardbitten, cynical character. He will shout with ecstasy over a win, and curse like a drill sergeant at a bad ride. You do not often make him cry. But that day there were tears enough in the stands at Aqueduct.

On a raw but sunny day, 32,900 people had packed the place to see Big Red for the last time. Here, where he had first carried the blue and white racing silks of Meadow Farm, he made his final bow to the public who had followed him from the beginning—the public who had made him their hero.

Eddie Sweat led Secretariat through the approach tunnel under the stands to the saddling area. Charlie Davis rode alongside them on lead pony Billy Silver.

"He knew there was sump'n wrong," said Eddie. "There wasn't no other horses, and it made him kinda nervous, you know."

They were met in the paddock by Penny, Lucien, Ron, Elizabeth Ham, the Chenery clan, and an army of notables from the New York Racing Association. And, of course, for the last time, by the press corps who had traveled the long road with him. The atmosphere was charged with emotion. Jimmy Kilroe, the respected California racing secretary observed, "I think he absolutely revitalized racing." He paused and then continued, "We must believe in something." Jack Krumpe, president of the New York Racing Association, said reverently, "He was a power that transcended racing. You didn't have to know *anything* about racing to appreciate that great mass of power, that beauty."

While Eddie and Charlie led a restless Secretariat around the walking ring, there was an official presentation of gifts and memorabilia to all those who had been involved in Big Red's career.

Farewell: Secretariat Day at Aqueduct, November 6, 1973.

Parading to the applause of his public.

Finally, Penny Tweedy, bundled in a fur coat and clutching a bouquet of roses, stepped forward to a microphone to say good-bye on behalf of her great horse. Her voice breaking with emotion and her eyes welling with tears, she said:

"The most wonderful thing we do have is the memory of Secretariat in his moments of triumph. We have also been proud of him in his moments of defeat.

"Having a horse like Secretariat is something that you pray might happen to you once in a lifetime, and we've all loved every minute of it.

"But I wanted to say something else. I wanted to thank all of you who have cared so much about this horse, who have been so loyal in supporting him, who've given us, the people that take care of Secretariat, such wonderful expressions of your warmth and affection for him.

"And for all of us, I say, thank you to *you.*"

That was it. The crowd was totally silent. Their big horse was to appear on the track one more time. In the stillness, Lucien Laurin began to saddle the now fidgeting Secretariat. Eddie stood at his colt's head, one hand firmly holding him in place, the other gently rubbing his nose. The saddling completed, Ron Turcotte stepped forward for his last leg up on the big red horse who had "floated" him to so many spectacular triumphs.

Horse and rider, led by Eddie Sweat, started for the track. As they left the paddock, two small, tearful girls held up a sign over the fence along the path: "Good-bye, Secretariat. We love you."

Eddie stepped on the track and released the chain snap to free Big Red. As Ron and Secretariat moved off the silence in the stands exploded into turbulent applause.

"*The Horse* is on the track," came over the loudspeaker from announcer Dave Johnson.

To the resounding cheers of heartfelt farewells, Ron jogged Secretariat up to the quarter pole and back the length of the stands. For the last time, Big Red entered the winner's circle, and, for the last time, a wreath of flowers was thrown over his saddle.

Lucien Laurin remembers, "I looked up in those stands at all those people cheering him, and I thought, they are never going to see another one like him."

Then he chuckled in that delightful way of his, "I thought it was a wonderful going away party, but I guess I loused it up. My eyes watered and my voice choked up. As for Secretariat, he got mad when he realized he wasn't going to run. He knew this when he came back to the winner's circle without a race. Mrs. Tweedy moved in to pose with him, holding her bouquet, and he was so mad he tried to eat the flowers."

Ron took the racing saddle off his big horse and affectionately slapped him on the flank. Eddie threw the blue and white wool cooler over him. With Charlie and pony Billy Silver beside them, he led Secretariat away, patting him on his withers.

As the little group made their way down the track for the last time, a large cloud suddenly appeared in what had been a clear sky. Its shadow entirely darkened the stands. But in the distance, some of Secretariat's copper coat could still be seen, shining in the sun.

Going off the race track for the last time.

179

NINE

To the Land of His Forefathers

There was now one final, sentimental journey. At 10:30 A.M., Sunday, November 11, 1973, a handful of people gathered at Belmont Park to witness the departure of Secretariat and Riva Ridge for Claiborne Farm. To forestall mobs of press and public, the journey had been planned with the secrecy of a wartime troop movement. Among the well-wishers was Ron Turcotte with his family, several of the NYRA's top officials, and some horsemen who just happened on the scene.

As Eddie Sweat went into the stalls to put on the two champions' shipping blankets, the horses acted strangely nervous. They sensed this was not routine. Their training schedules had been cut down to a minimum since Secretariat's Canadian race, and they knew they were not being shipped to a race. Lucien cocked his head over toward the two stalls and remarked with a trainer's pride, "Both these horses are going to stud perfectly sound." Secretariat, at only three, was also going as the fourth richest race horse in history, with total winnings of $1,316,808.

The van arrived. As Eddie led Secretariat to the ramp, the big colt, normally a docile loader, balked. He twisted his head back toward the row of sheds as though he knew he was leaving for good. Then he turned back and calmly walked into the van. Riva Ridge, usually a placid gentleman of a horse, was nervous and agitated going up the ramp. Eddie spoke softly into Secretariat's ears, "You ain't goin' to no race now, Red, you goin' to a new place to have your children."

Eddie had been up all night with a stomach virus and was still not feeling well. I asked him where Charlie Davis was. "He's in the bunk house in the bed an' won't come out. He doesn't want to see 'em go."

181

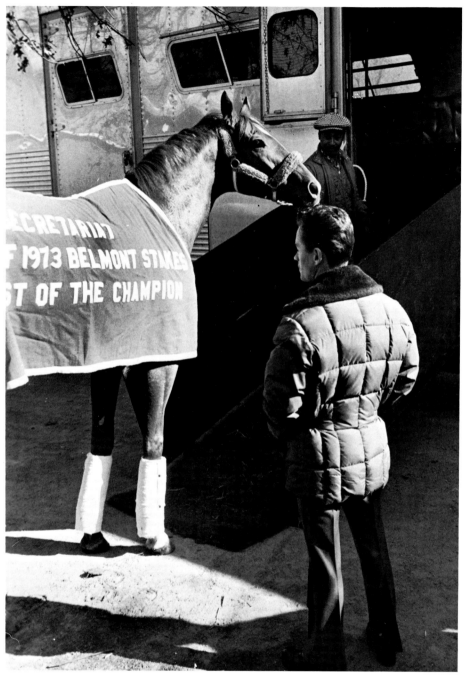

Turcotte watches a legend depart.

11 A.M.: The convoy moved out. Both horses, always good shippers, fretted badly in the van. Eddie had to move constantly from one to the other, comforting each with reassuring rubs and soft words. Lucien Laurin, in a car trailing the van, said later that he felt as though he was following a hearse, not a horse van. "That's how bad I felt." This from the same man who once told a reporter, "I'll be happy when it's all over."

A blue and white chartered airplane was waiting at the airport. Although the plane's colors were simply those of the airline, at this point it somehow seemed a grand and deliberate gesture.

By now, both horses had calmed down and went up the ramp onto the plane with no trouble. Following them were Penny Tweedy, Lucien Laurin, Elizabeth Ham, Eddie Sweat, a three-man film crew from the NYRA, the two Murty men, Bill Nack (a sportswriter), myself, the pilot, co-pilot, and the crew.

Murty Brothers, professional horse air cargo men, did their usual superb job readying the portable stalls and the horses in them for the flight. When all stays and braces were in place, the doors were closed. The plane started to taxi onto the runway for takeoff. Penny Tweedy, declining along with everyone else to take a seat with safety belts, braced herself and stood by Riva Ridge. The two prop jet engines roared, there was the feeling of increasing speed, and then we were suddenly airborne.

12:15 P.M.: It had been a smooth takeoff. Secretariat had put his head under Eddie's arm as the plane had begun its rush down the runway. "It's okay, Red, I'm here. We've done this all before."

Once airborne, everyone relaxed. Murty Brothers had set up a table behind Secretariat's stall. Now they put out iced champagne, Russian vodka, good Kentucky bourbon, and box lunches. "This is a Murty champagne flight," said Mr. Murty. "Not our usual thing, but when you carry two fellas like these it calls for something different."

I sat down next to Penny Tweedy in one of the seats set up in the rear of the cargo area. She pointed at the two stalls in front of us, one on either side, enclosed in the great dark tube of the plane's fuselage. "See those two stalls in that big dark tunnel? That's just the way my life has been for two years now, compressed into a confined area taken up primarily by those two horses. It's hard to believe it's all over."

As the engines droned on, Riva Ridge began to fret. The equally fretting Lucien Laurin who, like Eddie, had a touch of virus and a terrible cold to boot, fed Rolaids to Riva and himself. Eddie, standing with the now placid Secretariat, switched stations to soothe the increasingly nervous Riva. Eddie, whose stomach continued to be in such poor shape that he turned down the lavish Murty lunch, never once left his two charges.

While Eddie was calming Riva, Elizabeth Ham, looking soft and motherly in her Persian lamb coat and mink hat, stood by Secretariat, crooning to him as she gently patted him. Her namesake had come a long, long way since her first comments on the colt "you just have to like" had been entered in her Meadow Farm notebook.

The pilot, Neff Dee, stepped back into the cabin of the plane to have a look at his distinguished passengers. He commented that he had flown Secretariat three times and

Ron busses Secretariat goodbye.

183

Big Red takes a reassuring grip on Eddie's jacket as the plane takes off.

that the big colt had always been the ideal passenger. Then, he invited anyone who wished to join the crew to come to the cockpit for a view. Miss Ham, always keen for a good ride, joined him.

It was a beautiful day for flying and an incredibly smooth flight. The perfect journey to their new home for the two champions.

The plane began a gradual descent and, almost without its passengers realizing it, touched down in a feather-soft landing at Lexington's Bluegrass Field.

2:10 P.M.: The plane taxied to a halt and the cargo doors were opened to reveal that the horses' shipping secret had been slightly less well guarded in Kentucky. A modest crowd of 200 or 300, mostly local press and amateur photographers, was waiting. But they were quiet and well behaved. Penny Tweedy, tired and emotionally on edge, declined interviews.

At the bottom of the ramp was a tense Seth Hancock. He immediately took charge of the entire operation, directing the transfer of the two colts from the plane through the crowd to the van. "I won't relax until I see them

184

safe in those stalls at the farm," he replied when someone quipped that he could breathe easy now.

A police escort, lights flashing, accompanied the two vans to Claiborne. Special passes had been issued to the cars permitted in past the main gate.

Arriving first, we were able to watch the two vans move slowly up the long farm lane. Secretariat, who was unloaded first, was full of steam, jumping around and snorting. He was led now not by Eddie Sweat, but by Claiborne's stud manager, Lawrence Robinson, who was having quite a time trying to hold on to the powerful horse. Secretariat at one point managed to swing around and cowkick his new handler in the behind. Eddie Sweat stood to one side watching critically. Secretariat cocked his head over to Eddie as if to ask, "Is it okay? Are you there?"

He was led off to one of the immaculate stallion barns and into a stall. The stall of his late sire, Bold Ruler. There were two brass plaques on the door; one said, "Bold Ruler," the other, "Secretariat, Triple Crown Winner." Eddie had followed the parade and watched as Seth Hancock personally unwrapped the shipping bandages from the six-million-dollar legs.

Eddie stood by and gave advice on what to expect from Secretariat in the stable: how he behaved, how he ate, what he was afraid of, what he liked. His baby. Claiborne's baby now. And Claiborne's people listened.

Then Riva Ridge was unloaded, and the procedure was repeated. His was the stall next to Secretariat's. The two champions would still be together.

Seth Hancock visibly relaxed and began to smile. Home safe. They were in his keeping now. The Meadow people looked wist-

Eddie watches over Secretariat on the flight to Kentucky.

185

Claiborne, Secretariat's new home.

fully into the stalls that held such a big part of their lives and murmured comforting words to the two bewildered horses.

Seth showed Penny where Secretariat would live and be turned out in the fields. Then he took Eddie on the same tour. Eddie leaned on the fence and peered through the rails, critical, approving. Seth seemed to understand what Eddie was feeling—perhaps something akin to parting with one's own child.

Penny Tweedy and Elizabeth Ham bent down to read the plaques on the stable door. Eddie and Lucien stood off to one side. For the moment, the two men were no longer trainer and groom, but just two men sadly sharing the end of a wonderful part of their lives. They also had mutually dreadful colds.

The crowd began to drift away, and gradually all was quiet.

Eddie Sweat stood alone by the farm lane, his plaid suitcase by his side. Eddie, usually so cool and unshakable, was wiping away a tear.

It was finished.

And so, Secretariat, the Horse of the Century, stepped out of racing and into history. Hopefully, a long and successful career as a sire will complete his destiny, but the sight of that shining red horse blazing down to the wire will be sorely missed by everyone who ever saw him. Now, like Eddie Sweat, they have to look forward to his "little children."

May they be big and strong and wonderful like you, Secretariat.

186

Eddie Sweat will miss him most of all.

187

Grazing in the rain at Clai

TEN

SIXTEEN YEARS AT CLAIBORNE

He Struck with Lightning Bolts

Eddie Sweat was granted his wish. He lived to see Secretariat's "little children" put their own stamp on racing. He even watched the great horse's grandchildren do it as well. But we can only guess at the full and ultimate impact of Secretariat's bloodline on the sport; at the power of that mighty heart to carry itself down through the coming generations of thoroughbreds. We have seen, already, blinding flashes of brilliance from his progeny, and there are strong indications that the influence of Big Red will be with us, on the racetracks of the world, long into the 21st Century.

To the time of his death, Secretariat's breeding career was constantly lit by sons and daughters of quite remarkable speed. Although, at the very beginning, it seemed he might never get off the ground in his new occupation. After he and Riva Ridge arrived at Claiborne Farm in the Fall of 1973, they were allowed what was considered an appropriate time to "let down" from racing, and for the vets to conduct preliminary breeding examinations.

The initial sperm counts for both horses indicated some dismal signs. There were immediate fears that Secretariat might be infertile, or a "shy breeder." The word leaked out, and it was grim news to all who revered the horse who had given America a real-life hero when the world was so woefully in need of one. His followers, both inside the racing world and beyond had blithely allowed themselves to assume that Secretariat would readily recreate his own greatness—an achievement which is rare indeed among even ordinary stallions, never mind one with a race-record as awesome as Secretariat's.

The press pundits had a field day. Sports

Illustrated featured a devastating commentary entitled: "They Used To Call Him Sexy," which drew dire conclusions, principally that Secretariat's chances of becoming a successful sire resembled those of the fabled snowball in Hell.

The great horse would prove them as wrong as they were critical, because there was nothing wrong with him at all—save for the understandable requirement of some time to recuperate from a grueling 1973 campaign. Secretariat had withstood training and racing demands which few horses in history could have met. The pressure on Penny Tweedy and Lucien Laurin to give America and the world of racing the stream of victories it craved and demanded from their Champion had been tremendous. By November everyone was feeling the strain, not least Secretariat himself. What went largely unheralded after the scare over initial breeding test problems was that Secretariat in December, not eight weeks off the racetrack, got two out of three test mares in foal, both of which went full-term and produced live foals.

One of those mares was a handsome registered Appaloosa, owned by Claiborne Farm manager William Taylor. Her name was Leola, and she was frequently used as a nurse mare to provide milk for orphan foals. Taylor decided to let her be bred by Secretariat to determine the new stallion's fertility. To the world of thoroughbred racing both Leola and her forthcoming foal were regarded with massive indifference. The only aspect of the mating which mattered to them was Secretariat's ability to be a father. This rather callous attitude was not however reflected in the world of the Appaloosa, in which Leola was coveted for her own bloodlines. An out-standing example of the Appaloosa breed of her time, she had brought a record price in Houston in 1963.

Among her admirers was Jack Nankivil, the tall, cowboy-hatted owner of Sahaptin Farms located high on the bluffs overlooking the Mississippi River in Winona, Minnesota. Thoroughbred's elite may not have thought much of it, but Nankivil saw this unusual mating as, potentially, a match made in heaven. He contacted Taylor and persisted until the two met to discuss the purchase of Leola. They became fast friends in the process, and Nankivil got the mare by way of a substantial sealed bid. It was risky, but Nankivil wasn't one to run from a good gamble. To be of value to him, Leola's foal would have to be male and Appaloosa-marked, suitable for registration to that breed.

Leola came through. She bore Secretariat's first foal—a colt who would be named First Secretary—at 12 minutes past midnight on Friday, November 15, 1974. "Just for the colt to be born with a 'blanket' (the characteristic mottled coloring over an Appaloosa's hind-quarters) and three socks, was a miracle," recalled Nankivil's daughter Amy. "That was one happy night for us."

A big, leggy foal with beautiful bone, First Secretary grew to an imposing 17 hands. Other than his color and extra two inches in height, he was a splendid reflection of his sire. Literally tens of thousands of people came to see him, both at the farm, and on the only two occasions when he left it; once to Columbus, Ohio, and once as a two-year-old to lead the post-parade at the World-wide Appaloosa Futurity. Recognized and registered by the Appaloosa Horse Club of the United States, First Secretary went on to become a successful sire in his own domain.

Due to a mishap sustained when he slipped in his paddock and injured a hock, First Secretary never raced, but he produced numerous winners and speed record-breakers for racing in his breed class. Although he will never be credited in the hallowed records of the Jockey Club, Secretariat's first son is a credit to his sire and impressive testimony to the ability of the 1973 Triple Crown Champion to breed outstandingly beyond his own classic blood.

His fertility confirmed, Secretariat was allowed in 1974 to be booked for his first thoroughbred breeding season. His inaugural cover was to Mr. Walter Jefford's mare, My Card, by My Babu. In 1975 she bore a filly, Miss Secretariat. Secretariat went on to couple with a total of 36 mares in his initial season, many of them stakes winners (such as Chou Croute), and/or "blue hens" (the colloquial term for mares who have produced successful racehorses). Whatever reservations persisted about Secretariat's breeding potential, he was not given second-string matings by any means in his first year at stud. Of 30 foals born of his get, 28 lived and 24 raced. On their dams' side, Secretariat's first thoroughbred offspring carried the blood of such legendary racers as Buckpasser, Ribot, Acropolis, Nearctic, Lieutenant Stevens, My Babu, Gun Bow, Crimson Satan, Intentionally, Hail to Reason, Native Dancer, The Axe II, and Summer Tan. That first crop produced 15 winners and two stakes winners. He had not set racing on fire yet, but it was a more significant start than had been predicted by his detractors. And it got better. His progeny's first racing year (1977) produced a modest $106,680 in earnings, but in 1978 the figure jumped to $839,883.

Secretariat's second crop which was born in 1976 (37 foals) marked the first true light in the tunnel for Claiborne's Seth Hancock and the syndicate investors. It came in the form of a brilliant chestnut colt named General Assembly. Out of Exclusive Dancer, by Native Dancer, he was born to run, and run he did. Carrying Mr. and Mrs. Bertram Firestone's colors, he showed that he could blister a track in Grade I stakes at distances from seven furlongs to one and a quarter miles. In 1978 he cut a serious notch as a two-year-old, winning the Hopeful at Saratoga. He finished a strong second to Spectacular Bid in the 1979 Kentucky Derby, and then, literally, ran clean away with the classic Travers Stakes at Saratoga, winning by 15 lengths, and running the fastest 10 furlongs in the long history of the venerable New York State track—two minutes flat. He also equalled the track record of 1:21 flat in the seven-furlong Vosburg at Belmont Park, which, though equalled once again, still stands.

But it was at Saratoga where the name of General Assembly will be forever remembered. Here on the fast dirt-track which saw the defeat of Secretariat within a couple of months of his massive triumph in the Belmont, Bert Firestone's colt won FOUR times, twice at two, twice at three . . . as if in some furious attempt to avenge his father's humiliation at the hands of a horse called Onion in 1973.

It seemed almost poetic when Mr. and Mrs. Firestone decreed that General Assembly should stand at their stud in Ireland—Gilltown in the green heart of County Kildare, the same thoroughbred complex upon which Secretariat's immortal grandshire,

191

General Assembly at Saratoga.

Nasrullah, had been born and raised 30 years before. When General Assembly arrived from America, "home" to Kildare on Thursday, November 29, 1979—the best son, of the best son, of the best son of Nasrullah—lifelong Irish grooms stood and watched, some of them with tears rolling down their cheeks.

The 1976 crop also produced the impressive filly Terlingua, who, under the handling of D. Wayne Lukas really made them sit up and take serious notice on the west coast. This young lady could fly, and she won her first four starts in devastating style. In the $120,000 Del Mar Debutante Stakes she took nine lengths off a classy field; in the Hollywood Juvenile Championship she led all the way with the crack California classic colt, Flying Paster, more than two lengths back in her slip-stream. Had I been the editor of Sports Illustrated, I would have been doing some serious re-thinking about that derisive feature on Old Sexy not so many years previously.

Secretariat's 1977 crop included the stakes-winning colt, Globe, winner of the prestigious Excelsior and Grey Lag Handicaps in New York. His 1978 get produced the stakes-winning Swoon (San Marino Handicap).

But in 1982 Secretariat wrote himself another serious place in the American Stud Book with a filly whose name would be edged in gold. She arrived among his crop of 39 foals (which included seven stakes winners). She was grey in color, from Great Lady M, by Icecapade, and she was to turn racing inside out. They called her Lady's Secret. Owned by the enthusiast Eugene Klein, and trained by the able D. Wayne Lukas, she went on to become 1986 Horse of the Year, Champion Mare, and the world's leading money-winning mare. Along the way she captured the Grade I Breeder's Cup Distaff, and the Grade I Whitney Handicap against colts at Saratoga. I remember watching her win this latter race by almost five lengths. Thirteen years had passed since her sire, ailing but still game, had been put into the deep inside-rail going and failed to catch Onion. And now here was his daughter, in the same race,

1986 Horse of the Year—Lady's Secret.

over the same historic ground, sprinting clear with the roar of the huge Saratoga crowd in her ears. "Son of a gun," I muttered, to no one in particular. "That's gotta be one for Pop."

Like General Assembly, and Terlingua, Lady's Secret seemed at times to be touched by the near-mystical lightning of her sire. Later in that same 1986 season she electrified the crowd at Belmont Park, winning the Grade I Maskette Stakes by seven lengths, and two weeks later the $200,000 Grade I Ruffian Handicap by eight. She was winning both for the second time, adding to her enormous stakes haul of the Santa Margarita Handicap, the Beldame (twice), the Shuvee Handicap (all Grade I); the Grade II stakes Molly Pitcher, Test, Ballerina, El Encino, Moccasin, Prima Donna, Bowl of Flowers,

Rose Stakes, Hail Hilarious, Regret Handicap, and the Wavy Waves Stakes at Saratoga (I doubt the old Spa will ever be entirely free of the ghost of Big Red). Altogether Lady's Secret won 25 of 45 starts (22 of them stakes). She was second in nine, and third in three. She was never out of the money. And she earned a colossal $3,021,325.

Secretariat's 1982 crop also produced Fiesta Lady, another impressive stakes-winning filly who included victory in the 1984 Matron at Belmont in her solid 50% placing record. The pundits were by now becoming noticeably withdrawn in their negativism about Secretariat. And although there were still murmurs that he was "falling short of expectations," I wonder how many people really stopped to think about the millions-to-one odds of reproducing immortality, from mares who were after all, merely mortal.

During all of this time, Claiborne Farm had become a Mecca for the Secretariat faithful. The staff was almost overcome by the stream of visitors, and had literally to set up a separate division of the office to accomodate the influx of people who loved the great horse, and wanted their children to be able to say that they had seen "him." Stud manager Lawrence Robinson and Bobby Anderson, Secretariat's regular handler, took on some formidable extra duties as keepers of an idol. Secretariat, as he had in his racing days, took it pretty much in his stride. Cameras and admirers were familiar to him, and even as an active stallion, he retained his basic good nature. He did not become "studdish" or aggressively mean, as some stallions are apt to do. He remained "the people's horse," and oh, how they did love him. I know we could

193

never count the children who can number themselves among those who saw and touched him, even given Claiborne's impeccable record keeping.

In April 1985 the kind little horse with the big heart, Riva Ridge, Secretariat's lifelong stablemate, died of a heart attack there at Claiborne. With Lady's Secret not yet into her powerful stride as a three year old, Riva's death caused particular sadness at the farm. Because Seth Hancock, with all of his conservative humility, was assailed by feelings of heavy responsibility to those who had helped bring about the huge syndication for Meadow Stable. There were times when he believed that Riva Ridge might possibly be the stronger influence of the two, given Secretariat's propensity to hit with only rarified lightning bolts. And it was the most terrible loss when Riva died. He had given 10 times his size to racing.

In the 1985 and 1986 seasons, however, Secretariat's produce increased their annual earnings to $2,461,162 and $2,547,791 respectively. Secretariat was earning his keep. His 1985 crop produced a colt who would seal his worth as a stallion. Risen Star, a nearly-black colt out of Ribbon, by His Majesty, performed as his name suggested. He rose fast, and big-time, and he had been touched by the burning flame of his sire. He stormed to victory in the 1988 Preakness, and went on to win the Belmont Stakes by 10 lengths, with an authority which stated for all—"I am my father's son."

Two years later, on the other side of the world, Secretariat's "lightning" struck home again. Kingston Rule, a big chestnut horse with two white front feet, stormed to victory in Australia's greatest race, the Melbourne Cup, smashing the course record for the two miles. Kingston Rule on that November day ran like his sire, bursting through deep in the stretch and drawing away at the wire. He was Kentucky-bred, by Secretariat from the classic Australian racemare Rose of Kingston.

Eddie Sweat's dream of seeing the Big Horse's grandchildren achieve greatness came to pass in 1984—but Eddie had to be content with watching the first and biggest moment on the television. Over in England, on the historic Epsom Downs, June 6, the 205th Derby was won in a desperate, driving short-head finish by Secreto, son of Northern Dancer, the first foal of Betty's Secret, by Secretariat. This was no victory by a colt who had been touched by lightning. This was a knock-down-drag-out battle, ending with the

Secreto winning the 1984 English Derby.

194

Risen Star (left) defeats Forty Niner in 1988 Lexington Stakes.

defeat of the brilliant favorite El Gran Senor, in a stretch-war which rivalled the famous dead-heat between St. Gatien and Harvester over the same course 100 years previously.

Eddie did however see another piece of history made in the story of Secretariat. America's 1984 Champion two-year-old was Chief's Crown, by Danzig from Six Crowns, the daughter of Secretariat and Chris Evert. Chief's Crown won six races that year, including the Saratoga Special, and the Hopeful, the Cowdin, the Norfolk and the Breeders' Cup Juvenile. Now Secretariat had truly arrived as a broodmare sire, and the following year it got better. Chief's Crown won the Swale, the Flamingo, the Blue Grass, was placed in all three Classics, and then won the Travers, and the Marlboro Cup at Belmont.

In 1988 Terlingua's daughter, Chapel of Dreams by Northern Dancer, won five good races and more than $500,000. The following year a member of Secretariat's 1980 crop, Weekend Surprise, owned by William Farrish and W.S. Kilroy, produced, to the cover of the Northern Dancer stallion Storm Bird, a classic colt for Dogwood Stable. They named him Summer Squall, and he went unbeaten in four starts as a two-year-old, winning in the family tradition both the Saratoga Special, and the Hopeful, just like his 'uncle' General Assembly, and his 'first cousin' Chief's Crown. And once more the faithful at Saratoga felt the memories of Big Red cascade upon them.

Summer Squall, the following season, won the 1990 Preakness under an easy hand-ride. It was not the biggest surprise in the world since BOTH of his grandsires had won

195

Chief's Crown winning the 1984 Hopeful at Saratoga.

winners, 723 wins, 1280 placings, and earnings of over $20 million.

But still his greatness in the minds of the world's racing public, and in the thoughts of those who simply remembered him as their Champion, was that which he had done as a racehorse. Nothing could ever compare to that big, formidable, red express train that thundered past field after field of the best thoroughbreds in the United States. There would always be only one Secretariat in the hearts of those who had felt their spirits lifted in the highest moments of this truly grandiose racehorse. There were times when he seemed to charge over everyone's concerns of the moment—casting aside the cares of Presidents, Royalty, world-movers and plain folk alike. Everyone loved Secretariat. He

the Preakness, but there were those of us who could not fight off the memory of Secretariat coming down this same stretch in 1973, as young Summer Squall stretched out for victory, and another claim for the family on the blanket of the black-eyed Susans.

The table of leading broodmare sires would henceforth contain the name of Secretariat on a nearly permanent basis.

Over the years, Secretariat's get also established themselves firmly on Canadian, European, Asian and South American Turf, both on the flat, and in—yes—steeplechasing. There was literally no part of the sport, or the globe, which Secretariat had not touched. No one could deny his legacy to the world of horses. In his total of 16 crops he had produced 659 foals. At the 1990 count he had 17 graded stakes winners, 46 stakes

Summer Squall winning the 1990 Preakness.

196

was that brief, wonderful eclipse which overshadowed the world's troubles, and made people believe again in miracles, even if just for a little while.

At 11:45 a.m. on October 4, 1989, a living legend was no more. Secretariat died, tragically, and ironically, as a result of laminitis, an incurable and painful degenerative disease of the inner tissues of the hoof. Those magnificently-tough feet which had crashed their way through mud, down the hard summer-stretches of the great dirt-tracks, and even across the fast, firm turf of Belmont and the softer grass of Woodbine, had finally failed him. His death was front page news practically everywhere on earth. The world knew that it had lost something rare. One commentator, Bennett Lieberman, observed in the New York Times: "He wasn't just a horse—he was Secretariat."

In the lovely paddock at Belmont Park there stands a bronze statue of Secretariat by the late John Skeaping, a man I am proud to have had as a friend. The work was commissioned in 1974 as a gift to racing by Mr. Paul Mellon, the great humanitarian, patron of the arts, and classic racehorse owner-breeder. Skeaping drew his image mainly from a photograph in this book, which I took just as Ron Turcotte moved his hands and sent the message to Secretariat to begin that memorable sweep around the field in the 1973 Preakness. It was a moment worthy to be cast in bronze.

The Bronze at Belmont Park.

197

Penny says goodbye to Secretariat. Trainer Lucien Laurin and sculptor Jim Reno look on.

They buried Secretariat at Claiborne Farm, close by his forefathers, Bold Ruler and Nasrullah, and other exalted stallions. Penny Chenery's last farewell did not really take place, however, until 6 p.m. on the afternoon of June 6, 1991 at the dedication of a life-sized statue of Secretariat. This work of art was executed with loving and meticulous research by Texas sculptor, Jim Reno, for the Kentucky Horse Park's International Museum of the Horse, in Lexington.

After the unveiling, Penny stood quietly for a few moments, and then she reached up on her toes, and she kissed the cold bronze muzzle. She tried to blink back the tears, but one escaped and ran down her cheek. I watched her brush it away with the back of her hand, just as Eddie Sweat had done outside Claiborne in 1973.

That's when I knew that Penny too had finally said goodbye to Secretariat.

198

Where They Are

Status at the time of this publication of principal persona, living or deceased, who are prominent in the cast of characters who make up the Secretariat story. The people whose lives he touched and who touched his life in turn.

Helen "Penny" Chenery (Penny Tweedy at the time of the main story)

Penny Chenery, remains a revered member of the thoroughbred world, and continued to breed and race Meadow Farm's thoroughbreds for some time after Secretariat's retirement. She and Jack Tweedy separated in 1973. When the Chenery family decided to sell Meadow Farm, Penny moved to Lexington, where she purchased Walnut Lane Farm and continued to breed thoroughbreds on a modest basis. She has since sold the farm and now resides in Lexington, Kentucky where she continues to remain an active and vocal supporter of the American Thoroughbred industry and causes related to the encouragement and welfare of the breed. She became President of the Grayson Foundation for Equine Research (originally formed in 1940) and remained at its head throughout the 1980's. In 1989 the Grayson Foundation merged with the Jockey Club and has since been known as the Grayson-Jockey Club Research Foundation, Inc. Penny's efforts and contributions to the Foundation have been significant, inspired by her dedication to finding the causes and a possible cure for the terrible affliction laminitis, an incurable and agonizing disease of the foot which ultimately led to Secretariat's death. Penny has also been a staunch, continuing supporter of The Kentucky Horse Park & Museum and its work to promote and support continued active interest in the Horse in Kentucky and America as a whole.

Ron Turcotte, who rode Secretariat to his Triple Crown victories

Born in New Brunswick, Canada, Ron Turcotte was one of 12 children. His father was a lumberjack, and Ron spent much of his early years developing his physical strength working in the tall treetops. In 1960, unemployed, he went to Toronto where an older brother was already riding racehorses. He got a job as a hot walker at famed Canadian owner E. P. Taylor's Windfield Farm and went on to ride races. He won his first race in 1962 and became Canada's leading rider in 1962 and 1963. His career continued in the U.S. In 1965, he won the Preakness on Tom Rolfe and in 1972 rode Riva Ridge to victories in the Kentucky Derby and Belmont Stakes. In 1973 he won the Triple Crown on Secretariat, and in doing so became the only jockey to win five Triple Crown races in two consecutive years. On July 13, 1978 Ron's relatively short but brilliant riding career ended tragically at Belmont park when his mount, Flag of Leyte Gulf went down just out of the starting gate. The fall paralyzed Ron from the waist down, but the incident only began a new phase in the tough Canadian's will to win. Overcoming years of pain and physical struggle, Ron's spirit and love of family carried him through. An insatiable reader with a love of learning, and an avid outdoorsman, Ron completed his education and continues an active life working in support of others handicapped and of the Jockeys' Guild Injured Jockey's Fund. He still lives in New Brunswick with his wife Gae where they raised four daughters and are now grandparents. In his riding career, Ron won over 3,000 races, including two Canadian Championships, The American Triple Crown, and a long list of North America's highest-ranking stakes races. Along the way, he was awarded "The Order of Canada" (the highest civilian honor of his native country), The American turf journalists' Big Sport of Turfdom Award, The George Woolf Memorial Award, The 1978 Canadian Man of The Year Award bestowed by The Sovereign Award Committee, and The Avelino Gomez Memorial Award. In addition, Ron has been inducted into seven Halls of Fame: The National Museum of Racing Hall of Fame (U.S.), The Canadian All Sport's Hall of Fame, The Canadian Racing Hall of Fame, The New Brunswick Sports Hall of Fame, The New York Sports Hall of Fame, The Long Island Sports Hall of Fame, and The Hawthorne Racing Hall of Fame.

Lucien Laurin, Secretariat's racing career trainer

Lucien Laurin is remembered by his peers in the world of horsemen as "The Complete Horseman, 'L'Entraineur Complet'." Born on March 18, 1912 outside Montreal, Quebec, Canada near St. Paul des Joliette, Lucien Laurin lost both parents when very young. He began riding racehorses at area tracks in 1929. He had a successful apprenticeship and went on to ride in the U.S. In 1938 he ran into trouble when he was ruled off at Narragansett Park in Rhode Island after a "battery" was found in his jacket. To the end, Lucien maintained someone had slipped the illegal device into his clothing

without his knowledge for an unknown motive. It was a terrible thing for a horseman who went on to a lifelong career stamped with a reputation for unquestioned integrity. After the suspension, he went on to exercise horses at Alfred G. Vanderbilt's Sagamore Farm in Maryland until he was reinstated by the Rhode Island Racing Commission three years later. Lucien remarked years later of the commission board, "everything I have I owe to them for clearing my name." Lucien went on to ride for one more year before excessive weight forced him out of the saddle.

Lucien was a perfectionist and demanded the best from his people and his horses. He was a stern taskmaster, but those who worked for him all felt they had gained from doing so. He separated from Meadow Stable in 1976 and soon after went into semi-retirement. Beginning in 1945, he trained a total of 36 major stakes winners, including Secretariat, Angle Light, Upper Case and the top sprinter Spanish Riddle. The last of his top performers was Clansman in 1985. In 1977, Lucien Laurin was inducted into the National Museum of Racing's Hall of Fame in Saratoga Springs, N.Y. and the following year was enshrined in the Canadian Horse Racing Hall of Fame. His son Roger carried on taking Secretariat's line to championship with Chief's Crown winning the inaugural Breeders' Cup Juvenile in 1984. On June 26, 2000, Lucien Laurin died at a Miami hospital after complications following hip surgery from injuries he sustained from a fall at his home in Key Largo, Florida. Lucien is survived by his wife Juliette, his son Roger and Roger's sons Robert and Richard. On June 12, his first great grandchild was born. Richard Laurin's son was christened Lucien.

Edward "Eddie" Sweat ("Shorty" to his friends), Secretariat's beloved and faithful groom and companion

After Secretariat, Eddie continued to work with Lucien Lauren, then later with Roger Laurin. Born on August 30, 1938 in Holly Hill, South Carolina, Eddie Sweat began working as a child, picking cotton and harvesting corn to help support his family. Seeing the horses on Lucien Laurin's nearby farm set the course of his life. The story from there is told in this book. Never did this author ever see horses and their groom more devoted to one another than were Eddie Sweat, Secretariat and Riva Ridge. It was nothing less than profound. Eddie continued to work at his life's love, the racetrack, until failing health forced him to leave his active service with Roger Laurin in 1998. He was treated for leukemia and kidney disease at North Shore Hospital in Manhasset, N.Y. where he passed away on April 17, 1998. His body was transported to his birthplace in South Carolina to lie at rest where his story began. The Jockey Club Foundation, out of respect for Eddie's place in racing history, assisted his family with the arrangements. Eddie is survived by his wife Linda, daughters Michelle and Tiffany, his son Marvin, and five grandchildren. His daughter Michelle recalled simply that his life was horses and he thought and talked of them all the time. As he wished, he lived to see the children and grandchildren of his two beloved charges. He saw them win, and he is now again together with his two great comrades.

Elizabeth Ham, Meadow Farm's able and devoted executive secretary in whose honor Secretariat was named

Ms. Ham, who served for some 35 years as executive secretary and personal assistant to Meadow Stable founder Christopher T. Chenery was a part owner of Secretariat by virtue of being one of the heirs to Chenery's estate. Ms. Ham never missed being present at one of Secretariat's races and was in attendance in all of the major decision making meetings concerning Meadow Farm and its race horses. Ms. Ham passed away on July 23, 2000 at an Amherst, Mass. nursing home. She was 94. She was survived by a nephew, Allan Doyle.

Howard Gentry, manager of Meadow Farm who supervised the birth of Secretariat

Howard Moss Gentry was born January 2, 1908 at "Ellerslie Farm" in Albemarle County (Va.). Raised as an all around horseman, he went on to be farm manager for Christopher Chenery at Meadow Farm and for 33 years supervised the breeding and raising of Meadow's illustrious thoroughbreds. He was a member of the Virginia Thoroughbred Breeders' Association and in 1973 was named Horseman of the Year. He retired in 1976 and moved with his family to Charlottesville. Howard Gentry died on September 24, 1999 at the age of 91.

R. M. "Bob" Bailes, Meadow Farm's yearling trainer

Bob Bailes remained at Meadow Farm and trained for several subsequent owners after the Chenerys sold Meadow. He died in 1997.

Merideth Bailes, Bob's son and the first person to mount Secretariat as a yearling

After leaving Meadow Farm, he went to Maryland where he trains racehorses.

Riva Ridge

Thirteen years after his death in 1985, the gallant little champion Riva Ridge was finally enshrined in the National Museum of Racing's Hall of Fame in 1988. Ron Turcotte remarked that, "it came about 20 years too late. He was every bit as good as the horses from his time until now. Except one."

John "Jack" Tweedy, Penny Chenery's late, former husband

Born July 31, 1921 in Porto Velo, Ecuador, where his father was working as a mining engineer for an American firm, Jack Tweedy grew up in New Jersey, graduated from St. Paul's School in New Hampshire and earned a college degree at Princeton and his law degree at Columbia Law School. In 1949 he married Helen B. "Penny" Chenery. The couple lived in Denver, Colorado and had four children. Tweedy's love for Colorado began with his training there in the 1940's with the Army's crack 10th Mountain Division based in Leadville. Ironically, after intensive training for warfare in Europe's Alpine Mountains, he served as an intelligence officer in the jungles of Burma. After World War II, he and friends from the 10th Mountain returned to Colorado where they joined to form the nucleus of Vail Associates, which in 1959 created the famed skiing resort town of Vail. His bride Penny Chenery shared his love of the outdoors. In 1971 he

left Denver to become an executive with the Oil Share Corp., later known as Tosco. In 1981 he returned to Denver where he retired. Jack and Penny Tweedy divorced in 1973, the year of Secretariat's triumphs. In 1980 Tweedy married Marjorie S. Sargent and spent their time between Colorado and their ranch in Montana. Tweedy, who was an avid skier and outdoorsman, was a trustee of the Colorado Nature Conservancy, one of the organizers of Colorado Outward Bound School and a trustee of the Rocky Mountain Center for the Environment. Jack Tweedy died in Denver on November 26 1999 after complications from a stroke. He was survived by his wife, two sons, two daughters, two stepsons, three stepdaughters and six grandchildren.

Hollis Chenery, Penny Chenery's brother who helped manage Secretariat's career after the death of his father in 1973

Dr. Hollis Chenery was born in Richmond and grew up in Doswell at Meadow Farm. A noted and respected economist who served as vice president of the World Bank and the Agency for International Development, he was a professor at Harvard. He earned bachelor degrees from the Universities of Arizona and Oklahoma and served in World War II as a captain in the Army Air Corps. He received master's degrees from the University of Virginia and California Institute of Technology and was awarded a Ph.D. by Harvard in 1950. He was a professor of Economics at Stanford, a member of the U.N. Economic Commission for Latin America, a Guggenheim fellow and assistant administrator of the U.S. Agency for International Development. He and his family made their home in Santa Fe, NM in 1994 following the death of his wife Mary. Dr. Chenery died at 75 on September 8, 1994 from recurrent pneumonia.

Margaret Carmichael, Penny Chenery's sister who participated in the management of Meadow Farm's racing stable after Christopher Chenery's death in 1973

Margaret Carmichael went to Tucson, Arizona in 1940 to attend the University of Arizona. She met and married Chester "Chet" Carmichael and continued to live in Arizona. In addition to raising her family, Ms. Carmichael was an active and successful commercial real estate investor and was well known for her significant philanthropy which included sizable contributions to the University of Arizona for Valley Fever medical research and equally generous donations to various church organizations which were active in helping people in the areas around Tucson and Sonoita. Margaret Carmichael passed away at the Tucson Medical Center on November 7th, 1993, just three days after her 74th birthday.

The children of Jack and Penny Tweedy (Chenery)

Ranging in age from 50 to 40, all live in the Denver, Colorado area. They are

- Sarah Manning who is a teacher. She and her husband David have a son Christopher, 13, who is an avid hockey player.
- Kate McGrath divorced and now a writer, teacher and retired lawyer. She has two daughters, Elena, 16, and Alicia, 14.
- John B. Tweedy who is a lawyer in Boulder, Colorado. He and his wife, the former

Dr. Beret Strong, a writer and film maker, have two children, Paige Elizabeth, 6, and Marcus, 4.

Seth Hancock, a son and heir of "Bull" Hancock who took over as director of Claiborne Farm and structured Secretariat's Syndication

Seth Hancock remains CEO of Claiborne Farm and continues to be a prominent figure in the world of thoroughbred breeding and racing.

Henry "Henny" Hoeffner, Lucien Laurin's able and devoted assistant trainer

Henny continued on as Lucien Laurin's assistant until Lucien retired from active training at the tracks and went with him for a time at Laurin's Branchdale training center in Holly Hill, South Carolina. He retired to Florida and currently lives in a seniors' community.

Roger Laurin, the son of Lucien Laurin who turned Secretariat over to his father to train

Several years after his fateful move of turning Meadow Stable's string over to his father in order to become private trainer to Ogden Phipps, Roger left the position and, for a time, life on the racetrack. He went to Florida where he took commercial pilot's training but later decided to once more return to racing. He once again trained a public stable and his charges included his able training of Secretariat's illustrious grandson Chief's Crown. Upon that horse's retirement to stud, Roger received a substantial bonus and a share of the stud service. He retired from training in 1985. Roger went on to found a trust fund for the children of jockey

Don Macbeth who died of cancer. Roger currently lives in Saratoga Springs, New York.

Ogden Phipps, owner of Secretariat's sire Bold Ruler and who was on the other side of the famous coin toss

Ogden Phipps continued on as a prominent owner and breeder and influence in the American Jockey Club. He still resides at his homes in Long Island and Florida.

Jimmy Gaffney, Secretariat's first exercise rider at the race track

Jimmy Gaffney continued to be active on the racetrack as a popular exercise rider for top stables. He went on to a position in the parimutuel department of the New York Racing Association. He currently lives on Long Island and winters in Wintergreen, Florida.

Charlie Davis, childhood friend of Eddie Sweat and chief exercise rider for Secretariat

After continuing to ride exercise for the Laurins for a number of years, Charlie left the racetrack to return to South Carolina where he took a position as a horse farm foreman. He currently lives in Camden, South Carolina.

Paul Feliciano, who rode Secretariat in his first race

Paul Feliciano continued to ride races at various American tracks. In 1998, while riding races in Nebraska, he became ill and died.

Eddie Maple, who rode Secretariat in his last race

After a long and successful race-riding career, Eddie Maple retired from racing. He currently lives in Huntington, Long Island, N.Y. near Cold Spring Harbor where he opened a successful antique and gift shop business.

Dr. Olive Britt, DVM, veterinarian to Meadow Farm who was in attendance after Secretariat's birth

Several years after the Chenery family sold Meadow Farm, Dr. Britt moved her practice from Doswell and established the Virginia Equine Clinic in Manakin-Savot, Va. Dr. Britt still continues to practice and to accompany the staff veterinarians on calls. She currently resides in Manakin-Savot.

Louis "Eel" Tillman, Secretariat's groom as a foal at Meadow Farm

Louis continued to work at Meadow Farm for a series of owners after the Chenerys sold it. Louis Tillman died in 1995.

Billy Silver, Secretariat's familiar and always present Appaloosa lead pony

Billy Silver was retired from racetrack life and went to a private farm to live out his life as a beloved member of his owner, Mary D. Arthur of Richmond, Ky. and her family.

Sham, the great horse who was Secretariat's arch rival for the Triple Crown

After retiring from racing because of a leg fracture, Sham went to stud at Leslie Combs renowned Spendthrift Farm in Lexington, Ky. where he had a highly successful breeding career. Sham died at the age of 23 on April 3, 1993 in his stall of an apparent heart attack. He is buried at Walmac Farm in Lexington, next door to Spendthrift.

Frank "Pancho" Martin, trainer of Sham

Frank Martin is still an active trainer based at Belmont Park and conditions the racing string owned by Mrs. Viola Sommer, widow of the late owner of Sham, Sigmund Sommer.

Allen Jerkens, the shrewd, ever watchful trainer who conditioned Onion and Prove Out to defeat Secretariat at Saratoga and Belmont in late summer 1973

Allen Jerkens still is a successful, active trainer and bases his public stable at Belmont Park in New York.

Alfred Gwynne Vanderbilt, the President of NYRA who presided over the famous coin toss that decided Secretariat's future

Alfred Vanderbilt remained a prominent owner, breeder and figure in American Thoroughbred racing until his death in 1999.

John "Jack" Landry, a senior vice president of Philip Morris International who conceived the Marlboro Cup Stakes race to honor Secretariat and Riva Ridge

Jack Landry continued on with Philip Morris International and remained active in racing through his activities with the company's sponsorship of the Marlboro Cup at Belmont Park. When legislation passed which forbade visible promotion of tobacco at such public events, the race was continued for several more years entitled simply "The Cup." It was discontinued in 1988. Landry left Philip Morris in 1987. He died in 1997.

Edward "E. T." McLean Jr., A fine racing official and ever a perfectionist who was the official manual timer at the 1973 Preakness

He had to long endure teasing from his peers because of cruelly unlucky circumstance. Because a drunken spectator broke the electronic timer during the race with a discarded bottle, McLean's manual call automatically became official. McLean, who was as excited as everyone else by seeing the great horse winning, missed punching his stopwatch by a fraction of a second, costing Secretariat his Preakness record and McLean's peace of mind for years to follow. However, the Maryland Jockey Club has finally awarded that record to Secretariat after years of review, study and debate. Mr. McClean continued in his capacity as an able racing official until his recent retirement. He now lives in South Carolina where he does extensive volunteer work with special education.

Jimmy "The Greek" Snyder, famous Las Vegas gambling odds maker who predicted Secretariat could not win the Kentucky Derby because of a "bad knee"

In 1980, Snyder was at dinner in Las Vegas with jockey Ron Turcotte and two well-known pro football players for Boston. Turcotte asked, "Jimmy, who told you that Secretariat had a bad knee before the Derby?" "Nobody," replied Snyder. "I started that rumor and it paid off. I won a bet at 5 to 1 on him. Otherwise, he'd have been even money!" Jimmy the Greek died in 1988.

Secretariat's Blood-Lines

Figures under names indicate in succession, number of years raced, starts, wins, and racing index. 1.00 is an average racing index; Bold Ruler therefore earned more than 82 times the average in the three seasons he raced.

SECRETARIAT, 1970
Bred by Meadow Stud in Virginia

BOLD RULER, 1954
Bred by Wheatley Stable
3, 33, 23, 82.50
Champion at 3
Seven-time leading U.S. sire
Sire of 69 stks wnrs

NASRULLAH, 1940
Bred by H. H. Aga Khan
2, 10, 5, 21.37 in Eng
Five-time leading U.S. sire
Sire of 101 stks wnrs
(eight classic wnrs)

NEARCO, 1935
Bred by Tesio-Incisa
2, 14, 14 in It, Fr
Three-time leading Eng sire
Sire of seven classic wnrs

PHAROS, 1920
Bred by 17th Lord Derby
4, 30, 14, 21.86 in Eng

NOGARA, 1928
Bred by Tesio-Incisa
Champion in Italy

MUMTAZ BEGUM, 1932
Bred by H. H. Aga Khan
1, 8, 2, 2.96 in Eng
Dam of four stks wnrs

BLENHEIM II, 1927
Bred by Lord Carnavon
2, 10, 5, 41.87 in Eng

MUMTAZ MAHAL, 1921
Bred by Lady Sykes
2, 10, 7, 40.70 in Eng

MISS DISCO, 1944
Bred by A. G. Vanderbilt
5, 54, 10, 5.95
Stakes winner
Dam of three stks wnrs
(one classic wnr)

DISCOVERY, 1931
Bred by W. J. Salmon Sr.
4, 63, 27, 41.83
Champion at 4, 5
Sire of 26 stks wnrs

DISPLAY, 1923
Bred by W. J. Salmon Sr.
6, 103, 23, 23.62

ARIADNE, 1926
Bred by W. J. Salmon Sr.
Unraced

OUTDONE, 1936
Bred by A. G. Vanderbilt
2, 21, 2, 1.89
Stakes winner
Dam of three stks wnrs

POMPEY, 1923
Bred by W. R. Coe
3, 35, 13, 24.60

SWEEP OUT, 1926
Bred by W. R. Coe
3, 35, 13, 4.07

SOMETHINGROYAL, 1952
Bred by Christopher T. Chenery
1, 1, 0, .00
Dam of four stks wnrs

PRINCEQUILLO, 1940
Bred by L. L. Lawrence
3, 33, 12, 18.34
Stakes winner
Twice leading U.S. sire
Sire of 64 stks wnrs
(two classic wnrs)

PRINCE ROSE, 1928
Bred by Lord Durham
3, 20, 16, 55.81 in Fr, Belg
Stakes winner
Leading sire in Fr
(two classic wnrs)

ROSE PRINCE, 1919
Bred by Jean Joubert
4, 38, 9, 54.92 in Fr, Eng

INDOLENCE, 1920
Bred by Lord Durham
2, 11, 1, .75 in Eng

COSQUILLA, 1933
Bred by Mrs. Cradock
3, 27, 7, 5.63 in Fr
Stakes winner
Dam of one stks wnr

PAPYRUS, 1920
Bred by Sir John Johnson
3, 17, 9, 36.81 in Eng

QUICK THOUGHT, 1918
Bred by National Stud
2, 11, 1, .60 in Eng

IMPERATRICE, 1938
Bred by W. A. La Boyteaux
3, 31, 11, 9.24
Stakes winner
Dam of six stks wnrs
(one classic wnr)

CARUSO, 1927
Bred by W. R. Coe
3, 48, 12, 15.99
Stakes winner
Sire of four stks wnrs

POLYMELIAN, 1914
Bred by J. B. Joel
1, 8, 4, 2.89

SWEET MUSIC, 1917
Bred by W. R. Coe
3, 27, 4, 1.04

CINQUEPACE, 1934
Bred by Marshall Field
Unraced
Dam of one stks wnr

BROWN BUD, 1924
Bred by Fred Johnson
2, 22, 9, 35.58

ASSIGNATION, 1930
Bred by Marshall Field
Unraced

Log of a Champion

A full presentation of the log of Secretariat's training regimen from the colt's first day at the race track to the last. The log was compiled by William L. Nack, turf writer and author, with the assistance of trainer Lucien Laurin and assistant trainer Henry Hoeffner.

1972
JANUARY
20 Arrived at Hialeah from The Meadow Stud
21 Walk
22 Walk
23 Gallop
24 Gallop
25 Gallop
26 Gallop
27 Gallop
28 Gallop
29 Gallop
30 Gallop
31 Gallop
FEBRUARY
1 Gallop
2 Gallop
3 Gallop
4 Gallop
5 Gallop
6 Gallop
7 Gallop
8 Gallop
9 Gallop
10 Gallop
11 Gallop
12 Gallop
13 Gallop
14 Gallop
15 Gallop
16 Gallop
17 Gallop
18 Gallop
19 Gallop
20 Gallop
21 Gallop
22 Quarter-mile in :23$\frac{3}{5}$*
23 Walk
24 Gallop
25 Gallop
26 Quarter-mile in :24*
27 Walk
28 Gallop
29 Gallop
*Probably inaccurate, reflecting the time of the leader of Secretariat's set, Gold Bag, rather than Secretariat, who was beaten 15 lengths by Gold Bag the first time they worked together.
MARCH
1 Gallop
2 Gallop
3 Gallop
4 Gallop
5 Three-eighths in :36
6 Walk
7 Gallop
8 Gallop
9 Gallop
10 Three-eighths in :36
11 Walk
12 Gallop
13 Gallop
14 Gallop
15 Three-eighths in unrecorded time
16 Walk
17 Walk
18 Gallop
19 Gallop
20 Gallop
21 Gallop
22 Gallop
23 Gallop
24 Gallop
25 Gallop
26 Gallop
27 Three-eighths in :37
28 Walk
29 Gallop
30 Gallop
31 Gallop
APRIL
1 Three-eighths in :35$\frac{3}{5}$
2 Walk
3 Ship form Florida to Belmont Park
4 Walk
5 Walk
6 Gallop
7 Gallop
8 Gallop
9 Gallop
10 Three-eighths in :36$\frac{2}{5}$
11 Walk
12 Gallop
13 Gallop
14 Half-mile in :50$\frac{1}{5}$ in slop
15 Walk
16 Walk
17 Gallop
18 Stall (Secretariat had thrown rider and wrenched his back)
19 Walk (with boy)
20 Walk (with boy)
21 —
22 —
23 —
24 —
25 —
26 —
27 Jog
28 Jog
29 Jog
30 Gallop
MAY
1 Gallop
2 Gallop
3 Gallop
4 Gallop
5 Gallop
6 Gallop
7 Gallop
8 Gallop
9 Walk
10 Gallop
11 Gallop
12 Gallop
13 Gallop
14 Quarter-mile in unrecorded time
15 Walk
16 Gallop
17 Gallop
18 Three-eighths in :37
19 Walk
20 Walk
21 Gallop
22 Gallop
23 Three-eighths in :35$\frac{4}{5}$
24 Walk
25 Walk
26 Gallop
27 Gallop
28 Three-eighths in :36
29 Walk
30 Gallop
31 Gallop
JUNE
1 Half-mile in :48$\frac{4}{5}$ in slop
2 Walk
3 Walk
4 Gallop
5 Gallop
6 Half-mile in :47$\frac{3}{5}$
7 Walk
8 Gallop
9 Gallop
10 Half-mile in :48$\frac{1}{5}$
11 Walk
12 Walk
13 Gallop
14 Gallop
15 Five-eighths in 1:00$\frac{1}{5}$
16 Walk
17 Walk
18 Gallop
19 Gallop
20 Three-eighths in unrecorded time
21 Walk
22 Gallop
23 Gallop
24 Three-quarters in 1:12$\frac{4}{5}$
25 Walk
26 Walk
27 Gallop
28 Gallop
29 Three-eighths in :35
30 Walk
JULY
1 Walk
2 Gallop
3 Gallop
*4 ran fourth in first start, beaten 1$\frac{1}{4}$ lengths in 1:05 for 5$\frac{1}{2}$ furlongs at Aqueduct
5 Walk
6 Walk
7 Walk
8 Gallop
9 Gallop
10 Three-eighths in :35$\frac{2}{5}$
11 Walk
12 Gallop
13 Gallop
14 Three-eighths in :36 on sloppy track
15 Broke Maiden at Aqueduct in 1:10$\frac{3}{5}$, winning by six
16 Walk
17 Walk
18 Gallop
19 Gallop
20 Gallop
21 Three-eighths in :35
22 Walk
23 Gallop
24 Gallop
25 Five-eighths in unrecorded time
26 Walk
27 Gallop
28 Gallop
29 Three-eighths at Saratoga in :35
30 Walk
*31 Won allowance race by 1$\frac{1}{2}$ lengths at Saratoga, six furlongs in 1:10$\frac{4}{5}$
AUGUST
1 Walk
2 Walk
3 Gallop
4 Gallop
5 Gallop
6 Gallop
7 Half-mile in :48
8 Walk
9 Gallop
10 Gallop
11 Five-eighths in :59
12 Walk
13 Walk
14 Gallop
15 Gallop
*16 Won Sanford Stakes by three lengths, six furlongs in 1:10
17 Walk
18 Walk
19 Walk
20 Gallop
21 Gallop (twice around)
22 Half-mile in :46$\frac{2}{5}$
23 Walk
24 Gallop
25 Gallop
*26 Won Hopeful Stakes by five lengths in 1:16$\frac{1}{5}$ for 6$\frac{1}{2}$ furlongs
27 Walk
28 Walk
29 Walk
30 Gallop
31 Gallop
SEPTEMBER
1 Gallop
2 Gallop
3 Five-eighths in 1:03$\frac{1}{5}$ at Belmont Park
4 Walk
5 Gallop
6 Gallop
7 Seven-eighths in 1:24
8 Walk
9 Walk
10 Gallop
11 Gallop
12 Five-eighths in :22$\frac{4}{5}$, :46, and :58, up in 1:11$\frac{4}{5}$*
13 Walk
14 Gallop
15 Gallop
*16 Won Futurity Stakes at Belmont Park by 1$\frac{3}{4}$ lengths in 1:16$\frac{2}{5}$ for 6$\frac{1}{2}$ furlongs
17 Walk
18 Walk
19 Walk
20 Gallop
21 Gallop
22 Gallop
23 Gallop
24 Five-eighths in 1:01$\frac{4}{5}$
25 Walk
26 Walk
27 Gallop
28 Gallop
29 Seven-eighths in 1:27$\frac{3}{5}$
30 Walk
*Ron Turcotte hit Secretariat and went faster than Lucien wanted him to go. ''He's just a baby, Ronnie, ''Lucien scolded. ''You're asking too much of him.''
OCTOBER
1 Gallop
2 Gallop
3 Gallop
4 One mile in 1:36$\frac{2}{5}$, up in 1:5
5 Walk
6 Walk
7 Gallop
8 Gallop
9 Five-eighths in :25$\frac{3}{5}$, :50$\frac{4}{5}$, a 1:03, up in 1:15$\frac{4}{5}$
10 Walk
11 Gallop
12 Gallop (five-eighths in 1:04 d 1$\frac{1}{2}$ mile gallop)
13 Gallop
*14 Won Champagne Stakes by tv lengths in 1:35 for one mile. Disqualified.
15 Walk
16 Gallop
17 Gallop
18 Gallop
19 Gallop
20 Gallop
21 Three-eighths in :36$\frac{3}{5}$, up in
22 Walk
23 Ship to Laurel and walk
24 Five-eighths in 1:00
25 Walk
26 Gallop
27 Gallop
*28 Won Laurel Futurity by eight lengths in 1:42$\frac{4}{5}$ for 1$\frac{1}{16}$ mile
29 Ship back to Belmont and wa
30 Walk
31 Walk
NOVEMBER
1 Gallop
2 Gallop
3 Walk and ship to Garden Stat
4 Gallop
5 Gallop
6 Three-quarters in 1:18$\frac{4}{5}$
7 Walk
8 Gallop
9 Gallop
10 Seven-eighths in 1:25$\frac{4}{5}$
11 Walk
12 Walk
13 Gallop
14 Gallop
15 Half-mile in :48$\frac{2}{5}$ around dogs mud
16 Walk
17 Gallop
*18 Won Garden State Stakes by 3 lengths in 1:44$\frac{2}{5}$ for 1$\frac{1}{16}$ miles
19 Walk
20 Walk
21 Walk
22 Gallop
23 Gallop
24 Gallop
25 Gallop
26 Walk
27 Walk and ship to Hialeah from Belmont Park
28 Walk
29 Gallop
30 Gallop

BER
lk
llop
lk
llop
llop (twice around)
lk
lk
lk
ed for a splint
lk
lk
lk
lk
lk
lk
lk
lk
lk
lk
lk
lk
lk
lk
(five or ten minutes inside
ed)
(five or ten minutes inside
ed)
(five or ten minutes inside
ed)
llop
llop
llop
llop
llop

RY
llop
llop
llop (twice around)
llop (once)
llop (twice)
llop (once)
llop (once)
llop (twice)
llop (once)
llop (once)
llop (twice)
llop (once)
llop (twice)
llop (once)
ree-eighths in :37
lk
llop
llop
llop
ree-eighths in :35⅕, up in :49
lk
llop
llop
lf-mile in :23⅖ and :47⅗, up in
00⅗
lk
lk
llop
llop
llop
lf-mile in :49
lk
ARY
llop
llop
ve-eighths in 1:01⅗
lk
llop
llop
ve-eighths in :34⅖, :46⅖, and
8⅗, up in 1:12
lk
lk
llop
llop
ree-quarters in 1:11⅖
lk

14 Gallop
15 Gallop
16 Gallop
17 Seven-eighths in 1:25⅖
18 Walk
19 Walk
20 Gallop
21 Gallop (twice around)
22 Gallop (once)
23 Seven-eighths in 1:26
24 Walk
25 Gallop
26 Gallop
27 Gallop (twice)
28 Seven-eighths in :23⅘, :47, and 1:23⅖

MARCH
1 Walk
2 Walk
3 Gallop
4 Gallop
5 Gallop
6 Gallop
7 One mile in 1:40⅗ at Hialeah
8 Walk
9 Gallop (twice around)
10 Walk and ship from Hialeah to Belmont Park
11 Walk
12 Gallop
13 Gallop
14 Three-eighths in :11⅕, :21⅘, and :32⅗
15 Walk
16 Gallop
*17 Won Bay Shore Stakes by 4½ lengths in 1:23⅕ for seven furlongs
18 Walk
19 Walk
20 Gallop
21 Gallop
22 Gallop
23 Half-mile in :48
24 Walk
25 Gallop
26 Gallop
27 Gallop
28 One mile in :24⅗, :48, 1:11⅘, and 1:35⅖, up in 1:48⅘
29 Walk
30 Walk
31 Gallop

APRIL
1 Gallop (twice around)
2 Gallop
3 Five-eighths in :26, :38⅘, and 1:03, up in 1:15⅘
4 Walk
5 Gallop
6 Gallop
*7 Won Gotham Stakes by three lengths in 1:33⅖ for one mile (equaled track record)
8 Walk
9 Walk
10 Walk (with boy)
11 Gallop
12 Gallop
13 Half-mile in :49
14 Walk
15 Gallop
16 Gallop
17 One mile in :28⅕, :52, 1:17⅘, and 1:42⅖
18 Walk
19 Gallop
20 Gallop
*21 Third in Wood Memorial behind winner's nine furlongs in 1:49⅘, beaten four lengths
22 Walk
23 Walk and ship to Louisville
24 Walk
25 Gallop
26 Gallop
27 Three-quarters in 1:12⅗
28 Walk
29 Gallop
30 Gallop

MAY
1 Gallop
2 Five-eighths in :23⅘, :35, :47, and :58⅗
3 Walk
4 Gallop
*5 Won Kentucky Derby by 2½ lengths in 1:59⅖ for 1¼ miles (new track record), with successive quarters in :25⅕, :24, :23⅘, :23⅖, and :23
6 Walk
7 Walk
8 Walk
9 Gallop at Pimlico
10 Gallop
11 Gallop
12 Gallop
13 Five-eighths in :22⅗, :45⅕, and :57⅖, up in 1:10
14 Walk
15 Gallop
16 Gallop
17 Gallop
18 Gallop
*19 Won Preakness Stakes by 2½ lengths in unofficial 1:53⅖ (which would have been new track record), 1:54⅖ officially
20 Walk and ship to Belmont Park
21 Walk
22 Walk
23 Gallop (once around)
24 Gallop
25 Gallop
26 Gallop
27 Three-quarters in 1:12⅕, up in 1:25
28 Walk
29 Gallop (once around)
30 Gallop (once)
31 Gallop (once)

JUNE
1 One mile in :12, :23⅘, :47, 1:11, and 1:34⅘, up in 1:48⅖
2 Walk
3 Walk
4 Gallop
5 Gallop
6 Half-mile in :46⅖
7 Walk
8 Walk
*9 Won Belmont Stakes by 31 lengths in 2:24 (new American record), via fractions of :23⅗, :46⅕, 1:09⅘, 1:34⅕, and 1:59 and successive furlongs in :12⅕, :11⅖, :11⅖, :11⅕, :12, :11⅗, :12⅕, :12⅕, :12, :12⅘, :12⅕, and :12⅘
10 Walk
11 Walk
12 Walk
13 Gallop
14 Gallop
15 Gallop
16 Gallop
17 Walk
18 Gallop
19 Gallop (twice around)
20 Gallop
21 Five-eighths in :58⅘
22 Walk
23 Walk
24 Gallop
25 Gallop (twice)
26 Gallop
27 Five-eighths in :58⅕
28 Walk
29 Walk
*30 Won Arlington Invitational Stakes by nine lengths with nine furlongs in 1:47, racing 15 feet off rail around two turns

JULY
1 Walk
2 Walk
3 Walk
4 Gallop
5 Gallop
6 Gallop
7 Gallop
8 Walk
9 Gallop
10 Three-quarters in :24⅗, :49, and 1:13⅗
11 Walk
12 Gallop
13 Gallop (twice)
14 Gallop (twice)
15 Gallop
16 Seven-eighths in :25, :49⅗, 1:13⅖, and 1:25, up in 1:38
17 Walk
18 Gallop
19 Gallop
20 Gallop
21 One mile in 1:38
22 Walk
23 Walk
24 Gallop
25 Gallop (twice around)
26 Gallop
27 One mile in 1:34
28 Walk
29 Walk
30 Gallop
31 Gallop

AUGUST
1 Half-mile in :48⅕
2 Walk
3 Gallop
*4 Second to Onion in Whitney Stakes, beaten one length in 1:49⅕
5 Walk
6 Walk
7 Walk
8 Gallop (once around)
9 Gallop (once)
10 Gallop
11 Walk
12 Walk
13 Walk
14 Walk
15 Walk
16 Gallop
17 Gallop
18 Gallop
19 Gallop
20 Walk
21 Walk
22 Walk
23 Walk
24 Walk
25 Walk
26 Jog
27 Gallop
28 Gallop
29 Gallop
30 Five-eighths in :24, :48⅖, and 1:00⅗, up in 1:14⅖
31 Walk

SEPTEMBER
1 Gallop
2 Gallop
3 Seven-eighths in 1:24⅘
4 Walk
5 Gallop
6 Gallop
7 One mile in :24⅗, :48, 1:12, and 1:37, up in 1:50
8 Walk
9 Gallop
10 Gallop
11 Gallop
12 Five-eighths in :22⅗, :45, and :57, up in 1:08⅘
13 Walk
14 Gallop
*15 Won Marlboro Cup by 3½ lengths in 1:45⅖ for nine furlongs (new American and world record)
16 Walk
17 Walk
18 Walk
19 Gallop
20 Gallop
21 Half-mile on grass in 48⅗, dogs up
22 Walk
23 Gallop
24 Gallop
25 One mile on grass, dogs up, in :26, 1:14⅕, and 1:38, up in 2:03
26 Walk
27 Gallop
28 Gallop
*29 Second to Prove Out in Woodward Stakes, beaten 4½ lengths in 2:25⅘ for 12 furlongs
30 Walk

OCTOBER
1 Walk
2 Gallop
3 Gallop
4 Gallop
5 Five-eighths in :22⅖, :45, and :56⅘, up in 1:09
6 Walk
7 Gallop
*8 Won Man o'War Stakes by five lengths in 2:24⅘ for 1½ miles on grass (new course record)
9 Walk
10 Walk
11 Walk
12 Gallop
13 Gallop
14 Gallop
15 Three-quarters in :23⅘, :48, and 1:11⅗, up in 1:23⅘
16 Walk
17 Gallop
18 Gallop
19 One mile in 1:37, up in 1:49⅘
20 Walk
21 Walk
22 Gallop
23 Gallop in Canada
24 Gallop
25 Five-eighths at Woodbine, around plastic fence set 28 feet from hedge, in :45⅘ and :57⅗
26 Walk
27 Gallop
*28 Won Canadian International Stakes by 6½ lengths in 2:41⅘ for 1⅚ miles
29 Walk and ship back to Belmont Park
30 Walk
31 Walk

NOVEMBER
1 Walk (under tack)
2 Gallop
3 Jog
4 Walk
5 Jog (with tack)
6 Jog
7 Gallop
8 Walk
9 Jog
10 Jog
11 Walk
12 Ship from Belmont Park to Claiborne Farm

Stakes Winners Sired by Secretariat

Dactylographer, born 1975, colt—(England), William Hill Futurity.

Messina, born 1975, filly—Valdale Stakes.

General Assembly, born 1976, colt—Hopeful Stakes, Vosburg Stakes, Gotham Stakes, Travers Stakes, Saratoga Special Stakes.

Medaille d'Or, born 1976, colt—(Canada), Coronation Futurity.

Sifounas, born 1976, colt—(Italy), Prix Ellington Stakes.

Six Crowns, born 1976, filly—Meadow Queen Stakes.

Terlinqua, born 1976, filly—Hollywood Juvenile Championship Stakes, Hollywood Lassie Stakes, Del Mar Debutante Stakes, Santa Ynez Stakes, Nursery Stakes, Las Flores Handicap.

Tweak, born 1976, filly—Fair Lawn Stakes.

Cinegita, born 1977, filly—Railbird Stakes.

Globe, born 1977, colt—Excelsior Handicap, Grey Lag Handicap.

If This Be So, born 1977, colt—Evergreen Handicap, Henry P. Russell Handicap.

Office Wife, Born 1977, filly—Modesty Handicap.

Secretarial Queen, born 1977, filly—Ruth Lilly Stakes.

Secrettame, born 1978, filly—Shirley Jones Handicap.

Swoon, born 1978, colt—San Marino Handicap.

Viva Sec, born 1978, filly—Dark Mirage Stakes, Grey Flight Stakes.

Who's to Answer, born 1978, filly—Bed O' Roses Handicap.

D'Accord, born 1979, colt—Breeders' Futurity.

Golden Highlights, born 1979, filly—Sooner Stakes.

Lucky Legend, born 1979, colt—Glass House Handicap.

Romantico, born 1979, colt—Ventnor Stakes.

Satan's Secretary, born 1979, colt—Hoover Stakes, Loyalty Stakes.

Riviere Doree, born 1980, filly—(France), Prix Coronation.

Weekend Surprise, born 1980, filly—Schuylerville Stakes, Golden Rod Stakes, Pocahontas Stakes.

Ellington Hill, born 1981, filly—Coral Gables Stakes.

Fleet Secretariat, born 1981, filly—Burnsville Handicap.

Fiesta Lady, born 1982, filly—Matron Stakes, Del Mar Debutante Stakes.

Fine Spirit, born 1982, filly—Cascapedia Handicap.

Image of Greatness, born 1982, colt—San Felipe Handicap.

Lady's Secret, born 1982, filly—Breeders' Cup Distaff, Santa Margarita Invitational Handicap, Beldame Stakes (2), Whitney Handicap, Ruffian Handicap (2), La Canada Stakes, Maskette Stakes (2), Shuvee Handicap, Molly Pitcher Handicap, Test Stakes, Ballerina Stakes, El Encino Stakes, Moccasin Stakes, Prima Donna Stakes, Bowl of Flowers Stakes, Rose Stakes, Hail Hilarious Stakes, Regret Handicap, Wavy Waves Stakes.

Madame Secretary, born 1982, filly—Dolly Val Handicap.

Pancho Villa, born 1982, colt—Bay Shore Stakes, Silver Screen Handicap, National Sprint Championship, King's Bishop Stakes.

Subjective, born 1982, filly—Suffolk Downs Budweiser Breeders' Cup, Iris Stakes.

Clever Secret, born 1984, colt—Lamplighter Handicap, Aqueduct Handicap, Atherton Stakes.

Athyka, born 1985, filly—(France), Ciga Prix De L'Opera (2), Prix Chloe La Coupe, Prix Corrida, Prix Des Truleries.

Bluebook, born 1985, filly—(England and France), Gainsborough Stud Fred Darling Stakes, Princess Margaret Stakes, Prix De Seine-et-Oise.

Risen Star, born 1985, colt—Preakness Stakes, Belmont Stakes, Lexington Stakes, Louisiana Derby, Minstrel Stakes, Louisiana Derby Trial Stakes.

Summer Secretary, born 1985, colt—Beaugay Handicap, Atlantic City Budweiser Breeders' Cup Handicap.

Sweeping Change, born 1985, colt—Woodstock Stakes.

Kingston Rule, born 1986, colt—(Australia), Foster's Melbourne Cup, Landragin Wines, Moonee Valley Cup.

Pretty Secretary, born 1986, filly—(France), Grand Prix De Clairefontaine.

Secretaridge, born 1986, filly—Illinois Oaks.

Tiffany's Secret, born 1987, filly—(Canada), Canadian Oaks.

Fantastic Ways, born 1988, filly—Providencia Stakes.

Secret Imperatrice, born 1988, filly—Oak View Farm Handicap.

The charts for all of Secretariat's twenty-one races.

SECOND RACE

Aqueduct

JULY 4, 1972

5 ½ FURLONGS. (1.02 3/5) **MAIDEN SPECIAL WEIGHTS.** Purse $8,000. Colts and Gelding. 2-year-olds. Weights, 118 lbs.

Value of race $8,000, value to winner $4,800, second $1,760, third $960, fourth $480. Mutuel pool $307,033, OTB pool $27,050.

Last Raced		Horse	Eqt.	A.	Wt	PP	St	¼	½	Str	Fin	Jockey	Odds $1
22May72	^{4}Bel^{5}	Herbull	b	2	118	9	8	3^{1}	4^{2}	3^{1}	1^{nk}	Cordero A Jr	b-8.00
		Master Achiever		2	118	12	5	4^{2}	$3\frac{1}{2}$	1^{hd}	2^{1}	Belmonte E	a-12.30
28Jun72	^{3}Aqu^{2}	Fleet 'N Royal		2	118	7	1	7^{1}	7^{1}	$6\frac{1}{2}$	3no	Smith R C	3.60
		Secretariat	b	2	113	2	11	10^{2}	10^{2}	7^{3}	$4\frac{1}{2}$	Feliciano P^{5}	3.10
		Big Burn		2	118	1	10	$6\frac{1}{2}$	5^{3}	4^{2}	5^{hd}	Baeza B	6.80
		Burgeon	b	2	118	11	6	$8\frac{1}{2}$	6^{hd}	$5\frac{1}{2}$	6^{3}	Marquez C H	b-8.00
15Jun72	^{4}Bel^{2}	Count Successor		2	118	6	3	$1\frac{1}{2}$	$1\frac{1}{2}$	$2^{1\frac{1}{2}}$	7^{2}	Rotz J L	5.40
21Jun72	^{4}Aqu^{7}	Jacques Who		2	118	5	4	$9\frac{1}{2}$	9^{hd}	$9\frac{1}{2}$	8^{nk}	Venezia M	26.10
18May72	^{3}Bel^{9}	Rove		2	118	10	7	1^{2}	11^{2}	10^{5}	9^{2}	Cespedes R	27.50
		Knightly Dawn		2	118	8	2	2^{1}	2^{1}	8^{2}	$10^{3\frac{1}{2}}$	Baltazar C	a-12.30
		Strike The Line		2	118	3	12	12	12	$11\frac{1}{2}$	$11^{2\frac{1}{2}}$	Ruane J	34.50
		Quebec		2	118	4	9	5^{hd}	$8\frac{1}{2}$	12	12	Vasquez J	4.50

a-Coupled: Master Achiever and Knightly Dawn; b-Herbull and Burgeon.

Time, :22$\frac{2}{5}$, :46$\frac{1}{5}$, :58$\frac{4}{5}$, 1:05 (Against wind in backstretch.). Track fast.

$2 Mutuel Prices:

2-(L)-HERBULL (b-entry)	**18.00**	**8.80**	**4.80**
1-(O)-MASTER ACHIEVER (a-entry)		**11.60**	**5.40**
9-(G)-FLEET 'N ROYAL			**3.20**

dk b or br. c, by Herbager—Little Jupon, by Bull Lea. Trainer Cornell R. Bred by Calumet Farm (Ky).

IN GATE AT 2:02; OFF AT 2:02 1/2 EASTERN DAYLIGHT TIME. Start Good. Won Driving.

HERBÜLL, reserved behind the leaders while saving ground to the stretch, worked his way out between horses after entering the stretch and wore down MASTER ACHIEVER. The latter moved fast from the outside to make his bid leaving the turn, bore in approaching the final furlong and held on stubbornly. FLEET 'N ROYAL, outrun after breaking alertly, finished fast between horses. SECRETARIAT, impeded after the start, lacked room between horses racing into the turn, ducked to the inside after getting through into the stretch and finished full of run along the rail. BIG BURN, bothered following the start, came off the rail while moving on the turn and continued on with good courage. BURGEON rallied mildly while racing wide. COUNT SUCCESSOR was used up vying for the lead. ROVE broke through before the break and was always outrun. KNIGHTLY DAWN had nothing left after showing speed to the stretch. STRIKE THE LINE was knocked back after the start. QUEBEC ducked in sharply after the start, causing a jam, rushed into contention nearing the end of the backstretch and stopped badly.

Owners— 1, Calumet Farm; 2, Sommer S; 3, Winchell V H; 4, Meadow Stable; 5, Slim 'n None Stable; 6, Calumet Fm; 7, Bi Jay Acre Stable; 8, Wimp heimer J D; 9, Melton J P ; 10, Sommer S; 11, Elcee-H Stable; 12, Frelinghuysen H O H.

Trainers— 1, Cornell R; 2, Martin F; 3, Lake R P; 4, Laurin L; 5, Parisella J; 6, Cornell R; 7, Boland W; 8, Sedlacek W; 9, Walsh M G; 10, Martin F; 11, Erb D; 12 Yowell E.

Scratched—Bet On It (28Jun72^{4}Aqu^{5}); Intellectual Snob; Kinzua.

FOURTH RACE

Aqueduct

JULY 15, 1972

6 FURLONGS. (1.08 3/5) **MAIDEN SPECIAL WEIGHTS.** Purse $8,000. Colts and Geldings. 2-year-olds. Weights, 118 lbs.

Value of race $8,000, value to winner $4,800, second $1,760, third $960, fourth $480. Mutuel pool $265,879, OTB pool $41,362.

Last Raced		Horse	Eqt.	A.	Wt	PP	St	¼	½	Str	Fin	Jockey	Odds $1
4Jly72	^{2}Aqu^{4}	Secretariat	b	2	113	8	11	$6\frac{1}{2}$	$4\frac{1}{2}$	$1\frac{1}{2}$	1^{6}	Feliciano P^{5}	1.30
4Jly72	^{2}Aqu^{2}	Master Achiever		2	118	10	2	2^{1}	3^{1}	3^{3}	$2\frac{3}{4}$	Velasquez J	5.50
28Jun72	^{4}Aqu^{5}	Bet On It		2	118	9	1	1^{1}	$1^{1\frac{1}{2}}$	2^{1}	3^{4}	Rotz J L	5.90
		Scantling		2	118	11	9	$8\frac{1}{2}$	7^{3}	$6^{1\frac{1}{2}}$	$4\frac{3}{4}$	Arelliano J	37.10
20Jun72	^{2}Aqu^{2}	Impromptu	b	2	118	3	3	$3\frac{1}{2}$	$5^{1\frac{1}{2}}$	5^{hd}	5^{nk}	Guadalupe J	17.60
4Jly72	^{2}Aqu^{8}	Jacques Who	b	2	118	7	5	4^{1}	$2\frac{1}{2}$	4^{2}	$6\frac{1}{2}$	Venezia M	26.20
4Jly72	^{2}Aqu^{3}	Fleet 'N Royal		2	118	1	4	7^{1}	8^{4}	7^{1}	$7^{2½}$	Baeza B	3.30
28Jun72	^{3}Aqu^{5}	Irish Flavor	b	2	118	5	8	5^{3}	$6\frac{1}{2}$	8^{4}	8^{nk}	Baltazar C	27.20
		Monetary Crisis		2	118	6	7	$9\frac{1}{2}$	9^{5}	9^{1}	$9^{1\frac{1}{2}}$	Vasquez J	27.40
		Northstar Dancer		2	118	4	10	11	11	10^{8}	10^{14}	Ditmore A	18.40
8Jly72	^{3}Aqu^{13}	Perilous Serenade		2	118	2	6	10^{8}	$10^{1\frac{1}{2}}$	11	11	Gustines H	89.20

Time, :22$\frac{1}{5}$, :45$\frac{2}{5}$, 1:10$\frac{3}{5}$ (With wind in backstretch.). Track fast.

$2 Mutuel Prices:

9-(J)-SECRETARIAT	**4.60**	**3.00**	**2.60**
1-(L)-MASTER ACHIEVER		**5.00**	**3.80**
10-(K)-BET ON IT			**4.00**

Ch. c, by Bold Ruler—Somethingroyal, by Princequillo, Trainer Laurin L. Bred by Meadow Stable (Va).

IN GATE AT 3:09; OFF AT 3:09 1/2, EASTERN DAYLIGHT TIME. Start Good. Won Handily.

SECRETARIAT, rushed into contention after failing to break alertly caught the leaders while racing well out in the track nearing the final furlong and drew off with authority. MASTER ACHIEVER raced forwardly from the start, held on well while trying to get in a bit during the drive but was no match for the winner. BET ON IT weakened from his early efforts. SCANTLING raced very wide. IMPROMPTU was finished leaving the turn. JACQUES WHO, a factor to the stretch, flattened out. FLEET 'N ROYAL was always outrun. IRISH FLAVOR showed some early foot.

Owners— 1, Meadow Stable; 2, Sommer S; 3, Al-Jo Stable; 4, Elmendorf; 5, Ring G; 6, Wimpfheimer J D; 7, Winchell V H; 8, Audley Farm Stable; 9, Brookmeade Stable; 10, Milbar Stable; 11, Karutz W S.

Trainers— 1, Laurin L; 2, Martin F; 3, Parisella J; 4, Nickerson V J; 5, Martin J; 6, Sedlacek W; 7, Lake R P; 9, Baker F J; 9, Kelly T J; 10, Campo J P; 11, Barrera L S.

Scratched—Penrod (24Jun72^{4}Aqu^{6}); Burgeon (4Jly72^{2}Aqu^{6}); Knightly Dawn (4Jly72^{2}Aqu^{10}).

Exacta 9-1 Paid $22.40. Track exacta pool $317,460. OTB Exacta Pool $47,413.

FOURTH RACE

Saratoga

JULY 31, 1972

6 FURLONGS. (1.09 1/5) **ALLOWANCE.** Purse $9,000. 2-year olds which have never won two races. Weights, 118 lbs. Maidens, allowed 5 lbs.

Value of race $9,000, value to winner $5,400, second $1,980, third $1,080, fourth $540. Mutuel pool $90,448, OTB pool $50,675.

Last Raced		Horse	Eqt.	A.	Wt	PP	St	¼	½	Str	Fin	Jockey	Odds $1
15Jly72	^{4}Aqu^{1}	Secretariat	b	2	118	4	7	7	3^{4}	1^{hd}	$1^{1\frac{1}{2}}$	Turcotte R	.40
17Jly72	^{3}Aqu^{1}	Russ Miron	b	2	118	1	2	1^{hd}	1^{hd}	2^{3}	2^{7}	Marquez C H	8.50
17Jly72	^{2}Aqu^{1}	Joe Iz	b	2	118	5	3	$2^{1\frac{1}{2}}$	$2\frac{1}{2}$	3^{5}	$3^{2\frac{1}{2}}$	Rotz J L	11.70
8Jly72	^{8}Lib	Court Ruling	b	2	118	2	6	$4\frac{1}{2}$	4^{2}	4^{3}	$4^{1\frac{1}{2}}$	Patterson G	16.90
22Jly72	^{3}Aqu^{1}	Blackthorn	b	2	118	6	5	$3\frac{1}{2}$	5^{2}	5^{4}	$5^{6\frac{1}{2}}$	Venezia M	6.50
22Jly72	^{5}Aqu^{4}	Tropic Action		2	118	7	1	6^{1}	7	7	$6\frac{3}{4}$	Castaneda M	30.30
19Jly72	^{7}Aqu^{4}	Fat Frank	b	2	118	3	4	5^{hd}	$6\frac{1}{2}$	$6\frac{1}{2}$	7	Pineda R	9.90

Time, :23$\frac{1}{5}$, :46$\frac{2}{5}$, 1:10$\frac{4}{5}$ (With wind in backstretch.). Track fast.

$2 Mutuel Prices:

4-(D)-SECRETARIAT	**2.80**	**2.40**	**2.20**
1-(A)-RUSS MIRON		**5.00**	**5.20**
5-(E)-JOE IZ			**3.40**

Ch. c, by Bold Ruler—Somethingroyal, by Princequillo. Trainer Laurin L. Bred by Meadow Stable (Va).

IN GATE AT 3:06; OFF AT 3:06, EASTERN DAYLIGHT TIME. Start Good. Won Ridden out.

SECRETARIAT, unhurried early, moved to the leaders with a rush approaching the stretch and outfinished RUSS MIRON under good handling. The latter saved ground while vying for the lead and held on well to be second best. JOE IZ tired from his early efforts. COURT RULING, well placed while saving ground early, had nothing left after going a half. BLACKTHORN had brief speed. TROPIC ACTION was outrun after coming away alertly. FAT FRANK was finished early.

Owners—1, Meadow Stable; 2, Miron K L; L; 3, Straus J R; 4, Whitney C V; 5, Woodside Stud; 6, Lieberman J; 7, Rosoff A.

Trainers— 1, Laurin L; 2, Lake R P; 3, Pardue H C; 4, Poole G T; 5, McManus F J; 6, Buxton M A; 7, Preger M C.

SEVENTH RACE

Saratoga

AUGUST 16, 1972

6 FURLONGS. (1.09 1/5) **SANFORD.** $25,000 Added Fifty-Ninth Running. 2-year-olds. By subscription of $50 each, which shall accompany the nomination; $125 to pass the entry box; $125 to start, with $25,000 added. The added money and all fees to be divided 60% to the winner, 22% to second, 12% to third and 6% to fourth. Weights, 121 lbs. Starters to be named at the closing time of entries. A trophy will be presented to the owner of winner. Closed with 25 nominations.

Value of race $27,750, value to winner $16,650, second $6,105, third $3,330, fourth $1,665. Mutuel pool $124,583, OTB pool $76,548.

Last Raced		Horse	Eqt.	A.	Wt	PP	St	¼	½	Str	Fin	Jockey	Odds $1
31Jly72	^{4}Sar^{1}	Secretariat	b	2	121	2	5	5	4^{4}	$1\frac{1}{2}$	1^{3}	Turcotte R	1.50
19Jly72	^{7}Aqu^{1}	Linda's Chief		2	121	1	3	$3^{1\frac{1}{2}}$	$3\frac{1}{2}$	2^{2}	2^{6}	Baeza B	.60
9Aug72	^{4}Sar^{4}	Northstar Dancer	b	2	121	5	2	$2^{1\frac{1}{2}}$	1^{2}	4^{5}	$3^{3\frac{1}{2}}$	Cordero A Jr	a-8.00
31Jly72	^{3}Sar^{1}	Trevose		2	121	4	4	$1\frac{1}{2}$	$1\frac{1}{2}$	3^{hd}	$4^{2\frac{1}{2}}$	Belmonte E	a-8.00
7Aug72	^{7}Sar^{4}	Sailor Go Home	b	2	121	3	1	$4\frac{1}{2}$	5	5	5	Velasquez J	8.70

a-Coupled: Northstar Dancer and Trevose.

Time, :22$\frac{4}{5}$, :46$\frac{1}{5}$, 1:10 (Against wind in backstretch.). Track fast.

$2 Mutuel Prices:

5-(D)-SECRETARIAT	**5.00**	**2.40**
4-(C)-LINDA'S CHIEF	**2.40**	**2.40**

(No Show Wagering)

Ch. c, by Bold Ruler—Somethingroyal, by Princequillo. Trainer Laurin L. Bred by Meadow Stable (Va).

IN GATE AT 4:55; OFF AT 4:55, EASTERN DAYLIGHT TIME Start Good Won Ridden out

SECRETARIAT, sent up behind the leaders approaching the stretch, drove between TREVOSE and NORTHSTAR DANCER to reach the front nearing the final furlong and drew off while being ridden out. LINDA'S CHIEF, away alertly from the inside, was eased back to get to the outside midway along the backstretch, loomed boldly while racing wide into the stretch but was no match for the winner. NORTHSTAR DANCER, a forward factor to the upper stretch, faltered. TREVOSE saved ground while making the pace but had nothing left leaving the furlong grounds. SAILOR GO HOME fell back early.

Owners— 1, Meadow Stable; 2, Hellman N; 3, Milbar Stable; 4, Joalan Stable; 5, Wiersum F W

Trainers— 1, Laurin L; 2, Scotti A A; 3, Campo J P; 4, Campo J P; 5, Metcalf R.

Scratched—Biller's Brother (8Aug72^{5}Sar^{2}); Cades Cove (7Aug72^{7}Sar^{6}).

SEVENTH RACE
Saratoga
AUGUST 26, 1972

6 ½ FURLONGS. (1.15 3/5) **HOPEFUL STAKES.** $75,000 added Sixty-Eighth running. 2-year-olds. By subscription of $150 each, which shall accompany the nomination; $375 to pass the entry box, $375 to start with $75,000 added. The added money and all fees to be divided 60% to the winner, 22% to second, 12% to third and 5% to fourth. Weight 121 lbs. Starters to be named at the closing time of entries. Trophies will be presented to the winning owner, trainer and jockey. Closed with 32 nominations.

Value of race $86,550, value to winner $51,930, second $19,041, third $10,386, fourth $5,193. Mutuel pool $192,658, OTB pool $124,814.

Last Raced		Horse	Eqt.	A.	Wt	PP	St	¼	½	Str	Fin	Jockey	Odds $1
16Aug72	^{7}Sar^1	Secretariat	b	2	121	8	8	9	1^{hd}	1^4	1^5	Turcotte R	.30
19Aug72	^{8}Sar^1	Flight to Glory		2	121	9	1	5^1	3^1	2^2	2^{hd}	Pincay L Jr	25.20
7Aug72	^{7}Sar^1	Stop The Music		2	121	1	6	$3\frac{1}{2}$	$5\frac{1}{2}$	$3\frac{1}{2}$	3^2	Vasquez J	7.80
7Aug72	^{7}Sar^2	Step Nicely	b	2	121	4	4	$4\frac{1}{2}$	$8\frac{1}{2}$	6^5	$4^{1\frac{1}{2}}$	Baeza B	7.00
12Aug72	^{8}Lib^3	Torsion		2	121	7	9	$7\frac{1}{2}$	$4\frac{1}{2}$	4^{hd}	5^2	Belmont E	a-13.90
12Aug72	^{8}AP^2	Sunny South	b	2	121	3	3	1^3	2^{hd}	5^1	6^4	Gomez A	15.30
9Aug72	^{4}Sar^1	Branford Court	b	2	121	5	2	2^1	$6^{1\frac{1}{2}}$	8^6	7^{hd}	Velasquez J	14.00
16Aug72	^{7}Sar^4	Trevose		2	121	2	5	$6\frac{1}{2}$	$7\frac{1}{2}$	7^{hd}	8^5	Venezia M	a-13.90
12Aug72	^{6}Rkm^4	River Of Fire		2	121	6	7	8^1	9	9	9	Pineda R	79.20

a-Coupled: Torsion and Trevose.

Time, :22⅘, :46⅗, 1:09⅘, 1:15⅕ (No wind in backstretch). Track fast.

$2 Mutuel Prices:
7-(H)-SECRETARIAT 2.60 2.40 2.10
8-(I)-FLIGHT TO GLORY 8.40 4.00
2-(A)-STOP THE MUSIC 2.80

Ch. c, by Bold Ruler—Somethingroyal, by Princequillo. Trainer Laurin L. Bred by Meadow Stable (Va).

IN GATE AT 4.58; OFF AT 4:58 EASTERN DAYLIGHT TIME. Start Good. Won Handily.

SECRETARIAT, outrun away from the gate, looped his field on the turn to reach the front approaching the stretch and drew off with authority. FLIGHT TO GLORY went after SUNNY SOUTH rounding the turn but was no match for the winner and lasted for the place. STOP THE MUSIC, sent up along the inside soon after the start, had no place to go along the rail nearing the stretch, came out between horses for the drive and continued on gamely. STEP NICELY dropped back between horses at the turn and failed to seriously menace. TORSION moved fast to make a bid midway of the turn but lacked a further response. SUNNY SOUTH tired badly from his early efforts. BRANFORD COURT gave way leaving the turn. TREVOSE tired. RIVER OF FIRE wasn't able to keep pace after lacking room between horses nearing the end of the backstretch.

Owners— 1, Meadow Stable; 2, Wilcox Mrs A A; 3, Greentree Stable; 4, Hobeau Farm; 5, Buckland Fm; 6, Gilbride W P; 7, Rokeby Stable; 8, Joalan Stable; 9, Lake D.

Trainers— 1, Laurin L; 2, Yowell E; 3, Gaver J M; 4, Jerkens H A; 5, Campo J P; 6, Merrill F H; 7, Burch E; 8, Campo J P; 9, Bradley J M.

SEVENTH RACE
BELMONT
SEPTEMBER 16, 1972

6 ½ FURLONGS. (1.15 4/5) **FUTURITY,** $75,000 added Eighty Third running. 2-year-olds nominated to The Futurities of 1972 by a joint payment of $30 each. August 15, 1970. To continue eligibility, the following payments must be made to the New York Racing Association Inc. by December 1, 1971, $50 each; by August 1, 1972, $200 each. (Fillies which have been kept eligible for The Matron of 1972 may be made eligible for The Futurity of 1972 not later than August 1, 1972 upon payment of $250 each.) Starters to pay $1,500 additional with $75,000 added by The New York Racing Association Inc. of which $4,000 to the nominator of the winner; and to the nominator of the second and third horses, $2,000 and $1,000 respectively. The balance, together with one-third of the nominating fees to The Futurities of 1972 and all further eligibility and starting fees, to be divided 60%, 22%, 12% and 6% to the winners of the first, second, third and fourth horses respectively. Weight, 122 lbs. Starters to be named at the closing time of entires. A Gold Medallion trophy will be presented to the owner of the winner and trophies to the winning trainer and jockey. Closed August 15, 1970 with 1,085 nominations at $10 of which 509 remained eligible after December 1, 1971 paying an additional $50 each; 112 remained eligible after August 1, 1972 paying an additional $200 each.)

Value of race $144,200, value to winner $82,320, second $30,184, third $16,464, fourth $8,232: Nominator awards 1st $4,000, 2nd $2000, 3rd $1000. Mutuel pool $322,378, OTB pool $87,374. Minus show pools, Track $4,985; OTB $795.

Last Raced		Horse	Eqt.	A.	Wt	PP	St	¼	½	Str	Fin	Jockey	Odds $1
26Aug72	^{7}Sar^1	Secretariat	b	2	122	4	5	6^1	$5\frac{1}{2}$	1^2	$1^{1\frac{3}{4}}$	Turcotte R	.20
26Aug72	^{7}Sar^3	Stop The Music		2	122	6	2	5^2	4^1	4^4	2^5	Pincay L Jr	8.20
19Aug72	^{8}Mth^3	Swift Courier	b	2	122	3	1	1^1	1^{hd}	2^{hd}	$3^{2\frac{1}{2}}$	Cespedes R	a-14.90
2Sep72	^{4}Bel^1	Whatabreeze		2	122	5	6	2^1	2^2	$3\frac{1}{2}$	4^1	Velasquez J	6.80
2Sep72	^{8}ElP^1	Crimson Falcon	b	2	122	7	4	3^1	$3\frac{1}{2}$	$5\frac{1}{2}$	5^{hd}	Layland W	15.70
26Aug72	^{7}Sar^5	Torsion	b	2	122	2	7	7	7	6^4	6^4	Castaneda M	a-14.90
9Sep72	^{8}Atl^1	Gallant Knave		2	122	1	3	$4\frac{1}{2}$	6^2	7	7	Rotz J L	14.90

a-Coupled: Swift Courier and Torsion.

Time, :22⅗, :45⅗, 1:10, 1:16⅖ (Against wind in backstretch.). Track fast.

$2 Mutuel Prices:
3-(D)-SECRETARIAT 2.40 2.20 2.10
5-(F)-STOP THE MUSIC............. 3.00 2.10
1-(C)-SWEET COURIER (a-entry) 2.10

Ch. c, by Bold Ruler—Somethingroyal, by Princequillo, Trainer Laurin L. Bred by Meadow Stud Inc (Va).

IN GATE AT 4:53; OFF AT 4:53, EASTERN DAYLIGHT TIME. Start Good. Won Handily.

SECRETARIAT, unhurried following the start, moved boldly around horses to make his bid leaving the turn, quickly drew off nearing the final furlong and was never seriously threatened. STOP THE MUSIC was looking for room behind the leaders while moving approaching the stretch, swung out after straightening away for the drive and finished strongly to best the others. SWIFT COURIER tired from his early efforts. WHATABREEZE, rushed between horses to reach contention soon after the start, engaged SWIFT COURIER before going a half but had nothing left leaving the furlong grounds. CRIMSON FALCON, a factor to the stretch, flattened out. TORSION was never close. GALLANT KNAVE stopped badly.

Owners— 1, Meadow Stable; 2, Greentree Stable; 3, Elmendorf; 4, Elcee-H Stable; 5, Crimson King Farm; 6, Buckland Farm; 7, Appleton A I.

Trainers— 1, Laurin L; 2, Graver J M; 3, Campo J P; 4, Gauthier A; 5, Salmon P W Jr; 6, Campo J P; 7, Goldfine L. M.

SEVENTH RACE
Belmont
OCTOBER 14, 1972

1 MILE. (1.34⅖) **THE CHAMPAGNE 101ST RUNNING.** $125,000 Added. 2-year-olds. By subscription of $250 each, to accompany the nomination; $625 to pass the entry box; $625 to start, with $125,000 added, the added money and all fees to be divided 60% to the winner, 22% to second, 12% to third and 6% to fourth. 122 lbs. Starters to be named at the closing time of entires. The New York Racing Association to add THE CHAMPAGNE CHALLENGE CUP, to be won three times, not necessarily consecutively by the same owner before becoming his or her property. Trophies will also be presented to the winning owner, trainer and jockey. (Nominations closed Saturday, September 30 with 26 Nominations).

Value of race $145,500, value to winner $87,900, second $32,230, third $17,580, fourth $8,790. Mutuel pool $439,980, OTB pool $109,979.

Last Raced		Horse	Eqt.	A.	Wt	PP	St	¼	½	¾	Str	Fin	Jockey	Odds $1
16Sep72	^{7}Bel^1	Secretariat	b	2	122	4	12	$11\frac{1}{2}$	$9^{1\frac{1}{2}}$	5^{hd}	$1\frac{1}{2}$	1^2	Turcotte R	[D] a-.70
4Oct72	^{7}Bel^2	Stop The Music		2	122	6	8	$8\frac{1}{2}$	8^3	6^2	3^2	2^2	Rotz J L	6.80
4Oct72	^{7}Bel^1	Step Nicely	b	2	122	3	11	$10\frac{1}{2}$	11^2	7^6	4^1	$3^{1\frac{1}{2}}$	Cordero A Jr	6.50
4Oct72	^{7}Bel^6	Puntilla		2	122	8	4	$6\frac{1}{2}$	$2\frac{1}{2}$	1^{hd}	$2\frac{1}{2}$	4^5	Baeza B	9.60
4Oct72	^{7}Bel^3	Linda's Chief	b	2	122	10	2	7^2	$3\frac{1}{2}$	2^2	5^2	$5^{1\frac{1}{2}}$	Pincay L Jr	8.20
25Sep72	^{5}Bel^1	Raise And Rule	b	2	122	11	1	9^4	$7\frac{1}{2}$	$4\frac{1}{2}$	6^5	6^5	Maple E	63.20
29Sep72	^{4}Bel^1	Scantling		2	122	9	10	12	10^{hd}	$8^{1\frac{1}{2}}$	7^3	7^5	Venezia M	45.80
4Oct72	^{7}Bel^4	Angle Light	b	2	122	1	7	1^1	1^2	3^1	8^3	$8^{1\frac{1}{2}}$	Baltazar C	a-.70
7Oct72	^{7}WO^{12}	Zaca Spirit	b	2	122	12	3	$4^{1\frac{1}{2}}$	$4\frac{1}{2}$	10^3	9^2	9^3	Ruane J	21.00
3Oct72	^{4}Bel^1	Expression	b	2	122	5	9	$5^{1\frac{1}{2}}$	$6^{1\frac{1}{2}}$	$9\frac{1}{2}$	10^4	10^5	Belmonte E	18.00
4Oct72	^{7}Bel^7	Rapid Sage	b	2	122	7	6	2^{hd}	5^{hd}	11^8	11^5	11^8	Woodhouse R	79.10
30Sep72	^{8}Mar^1	Osage River		2	122	2	5	$3\frac{1}{2}$	12	12	12	12	Howard R	54.70

[D] —Secretariat Disqualified and placed second.
a-Coupled: Secretariat and Angle Light.

Time, :22⅘, :45⅕, 1:09⅘, 1:35 (Crosswind in backstretch). Track fast.

$2 Mutuel Prices:
5-(F)-STOP THE MUSIC..............15.60 4.20 3.00
1-(D)-SECRETARIAT (a-entry) 2.60 2.20
3-(C)-STEP NICELY 3.20

Stop The Music—B. c, by Hall to Reason—Bebopper, by Tom Fool. Trainer Gaver J M. Bred by Greentree Stud Inc (Ky).

IN GATE AT 4.52; OFF AT 4:52, EASTERN DAYLIGHT TIME. Start Good. Won Driving.

SECRETARIAT, void of early foot, settled suddenly after going a half, circled horses while moving leaving the turn, bore in bumping STOP THE MUSIC just inside the final three-sixteenths, was straightened up under left-handed pressure and drew away while being strongly ridden. SECRETARIAT was disqualified and placed second. STOP THE MUSIC, was forced over on LINDA'S CHIEF when SECRETARIAT bore in, continued on gamely when clear but wasn't good enough. STEP NICELY launched a rally while racing wide approaching the stretch, loomed a threat near midstretch but failed to sustain his bid. PUNTILLA gained a narrow advantage soon after going five furlongs but failed to stay in a stiff drive. LINDA'S CHIEF moved fast from the oustdie to engage PUNTILLA nearing the turn but lacked a further response. SCANTLING was always outrun. ANGLE LIGHT, hustled to the front along the inside early, was finished after going three-quarters. ZACA SPIRIT gave way soon after going a half, as did EXPRESSION. RAPID SAGE tired badly from his early efforts. OSAGE RIVER stopped badly after showing brief speed.

Owners— 1, Meadow Stable; 2, Greentree Stable; 3, Hobeau Farm; 4, Cragwood Stable; 5, Hellman N; 6, Schiff J M; 7, Elmendorf; 8, Whittaker E; 9, Frostad G C; 10, De Cap Stable; 11, Sestak Roslyn B; 12, Wright E B.

Trainers— 1, Laurin L; 2, Gaver J M; 3 Jerkens H A; 4, Miller M; 5, Scotti A A; 6, Kelly T J; 7, Nickerson V J; 8, Laurin L; 9, Whitaker C D; 10, Frankel R; 11, O'Chade E A; 12, Smithwick A P.

Chart of Laurel Futurity

SEVENTH RACE
Laurel
OCTOBER 28, 1972

1 1/16 MILES. (1.42⅖) **THE LAUREL FUTURITY** $50,000 Added. 15th Running. 2-Year-Olds (Foals of 1970), nominated to the Futuries of 1972 by a joint payment of $30 each August 15, 1970. To continue eligibility, the following additional payments must be made to Laurel Race Course, Inc., P.O. Box 130, Laurel, Maryland 20810: BY December 1, 1972, $50 each; by June 1, 1972, $200 each. To pass the entry box $500. Starters to pay $500 additional. Laurel Race Course, Inc. to add $50,000 of which $2,500, $1,500 and $1,000 respectively to the nominators of the first, second and third horses. The balance, together with one-third of the nominating fees to The Futuries of 1972, and all further eligibility payments and starting fees, to be divided 65%, 20%, 10% and 5% to the owners of the first, second, third and fourth horses respectively. 122 lbs. Starters to be named through the entry box by the usual time of closing. Closed August 15, 1970 with 1085 nominations. 467 made the $50 payment December 1, 1971; and 213 made the $200 payment June 1, 1972. (No Supplementary Nominations.) The McLean Cup to the winner for one year. Trophies to the winning owner, trainer and jockey.

Value of race $133,300, value to winner $83,395, second $25,550, third $12,830, fourth $6,415; $2500 to 1st nominator, $1500 to 2d, $1000 to 3d. Mutuel pool $103,031, Minus place pool $181,815.

Last Raced		Horse	Eqt.	A.	Wt	PP	St	¼	½	¾	Str	Fin	Jockey	Odds $1
14Oct72	^{7}Bel^1	Secretariat	b	2	122	5	6	6	5^{16}	5^{10}	1^5	1^4	Turcotte R	a-.10
14Oct72	^{7}Bel^2	Stop The Music		2	122	1	4	$4^{2\frac{1}{2}}$	4^{hd}	3^1	2^4	2^4	Rotz J L	3.80
14Oct72	^{7}Bel^8	Angle Light		2	122	6	3	$3^{2\frac{1}{2}}$	$3^{2\frac{1}{2}}$	4^{hd}	4^5	3^1	Feliciano B M	a-.10
21Oct72	^{6}Aqu^1	Whatabreeze	b	2	122	2	2	2^4	$2^{2\frac{1}{2}}$	2^1	3^3	4^5	Broussard R	15.00
21Oct72	^{6}Kee^2	Rocket Pocket	b	2	122	3	1	1^3	1^5	1^1	5^4	5^1	Sibille R	30.40
21Oct72	^{7}Lri^4	The Lark Twist	b	2	122	4	5	$5^{1\frac{1}{2}}$	6	6	6	6	Davidson J	62.20

a-Coupled: Secretariat and Angle Light.

Time, :22⅘, :45⅘, 1:11⅖, 1:35⅕, 1:42⅘ Track sloppy.

$2 Mutuel Prices:
1-SECRETARIAT (a-entry) 2.20 2.10 2.10
2-STOP THE MUSIC................ 2.10 2.10
1-ANGLE LIGHT (a-entry) 2.20 2.10 2.10

Ch. c, by Bold Ruler—Somethingroyal, by Princequillo, Trainer Laurin L. Bred by Meadow Stud Inc (Va).

IN GATE AT 4:08; OFF AT 4:08, 1/2, EASTERN DAYLIGHT TIME. Start Good. Won Easily.

SECRETARIAT, unhurried at the start and carefully kept on the outside throughout, responded without the need of the whip when given rein leaving the backstretch, forged to the lead entering the stretch and won in hand. STOP THE MUSIC, also unhurried early, responded between horses leaving the backstretch, continued gamely in the stretch and was easily second best. ANGLE LIGHT responded leaving the backstretch, but could not keep pace with the first two in the stretch. WHATABREEZE, nearest the pace to the stretch, flattened out in the final furlong. ROCKET POCKET sprinted to a long lead before a quarter, increased his margin on the backstretch, but had little left for the stretch run. THE LARK TWIST was always outrun.

Owners— 1, Meadow Stable; 2, Greentree Stable; 3, Whittaker E; 4, Elcee-H Stable/ 5, Matherne C J; 6, Boyce L.

Trainers— 1, Laurin L; 2, Graver J M Jr.; 3, Laurin L; 4, Gauthier A; 5, Matherne C J; 6, Boyce L.

Scratched—Ribarno (12Oct72 ^{3}Bel^2).

EIGHTH RACE

Garden State

NOVEMBER 18, 1972

1 1/16 MILES. (1.41) 20th Running. **THE GARDEN STATE OF 1972—** $125,000 Added. 2-year-olds (Foals of 1970). By subscription of $25 each if made on or before August 16, 1971, or $40 each if made after August 16, 1971, and on or before December 15, 1971, fee to accompany the nomination or the entry shall be void. To remain eligible, the following cash payments must be made: March 15, 1972, $125 each; June 15, 1972, $250 each; $1,000 to pass the entry box and $1,000 to start. The Garden State Racing Association to add $125,000 (estimated gross value $275,000). The added money together with all nomination fees, eligibility payments, entry and starting fees for The Garden State of 1972 to be divided—60% to first, 20% to second, 10% to third 5% to fourth; with 5% for nominators' awards to be distributed as follows: 60% 7% to the nominator of the first, second, third and fourth horses respectively. A supplementary nomination made subsequent to an original that became ineligible, the nominators' award will be distributed to the original nominator. Weights; Colts and geldings, 122 lbs./ fillies, 119 lbs. (Starters to be named through the entry box at the closing time of entries.) Closed August 15, 1971 with 768 nominations at $25 each. Final closing December 15, 1971 with 146 nominations at $40 each of which 439 made second payment of $125 each on March 15, 1972 and 247 made payment of $250 each on June 15, 1972. Supplementary nominations may be made at the closing time of entries by payment of a fee of $10,000 each. The first finishers in the GARDEN STATE are automatically made eligible for the JERSEY DERBY OF 1973 as to the nominating fees.

Value of race $298,665, value to winner $179,199, second $59,733, third $29,866, fourth $14,934; Nominator awards $8,959.95; $2,986.65; $1,941.32; $1,044.33. Mutuel pool $185,759, Minus place pool $1.

Last Raced		Horse	Eqt.	A.	Wt	PP	St	¼	½	¾	Str	Fin	Jockey	Odds $1
28Oct72	^{7}Lrl^{1}	Secretariat	b	2	122	6	6	6	4^{hd}	$3^{1\frac{1}{2}}$	$1^{1\frac{1}{2}}$	$1^{3\frac{1}{2}}$	Turcotte R	a-.10
7Nov72	^{8}GS^{2}	Angle Light		2	122	3	1	2^{3}	2^{3}	1^{3}	2^{3}	$2^{1\frac{1}{2}}$	Turcotte R L	a-.10
7Nov72	^{8}GS^{3}	(S)Step Nicely	b	2	122	4	5	$5^{1\frac{1}{2}}$	6	$5^{1\frac{1}{2}}$	4^{2}	$3^{\frac{3}{4}}$	Tejeira J	8.00
7Nov72	^{8}GS^{1}	(S)Impecunious	b	2	122	5	3	3^{1}	3^{hd}	2^{hd}	3^{hd}	$4^{\frac{3}{4}}$	Moseley J W	D 8.10
7Nov72	^{9}GS^{4}	Knightly Dawn		2	122	2	4	4^{2}	5^{2}	6	5^{3}	5^{12}	Areilano J	35.90
28Oct72	^{10}Rin^{3}	Piamem		2	122	1	2	1^{hd}	1^{hd}	4^{hd}	6	6	Parra A	9.70

D -Impecunious Disqualified and placed fifth.
a-Coupled: Secretariat and Angle Light.
(S) Supplementary nomination.

Time, :24$\frac{1}{5}$, :47$\frac{2}{5}$, 1:12, 1:37$\frac{4}{5}$, 1:44$\frac{2}{5}$ Track fast.

$2 Mutuel Prices:
1-SECRETARIAT (a-entry) . . . . 2.20 2.10 —
1-ANGLE LIGHT (a-entry) . . . . 2.20 2.10 —
(No Show Wagering)

Ch. c, by Bold Ruler—Somethingroyal, by Princequillo. Trainer Laurin L. Bred by Meadow Stud Inc (Va).

IN GATE AT 3:59; OFF AT 3:59, EASTERN STANDARD TIME. Start Good. Won Handily.

SECRETARIAT, allowed to settle into stride, rallied boldly around horses on the final turn, gained command after straightening into the stretch and was in hand in the late stages. ANGLE LIGHT pressed the early pace closely, drew into a clear lead leaving the backstretch and was no match for his stablemate when challenged. STEP NICELY, unhurried for five furlongs, rallied when called upon but was unable to menace. IMPECUNIOUS could not stay with the leaders early while along the inside, came out midway of the final turn to bump KNIGHTLY DAWN, reached the runner up position entering the stretch and faltered. KNIGHTLY DAWN, in hand for a half, was caught between IMPECUNIOUS and SECRETARIAT at the five-sixteenths pole, was bumped by the former, fell back and could not menace. Following an objection lodged by jockey Jaime Arellano against the riders of SECRETARIAT and IMPECUNIOUS for alleged interference in the vicinity of the five-sixteenths pole, IMPECUNIOUS was disqualified and placed fifth. PIAMEM was sent through along the inside to gain the lead in the run to the clubhouse turn, could not shake off ANGLE LIGHT and tired.

Owners— 1, Meadow Stable; 2, Whittaker E; 3, Hobeau Farm; 4, Feinberg Mrs R L; 5, Sommer S; 6, Alfonso M.

Trainers— 1, Laurin L; 2, Laurin L; 3, Jerkens H A; 4, Handy G R; 5, Martin F; 6, Azpurua M.

SEVENTH RACE

Aqueduct

MARCH 17, 1973

7 FURLONGS. (1.20 1/5) **14TH RUNNING THE BAY SHORE.** $25,000 Added. 3-year-olds. By subscription of $50 each, which shall accompany the nomination; $125 to pass the entry box; $125 to start, with $25,000 added. The added money and all fees to be divided 60% to the winner, 22% to second, 12% to third and 6% to fourth. Weight 126 lbs. Non-winners of $50,000 allowed 3 lbs.; $25,000 twice, 5 lbs.; $15,000 twice in 1973, 8 lbs.; three races other than maiden or claiming, 11 lbs. Starters to be named at the closing time of entries. A trophy will be presented to the owner of the winner. (Closed Saturday, March 3 with 25 nominations)

Value of race $27,750, value to winner $16,650, second $6,105, third $3,330, fourth $1,665. Mutuel pool $344,718, OTB pool $87,324. Minus Show Pools—Track $5,198.81. OTB $977.96.

Last Raced		Horse	Eqt.	A.	Wt	PP	St	¼	½	Str	Fin	Jockey	Odds $1
18Nov72	^{9}GS^{1}	Secretariat	b	3	126	4	5	5^{2}	5^{3}	1^{hd}	$1^{4\frac{1}{2}}$	Turcotte R	.20
3Mar73	^{7}Aqu^{1}	Champagne Charlie		3	118	1	4	$4^{1\frac{1}{2}}$	3^{hd}	2^{hd}	$2^{2\frac{1}{2}}$	Venezia M	8.60
16Dec72	^{8}Lib^{1}	Impecunious	b	3	126	5	2	3^{2}	$2^{\frac{1}{2}}$	4^{5}	3^{hd}	Moseley J W	13.50
3Mar73	^{7}Aqu^{3}	Actuality		3	118	3	1	2^{1}	4^{1}	$3^{\frac{1}{2}}$	4^{6}	Woodhouse R	10.20
8Mar73	^{5}Aqu^{1}	Torsion		3	115	6	6	6	6	5^{6}	5^{16}	Velasquez J	7.30
17Sep72	^{9}WO^{7}	Close Image		3	115	2	3	$1^{1\frac{1}{2}}$	$1^{1\frac{1}{2}}$	6	6	Maple E	29.40

Time, :22$\frac{1}{5}$, :44$\frac{4}{5}$, 1:10, 1:23$\frac{1}{5}$ (With wind in backstretch.). Track sloppy.

$2 Mutuel Prices:
4-(D)-SECRETARIAT 2.40 2.20 2.10
1-(A)-CHAMPAGNE CHARLIE 3.40 2.10
5-(E)-IMPECUNIOUS 2.10

Ch. c, by Bold Ruler—Somethingroyal, by Princequillo. Trainer Laurin L. Bred by Meadow Stud Inc (Va).

IN GATE AT 4:39; OFF AT 4:39 EASTERN STANDARD TIME. Start Good for all but TORSION. Won Ridden Out.

SECRETARIAT bumped with TORSION soon after leaving the chute, commenced to rally nearing the end of the backstretch, was steadied along behind the leaders while looking for room rounding the turn, drove between horses to make his run after entering the stretch and drew away while being ridden out. SECRETARIAT went out a mile in 1:37$\frac{2}{5}$. A foul claim against the winner by the rider of IMPECUNIOUS, for alleged interference through the stretch, was not allowed. CHAMPAGNE CHARLIE, never far back, joined the leaders from the outside entering the stretch and continued on with good energy to be second best. IMPECUNIOUS made a bid approaching the stretch, was caught in close quarters between horses nearing the final furlong and gave way. ACTUALITY moved through along the inside to gain a narrow lead nearing the stretch, came out slightly after straightening away from the drive and faltered under pressure. TORSION was always outrun after going in the air at the start. CLOSE IMAGE stopped badly after showing good early foot.

Owners—1, Meadow Stable; 2, Wimpfheimer J D; 3, Feinberg Mrs R L; 4, Tartan Stable; 5, Buckland Farm; 6, Campeau Yves.

Trainers—1, Laurin L; 2, Sedlacek W; 3, Handy G R; 4, Schulhofer F S; 5, Campo J P; 6, Pion R.

SEVENTH RACE

Aqueduct

APRIL 7, 1973

1 MILE. (1.33 2/5) 21st Running. **THE GOTHAM.** $50,000 Added 3-year-olds. By subscription of $100 each, which shall accompany the nomination; $250 to pass the entry box; $250 to start, with $50,000 added. The added money and all fees to be divided 60% to the winner. 22% to second, 12% to third and 6% to fourth. Weight 122 lbs. Winners of a race of $75,000 twice, 4 lbs. additional. Non-winners of $50,000, allowed 3 lbs.; $25,000, 5 lbs.; $15,000 in 1973, 8 lbs. Starters to be named at the closing time of entries. Trophies will be presented to the winning owner, trainer and jockey. Closed Saturday March 24 with 23 Nominations.

Value of race $55,550, value to winner $33,330, second $12,221, third $6,666, fourth $3,333. Mutuel pool $403,763, OTB pool $140,792. Minus Show Pools, Track $14,900.89, OTB $2,534.58.

Last Raced		Horse	Eqt.	A.	Wt	PP	St	¼	½	¾	Str	Fin	Jockey	Odds $1
17Mar73	^{7}Aqu^{1}	Secretariat	b	3	126	3	4	$3^{\frac{1}{2}}$	1^{hd}	1^{2}	$1^{\frac{1}{2}}$	1^{3}	Turcotte R	.10
17Mar73	^{7}Aqu^{2}	Champagne Charlie		3	117	5	1	$4^{\frac{1}{2}}$	3^{1}	2^{3}	2^{10}	2^{10}	Venezia M	10.50
17Mar73	^{4}Aqu^{2}	Flush		3	117	4	5	6	6	$5^{\frac{1}{2}}$	$3^{\frac{1}{2}}$	$3^{2\frac{1}{2}}$	Ussery R	28.60
16Mar73	^{7}Aqu^{1}	Dawn Flight		3	114	1	3	1^{1}	$2^{\frac{1}{2}}$	3^{2}	$4^{1\frac{1}{2}}$	$4^{1\frac{1}{2}}$	Santiago A	5.90
31Mar73	^{6}Aqu^{1}	Harrison Kid	b	3	114	6	2	2^{hd}	4^{4}	4^{4}	5^{6}	$5^{4\frac{1}{2}}$	Arellano J	15.10
28Mar73	^{6}Pim^{1}	King Calabrese		3	114	2	6	57	5^{4}	6	6	6	Maple E	29.60

Time, :23$\frac{1}{5}$, :45$\frac{1}{5}$, 1:08$\frac{3}{5}$, 1:33$\frac{2}{5}$ (With Wind in backstretch). Track fast.
Equals track record

$2 Mutuel Prices:
3-SECRETARIAT 2.20 2.10 2.10
5-CHAMPAGNE CHARLIE 2.60 2.10
4-FLUSH 2.10

Ch. c, by Bold Ruler—Somethingroyal, by Princequillo. Trainer Laurin L. Bred by Meadow Stud Inc. (Va).

IN GATE AT 4.52 EASTERN STANDARD TIME Start Good. Won Ridden out

SECRETARIAT, away in good order, ducked to the inside to join the leaders before going three furlongs, opened a clear lead while saving ground around the turn, was roused when challenged by CHAMPAGNE CHARLIE after entering the stretch and drew off under a hand ride. CHAMPAGNE CHARLIE broke alertly, was carried out by DAWN FLIGHT at the turn, moved fast to go after SECRETARIAT into the stretch but was no match for that one while easily besting the others. FLUSH, void of early foot, passed only tired horses. DAWN FLIGHT showed good early foot, bore out into CHAMPAGNE CHARLIE at the turn, gave way readily thereafter and was finished when jockey Santiago lost his whip after entering the stretch. Foul claims against CHAMPAGNE CHARLIE and DAWN FLIGHT, by the rider of HARRISON KID, for alleged interference at the turn, were not allowed. HARRISON KID gave up soon after going a half. KING CALABRESE, hustled into contention along the inside early, was finished before going a half.

Owners— 1, Meadow Stable; 2, Wimpfheimer J D; 3, Buckland Farm; 4, Elmendorf; 5, Rosoff A; 6, Hutton L.

Trainers— 1, Laurin L; 2, Sedlacek W; 3, Campo J P; 4, Nickerson V J; 5, Preger M C; 6, Currier E T.

Scratched— Step Nicely (29Mar73^{7}Aqu^{1})

SEVENTH RACE

Aqueduct

APRIL 21, 1973

1 1/8 MILES. (1.47 1/5) 49th Running **THE WOOD MEMORIAL** Purse $100,000 Added. 3-year-olds. By subscription of $200 each, which shall accompany the nomination; $500 to pass the entry box; $500 to start, with $100,000 added. The added money and all fees to be divided 60% to the winner, 22% to second, 12% to third and 6% to fourth. Weight 126 lbs. Starters to be named at the closing time of entries. Trophies will be presented to the winning owner, trainer and jockey. Closed with 27 nominations.

Value of race $144,900, value to winner $68,940, second $25,278, third $13,788, fourth $6,894. Mutual pool $448,023, OTB pool $126,822.

Last Raced		Horse	Eqt.	A.	Wt	PP	St	¼	½	¾	Str	Fin	Jockey	Odds $1
31Mar73	^{9}FG^{3}	Angle Light		3	126	8	1	1^{1}	$1^{1\frac{1}{2}}$	$1^{1\frac{1}{2}}$	$1^{1\frac{1}{2}}$	1^{hd}	Vasquez J	c-.30
31Mar73	^{8}SA^{1}	Sham	b	3	126	2	2	$2^{1\frac{1}{2}}$	2^{2}	2^{2}	2^{2}	2^{4}	Velasquez J	2.60
7Apr73	^{7}Aqu^{1}	Secretariat	b	3	126	6	7	7^{2}	$6^{1\frac{1}{2}}$	5^{3}	4^{hd}	$3^{\frac{1}{2}}$	Turcotte R	c-.30
29Mar73	^{7}Aqu^{1}	Step Nicely	b	3	126	7	4	5^{hd}	$4^{\frac{1}{2}}$	$4^{1\frac{1}{2}}$	5^{6}	$4^{\frac{3}{4}}$	Cordero A Jr	15.80
14Apr73	^{6}Aqu^{1}	Champagne Charlie		3	126	3	5	$3^{1\frac{1}{2}}$	$3^{1\frac{1}{2}}$	$3^{\frac{1}{2}}$	3^{2}	5^{6}	Venezia M	13.00
7Apr73	^{7}Aqu^{3}	Flush		3	126	1	6	8	8	8	6^{4}	6^{7}	Ussery R	b-38.20
31Mar73	^{9}FG^{1}	Leo's Pisces		3	126	5	3	$4^{\frac{1}{2}}$	7^{6}	6^{hd}	7^{1}	7^{3}	Baltazar C	37.90
31Mar73	^{8}Aqu^{5}	Expropriate	b	3	126	4	8	6^{1}	$5^{\frac{1}{2}}$	7^{5}	8	8	Adams L	b-38.20

b-Coupled: Flush and Expropriate; c-Angle Light and Secretariat.

Time, :24$\frac{3}{5}$, :48$\frac{1}{5}$, 1:12$\frac{1}{5}$, 1:36$\frac{4}{5}$, 1:49$\frac{4}{5}$ (Wind in backstretch). Track fast.

$2 Mutuel Prices:
3-(K)-ANGLE LIGHT (c-entry) . . . . 2.60 2.10 —
1-(C)-SHAM . . . . 2.10 —
3-(H)-SECRETARIAT . . . . 2.60 2.10 —

B. c, by Quadrangle—Pilot Light by Jet Action. Trainer Laurin L. Bred by Noonan & Runnymede Farm (Ky).

IN GATE AT 4:54 OFF AT 4:54 EST Start Good Won Driving

ANGLE LIGHT saved ground after quickly sprinting clear made the pace under good handling, settled into the stretch with a clear lead and responded gamely to last over SHAM. the latter prompted the pace throughout and finished strongly, narrowly missing. SECRETARIAT, unhurried early, commenced to rally while racing outside horses on the backstretch, continued wide into the stretch, lugged in slightly nearing the final furlong and failed to seriously menace the top pair. STEP NICELY, in close quarters between horses on the first turn, raced within easy striking to the upper stretch but lacked the needed late response. CHAMPAGNE CHARLIE, well placed early, made a run along the rail at the far turn, eased to the outside nearing the stretch but weakened during the drive. FLUSH was without speed. LEO'S PISCES was through early. EXPROPRIATE, hustled along after breaking slowly, lacked room along the rail midway of the first turn and was finished after going a half.

Owners— 1, Whittaker E; 2, Sommer S; 3, Meadow Stable; 4, Hobeau Farm; 5, Wimpfheimer J D; 6, Buckland Farm; 7, Taub J; 8, Buckland Farm.

Trainers— 1, Laurin L; 2, Martin F; 3, Laurin L; 4, Jerkens H A; 5, Sedlacek W; 6, Campo J P; 7, Paley H; 8, Campo J P.

Scratched—Knightly Dawn (14Apr73^{6}Aqu^{4}); Beautiful Music (21Mar73^{6}SA^{1}); Settecento (14Apr73^{6}Aqu^{2}).

Kentucky Derby Chart

NINTH RACE

Churchill

MAY 5, 1973

1 ¼ MILES. (2.00) 99th Running **KENTUCKY DERBY.** $125,000 added. 3-year-olds. By subscription of $100 each in cash which covers nomination for both the Kentucky Derby and Derby Trial. All Nomination fees to Derby Winner, $2,500 to pass entry box, Thursday, May 3, $1,500 additional to start, $125,000 added, of which $25,000 to second, $12,500 to third, $6,250 to fourth, $100,000 guaranteed to Winner (to be divided equally in event of a dead heat). Weight 126 lbs. Starters to be named through the entry box Thursday, May 3, at time of closing. The owner of the winner to receive a gold trophy. Closed Thursday, February 15, 1973 with 218 Nominations.

Value of race $198,800, value to winner $155,050, second $25,000, third $12,500, fourth $6,250. Mutuel pool $3,284,962.

Last Raced		Horse	Eqt.	A.	Wt	PP	St	¼	½	¾	Str	Fin	Jockey	Odds $1
21Apr73	$^{7}Aqu^{3}$	Secretariat	b	3	126	10	11^{hd}	$6^{\frac{1}{2}}$	5^{1}	$2^{1\frac{1}{2}}$	$1^{\frac{1}{2}}$	$1^{2\frac{1}{2}}$	Turcotte R	a-1.50
21Apr73	$^{2}Aqu^{2}$	Sham	b	3	126	4	5^{1}	3^{2}	2^{1}	$1^{\frac{1}{2}}$	2^{6}	2^{8}	Pincay L Jr	2.50
26Apr73	$^{6}Kee^{2}$	Our Native	b	3	126	7	$6^{\frac{1}{2}}$	$8^{1\frac{1}{2}}$	8^{1}	5^{hd}	3^{hd}	$3^{\frac{1}{2}}$	Brumfield D	10.60
26Apr73	$^{6}Kee^{5}$	Forego		3	126	9	$9^{1\frac{1}{2}}$	$9^{\frac{1}{2}}$	$6^{\frac{1}{2}}$	6^{2}	$4^{\frac{1}{2}}$	$4^{2\frac{1}{2}}$	Anderson P	28.60
28Apr73	$^{7}CD^{2}$	Restless Jet		3	126	1	$7^{1\frac{1}{2}}$	7^{hd}	$10^{1\frac{1}{2}}$	$7^{1\frac{1}{2}}$	$6^{1\frac{1}{2}}$	$5^{2\frac{1}{2}}$	Hole M	28.50
28Apr73	$^{7}CD^{1}$	Shecky Greene	b	3	126	11	$1^{1\frac{1}{2}}$	1^{3}	$1^{1\frac{1}{2}}$	3^{3}	5^{1}	$6^{1\frac{1}{2}}$	Adams L	b-5.70
26Apr73	$^{6}Kee^{6}$	Navajo	b	3	126	5	$10^{1\frac{1}{2}}$	10^{1}	11^{4}	$8^{1\frac{1}{2}}$	8^{2}	7^{hd}	Soirez W	52.30
26Apr73	$^{6}Kee^{7}$	Royal and Regal		3	126	8	3^{1}	4^{3}	4^{3}	4^{1}	$7^{1\frac{1}{2}}$	$8^{3\frac{1}{2}}$	Blum W	28.30
26Apr73	$^{6}Kee^{1}$	My Gallant	b	3	126	12	8^{hd}	$11^{1\frac{1}{2}}$	12^{3}	11^{2}	$10^{\frac{1}{2}}$	9^{hd}	Baeza B	b-5.70
21Apr73	$^{7}Aqu^{1}$	Angle Light		3	126	2	4^{hd}	$5^{1\frac{1}{2}}$	7^{1}	$10^{1\frac{1}{2}}$	$9^{1\frac{1}{2}}$	$10^{1\frac{3}{4}}$	LeBlanc J O	a-1.50
1May73	$^{8}CD^{5}$	Gold Bag	b	3	126	13	2^{hd}	2^{hd}	$3^{\frac{1}{2}}$	9^{1}	11^{1}	11^{hd}	Fires E	68.30
28Apr73	$^{7}CD^{6}$	Twice A Prince	b	3	126	6	13	13	13	13	12^{2}	$12^{1\frac{1}{2}}$	Santiago A	62.50
26Apr73	$^{6}Kee^{3}$	Warbucks		3	126	3	12^{1}	12^{3}	9^{hd}	$12^{1\frac{1}{2}}$	13	13	Hartack W	7.20

a-Coupled: Secretariat and Angle Light; b-Shecky Greene and My Gallant.

Time, :23$\frac{2}{5}$, :47$\frac{2}{5}$, 1:11$\frac{4}{5}$, 1:36$\frac{1}{5}$, 1:59$\frac{2}{5}$ Track fast.

New Track Record.

$2 Mutuel Prices:

1-SECRETARIAT (a-entry)	**5.00**	**3.20**	**3.00**
5-SHAM		**3.20**	**3.00**
8-OUR NATIVE			**4.20**

Ch. c, by Bold Ruler—Somethingroyal, by Princequillo, Trainer Laurin L. Bred by Meadow Stud Inc (Va).

IN GATE AT 5:37; OFF AT 5:37, EDT. Start Good. Won Handily.

SECRETARIAT relaxed nicely and dropped back last leaving the gate as the field broke in good order, moved between horses to begin improving position entering the first turn but passed rivals from the outside thereafter. Turcotte roused him smartly with the whip in his right hand leaving the far turn and SECRETARIAT strongly raced to the leaders, lost a little momentum racing wide into the stretch where Turcotte used the whip again, but then switched it to his left hand and merely flashed it as the winner willingly drew away in record breaking time. SHAM, snugly reserved within striking distance after brushing with NAVAJO at the start, raced around rivals to the front without need of rousing and drew clear between calls entering the stretch, was under a strong hand ride after being displace the last furlong and continued resolutely to dominate the remainder of the field. OUR NATIVE, reserved in the first run through the stretch, dropped back slightly on the turn, came wide in the drive and finished well for his placing. FOREGO, taken to the inside early, veered slightly from a rival and hit the rail entering the far turn, swung wide entering the stretch and vied with OUR NATIVE in the drive. RESTLESS JET saved ground in an even effort. SHECKY GREENE easily set the pace under the light rating for nearly seven furlongs and faltered. NAVAJO was outrun. ROYAL AND REGAL raced well for a mile and had nothing left in the drive. MY GALLANT was not a factor. ANGLE LIGHT gave way steadily in a dull effort and was forced to check when crowded by GOLD BAG on the stretch turn. GOLD BAG had good early speed and stopped. TWICE A PRINCE reared and was hung in the gate briefly before the start and then showed nothing in the running. WARBUCKS was dull.

Owners— 1, Meadow Stable; 2, Sommer S; 3, Pritchard Mrs M J & Resseguet Jr; 4, Lazy F Ranch; 5, Elkwood Farm; 6, Kellman J; 7, Stevenson & Stump; 8, Aisco Stable; 9, Appleton A I; 10, Whittaker E; 11, Gottdank & Sechrest; 12, Elmendorf; 13, Elzemeyer E E.

Trainers— 1, Laurin L; 2, Martin F; 3, Resseguet W J Jr; 4, Ward S W; 5, Thorton C; 6, Goldfine L M; 7, Keefer J; 8, Croll W A Jr; 9, Goldfine L M; 10, Laurin L; 11, Sechrest Randy; 12, Campo J P; 13, Combs D.

Preakness Stakes Chart

EIGHTH RACE

Pimlico

MAY 19, 1973

1 $\frac{3}{16}$ MILES. (1.54) Ninety-eighth Running **PREAKNESS.** $150,000 Added. 3-year-olds. By subscription of $100 each, this fee to accompany the nomination. $1,000 to pass the entry box, starters to pay $1,000 additional. All eligibility, entrance and starting fees to the winner, with $150,000 added, of which $30,000 to second, $15,000 to third and $7,500 to fourth. Weight 126 lbs. A replica of the Woodlawn Vase will be presented to the winning owner to remain his or her personal property. Closed Thursday, February 15, 1973 with 194 Nominations.

Value of race $182,400, value to winner $129,900, second $30,000, third $15,000, fourth $7,500. Mutuel pool $922,989.

Last Raced		Horse	Eqt.	A.	Wt	PP	St	¼	½	¾	Str	Fin	Jockey	Odds $1
5May73	$^{9}CD^{1}$	Secretariat	b	3	126	3	6	$4^{\frac{1}{2}}$	$1^{\frac{1}{2}}$	$1^{2\frac{1}{2}}$	$1^{2\frac{1}{2}}$	$1^{2\frac{1}{2}}$	Turcotte R	.30
5May73	$^{9}CD^{2}$	Sham	b	3	126	1	4	$3^{3\frac{1}{2}}$	4^{3}	$2^{1\frac{1}{2}}$	2^{5}	2^{8}	Pincay L Jr	3.10
5May73	$^{9}CD^{3}$	Our Native	b	3	126	4	5	5^{hd}	5^{6}	4^{3}	3^{3}	3^{1}	Brumfield D	11.90
12May73	$^{6}Pim^{1}$	Ecole Etage	b	3	126	6	1	$1^{1\frac{1}{2}}$	2^{2}	$3^{\frac{1}{2}}$	4^{10}	4^{10}	Cusimano G	11.30
5May73	$^{7}Pen^{1}$	Deadly Dream	b	3	126	2	3	6	6	6	6	$5^{3\frac{1}{2}}$	Black A S	35.90
12May73	$^{6}Pim^{5}$	Torsion		3	126	5	2	$2^{\frac{1}{2}}$	3^{hd}	5^{14}	5^{3}	6	Feliciano B M	39.00

Time, :24$\frac{2}{5}$, :48$\frac{1}{5}$, 1:11$\frac{2}{5}$, 1:35$\frac{3}{5}$, 1:54$\frac{2}{5}$ Track fast.

(Daily Racing Form Time, 1:53$\frac{2}{5}$).

$2 Mutuel Prices:

3-SECRETARIAT	**2.60**	**2.20**	**2.10**
1-SHAM		**2.20**	**2.20**
4-OUR NATIVE			**2.20**

Ch. c, by Bold Ruler—Somethingroyal, by Princequillo, Trainer Laurin L. Bred by Meadow Stud Inc (Va).

IN GATE AT 5:40; OFF AT 5:40, EDT. Start Good. Won Handily.

SECRETARIAT broke well and was eased back and relaxed nicely as the field passed the stands the first time. He was guided outside two rivals entering the clubhouse turn and responding when Turcotte moved his hands on the reins, made a spectacular run to take command entering the backstretch. SECRETARIAT was not threatened thereafter and was confidently hand ridden to the finish. SHAM broke to the right and brushed with DEADLY DREAM leaving the gate, then drifted in and hit the rail entering the clubhouse turn. Pincay swung SHAM out entering the backstretch and roused him in pursuit of the winner but he could not threaten that rival in a game effort. OUR NATIVE, reserved between rivals early, rallied to gain the show. ECOLE ETAGE, hustled to the lead, gradually weakened after losing the advantage. DEADLY DREAM stumbled then was brushed by SHAM just after the break and was outrun thereafter. TORSION, stoutly rated early, could not menace when called upon. (The :25, :48 4/5, 1:12, 1:36 1/5 and 1:55 as posted by the electric timer during the running was invalidated after a 48-hour interval by a stewards' ruling, and the above time reported by official timer E. T. McLean, Jr. was accepted as official.)

Owners— 1, Meadow Stable; 2, Sommer S; 3, Pritchard Mrs M J & Resseguet Jr; 4, Bon Etage Farm; 5, Wide Track Farm; 6, Buckland Farm.

Trainers— 1, Laurin L; 2, Martin F; 3, Resseguet W J Jr; 4, Delp G G; 5, Worcester H E III; 6, Campo J P.

Scratched—The Lark Twist (14May73^{7}GS^{6}).

Belmont Stakes Chart

EIGHTH RACE

Belmont

JUNE 9, 1973

1 ½ MILES. (2.26$\frac{3}{5}$) 105th Running **THE BELMONT.** $125,000 added 3-year-olds. By subscription of $100 each to accompany the nomination; $250 to pass the entry box; $1,000 to start. A supplementary nomination may be made of $2,500 at the closing time of entries plus an additional $10,000 to start, with $125,000 added, of which 60% to the winner, 22% to second, 12% to third and 6% to fourth. Weights, Colts and Geldings 126 lbs. Fillies 121 lbs. Starters to be named at the closing time of entries. The winning owner will be presented with the August Belmont Memorial Cup to be retained for one year, as well as a trophy for permanent possession and trophies will be presented to the winning trainer and jockey. Closed Thursday, February 15, 1973 with 187 Nominations.

Value of race $150,200, value to winner $90,120, second $33,044, third $18,024, fourth $9,012. Mutuel pool $519,689, OTB pool $688,460.

Last Raced		Horse	Eqt.	A.	Wt	PP	¼	½	1	1¼	Str	Fin	Jockey	Odds $1
19May73	$^{8}Pim^{1}$	Secretariat	b	3	126	1	1^{hd}	1^{hd}	1^{7}	1^{20}	1^{28}	1^{31}	Turcotte R	.10
2Jun73	$^{6}Bel^{4}$	Twice A Prince		3	126	5	4^{5}	4^{10}	3^{hd}	2^{hd}	3^{12}	$2^{\frac{1}{2}}$	Baeza B	17.30
31May73	$^{6}Bel^{1}$	My Gallant	b	3	126	3	3^{3}	3^{hd}	4^{7}	3^{2}	2^{hd}	3^{13}	Cordero A Jr	12.40
28May73	$^{8}GS^{2}$	Pvt. Smiles	b	3	126	2	5	5	5	5	5	$4^{\frac{3}{4}}$	Gargan D	14.30
19May73	$^{8}Pim^{2}$	Sham	b	3	126	6	2^{5}	2^{10}	2^{7}	4^{8}	$4^{1\frac{1}{2}}$	5	Pincay L Jr	5.10

Time, :23$\frac{3}{5}$, :46$\frac{1}{5}$, 1:09$\frac{4}{5}$, 1:34$\frac{1}{5}$, 1:59, 2:24, (Against wind in backstretch.). Track fast.

New Track Record.

$2 Mutuel Prices:

2-(A)-SECRETARIAT	**2.20**	**2.40**	**—**
5-(E)-TWICE A PRINCE		**4.60**	**—**
(No Show Wagering)			

Ch. c, by Bold Ruler—Somethingroyal, by Princequillo, Trainer Laurin L. Bred by Meadow Stud Inc (Va).

IN GATE AT 5:38; OFF AT 5:38, EDT. Start Good. Won Ridden out.

SECRETARIAT sent up along the inside to vie for the early lead with SHAM to the backstretch, disposed of that one after going three-quarters, drew off at will rounding the far turn and was under a hand ride from Turcotte to establish a record in a tremendous performance. TWICE A PRINCE, unable to stay with the leader early, moved through along the rail approaching the stretch and outfinished MY GALLANT for the place. The latter, void of early foot, moved with TWICE A PRINCE rounding the far turn and fought it out gamely with that one through the drive. PVT. SMILES showed nothing. SHAM alternated for the lead with SECRETARIAT to the backstretch, wasn't able to match stride with that rival after going three-quarters and stopped badly.

Owners—1, Meadow Stable; 2, Elmendorf; 3, Appleton A I; 4, Whitney C V; 5, Sommer S.

Trainers—1, Laurin L; 2, Campo J P; 3, Goldfine L M; 4, Poole G T; 5, Martin F.

Scratched—Knightly Dawn (28May73^{8}GS^{1}).

Arlington Invitational Chart

EIGHTH RACE

Arlington

JUNE 30, 1973

1 ⅛ MILES. (1.46$\frac{1}{5}$) **ARLINGTON INVITATIONAL.** Purse $125,000. Invitational race for 3-year-olds. Weight, 126 lbs. non-winners of $50,000 3 times since May 1, allowed 6 lbs.; $125,000 of which $75,000 to winner, $30,000 to second, $20,000 to third. Invitations closed Tuesday, June 26, 1973 with 4 acceptances.

Value of race $125,000, value to winner $75,000, second $30,000, third $20,000. Mutuel pool $224,505, Minus show pool $17,941.

Last Raced		Horse	Eqt.	A.	Wt	PP	St	¼	½	¾	Str	Fin	Jockey	Odds $1
9Jun73	$^{8}Bel^{1}$	Secretariat	b	3	126	4	4	1^{3}	1^{3}	$1^{2\frac{1}{2}}$	1^{6}	1^{9}	Turcotte R	.05
9Jun73	$^{8}Bel^{3}$	My Gallant	b	3	120	3	1	$2^{1\frac{1}{2}}$	$2^{2\frac{1}{2}}$	$2^{1\frac{1}{2}}$	$2^{\frac{1}{2}}$	2^{nk}	Perret C	f-5.70
16Jun73	$^{9}Tdn^{1}$	Our Native	b	3	120	1	2	3^{hd}	$3^{1\frac{1}{2}}$	3^{8}	3^{15}	3^{17}	Rini A	f-5.70
16Jun73	$^{7}AP^{2}$	Blue Chip Dan	b	3	120	2	3	4	4	4	4	4	Ahrens L	f-5.70

f-Mutuel field.

Time, :24$\frac{4}{5}$, :48, 1:11$\frac{1}{5}$, 1:35 1:47 Track fast.

$2 Mutuel Prices:

1-SECRETARIAT	**2.10**	**—**	**—**
(Win Wagering Only)			

Ch. c, by Bold Ruler—Somethingroyal, by Princequillo. Trainer Laurin L. Bred by Meadow Stud Inc (Va).

IN GATE AT 5:18; OFF AT 5:18, CDT. Start Good. Won Easily.

SECRETARIAT broke a bit slow from the outside, went three wide into clubhouse turn to gain command while under tight restraint. Moved inside once clear of rivals in mid turn and continued under a hold down backstretch, increased advantage coming out of stretch turn and was allowed to run freely final eighth when Ron Turcotte relaxed his hold. MY GALLANT away in good order, maintained even position for six furlongs, then was all out to hold OUR NATIVE safe in final quarter. OUR NATIVE raced in behind MY GALLANT, swung wide coming out of turn and just missed getting up for second. BLUE CHIP DAN was taken back early and gradually lost ground thereafter.

Owners—1, Meadow Stable; 2, Appleton A I; 3, Pritchard Mrs M J & Resseguet Jr; 4, Teinowitz P.

Trainers—1, Laurin L; 2, Goldfine L M; 3, Resseguet W J Jr; 4, Getz G J.

SEVENTH RACE

Saratoga

AUGUST 4, 1973

1⅛ MILES. (1.48⅕) 46th Running. **THE WHITNEY.** $50,000 Added. 3-year-olds and upward. By subscription of $100 each, which shall accompany the nomination; $250 to pass the entry box; $250 to start, with $50,000 added. The added money and all fees to be divided 60% to the winner, 22% to second, 12% to third and 6% to fourth. Weights, 3-year-olds, 119 lbs; older, 126 lbs. Non-winners of $65,000 twice at a mile and a furlong or over since August 18, allowed 2 lbs.; $35,000 three times at a mile in 1972-73, 4 lbs.; a sweepstakes in 1973, 7 lbs. Starters to be named at the closing time of entries. Trophies will be presented to the winning owner, trainer and jockey. (Nominations closed Saturday, July 21). (11 Nominations.)

Value of race $53,850, value to winner $32,310, second $11,847, third $6,464, fourth $3,231. Mutuel pool $115,742, OTB pool $84,089.

Last Raced		Horse	Eqt.	A.	Wt	PP	St	¼	½	¾	Str	Fin	Jockey	Odds $1
31Jly73	^{7}Sar^{1}	Onion		4	119	4	3	1^{2}	1^{1}	$1\frac{1}{2}$	1nd	1^{1}	Vasquez J	5.60
30Jun73	^{8}AP^{1}	Secretariat	b	3	119	3	4	4^{4}	3^{3}	$2^{1\frac{1}{2}}$	2^{5}	$2\frac{1}{2}$	Turcotte R	.10
22Jun73	^{7}Aqu^{2}	Rule by Reason		6	119	2	1	3^{2}	4^{6}	4^{5}	5	3^{2}	Santiago A	26.20
21Jly73	^{7}Aqu^{2}	True Knight		4	122	5	5	5	5	5	$3\frac{1}{2}$	4^{1}	Velasquez J	7.80
21Jly73	^{7}Aqu^{5}	West Coast Scout	b	5	126	1	2	2^{hd}	2^{hd}	3^{2}	4^{hd}	5	Belmonte E	22.00

Time, :24⅖, :47⅘, 1:11, 1:36, 1:49⅕ (With wind in backstretch.). Tract fast.

$2 Mutuel Prices: **4-(D)-ONION** . . . . **13.20 — —**
(Win Wagering Only)

Ch. g, by Third Martini—With A Flair, by Beau Gar. Trainer Jerkens H A. Bred by Hobeau Farm Inc (Fla).

IN GATE AT 4:48; OFF AT 4:48, EDT. Start Good. Won Driving.

ONION sprinted away to a clear lead around the first turn, made the pace under good rating and while remaining well out from the inner rail, responded readily when challenged by SECRETARIAT at the far turn, lugged in slightly just inside the final three-sixteenths, was quickly straightened away and proved best under brisk urging. SECRETARIAT knocked open the stall doors before the start, came away in good order, ducked to the inside after entering the backstretch, went up after ONION at the far turn, continued to race along the rail while dueling with that rival until the final sixteenth and weakened. RULE BY REASON, outrun after breaking alertly, was unable to keep pace with the leaders around the far turn, then finished full of run from the outside. TRUE KNIGHT, void of early foot, commenced to rally along the inside midway of the far turn, swung out for the drive but failed to sustain his bid. WEST COAST SCOUT, a forward factor until near the stretch, tired.

Owners— 1, Hobeau Farm; 2, Meadow Stable; 3, Walder M; 4, Darby Dan Farm; 5, Oxford Stable.

Trainers— 1, Jerkens H A; 2, Laurin L; 3, Campo J P; 4, Rondinello T L; 5, Marks M.

Scratched—Anono (28Jly73^{8}Aqu^{2}).

Chart of Marlboro Cup

SEVENTH RACE

Belmont

SEPTEMBER 15, 1973

1⅛ MILES. (1.46⅕) 1ST RUNNING **THE MARLBORO CUP HANDICAP.** Purse $250,000. By Invitation. Purse to be divided 60% to the winner, 22% to second, 12% to third and 6% to fourth. Weights Monday, September 10. Trophies to be presented to the winning owner, trainer and jockey.

Value of race $250,000, value to winner $150,000, second $55,000, third $30,000, fourth $15,000. Mutuel pool $595,169, OTB pool $325,311.

Last Raced		Horse	Eqt.	A.	Wt	PP	St	¼	½	¾	Str	Fin	Jockey	Odds $1
4Aug73	^{7}Sar^{2}	Secretariat	b	3	124	7	6	5^{4}	5^{4}	3^{2}	1^{2}	$1^{3\frac{1}{2}}$	Turcotte R	b-.40
21Aug73	^{7}Sar^{1}	Riva Ridge	b	4	127	6	2	2^{1}	2^{1}	$1\frac{1}{2}$	2^{6}	2^{2}	Maple E	b-.40
23Jly73	^{8}Hol^{1}	Cougar II		7	126	2	7	7	7	7	3^{1}	$3^{6\frac{1}{2}}$	Shoemaker W	a-4.00
8Sep73	^{7}Bel^{7}	Onion		4	116	3	4	$1\frac{1}{2}$	1^{hd}	2^{hd}	$4\frac{1}{2}$	$4^{2\frac{1}{2}}$	Velasquez J	14.30
25Aug73	^{8}Mth^{2}	Annihilate 'Em		3	116	4	3	$4^{1\frac{1}{2}}$	3^{hd}	4^{hd}	5^{2}	$5\frac{1}{2}$	Cordero A Jr	21.70
18Aug73	^{7}Dmr^{1}	Kennedy Road		5	121	5	1	3^{1}	4^{hd}	5^{5}	$6^{1\frac{1}{2}}$	6^{2}	Pierce D	a-4.00
21Jly73	^{7}Aqu^{1}	Key To The Mint	b	4	126	1	5	6^{6}	6^{4}	6^{1}	7	7	Baeza B	3.50

a-Coupled: Cougar II and Kennedy Road; b-Secretariat and Riva Ridge.

Time, :22⅗, :45⅗, 1:09⅕, 1:33 1:45⅖ (Against wind in backstretch.). Track fast.

New World Record.

$2 Mutuel Prices:

2-(G)-SECRETARIAT	**2.80**	**2.80**	**2.40**
2-(F)-RIVA RIDGE (b-entry)	**2.80**	**2.80**	**2.40**
2-(B)-COUGAR II (a-entry)			**3.00**

Ch. c, by Bold Ruler—Somethingroyal, by Princequillo. Trainer Laurin L. Bred by Meadow Stud Inc (Va).

IN GATE AT 4:50; OFF AT 4:50; EDT. Start Good. Won Ridden out.

SECRETARIAT, unhurried away from the gate, moved around horses to reach contention after going a half, drifted out a bit leaving the turn. headed RIVA RIDGE with three sixteenths remaining and drew away under brisk handling. RIVA RIDGE, prominent from the outset, took over when ready racing into the turn, remained well out in the track while making the pace into the stretch but wasn't able to stay with SECRETARIAT while holding COUGAR II safe. COUGAR II, off slowly, settled suddenly approaching the stretch, altered course when blocked attempting to split horses nearing midstretch and finished with good energy. ONION showed good early foot while racing well out from the rail but had nothing left for the drive. ANNIHILATE 'EM made a run along the inside approaching the end of the backstretch and was finished soon after going three-quarters. KENNEDY ROAD, steadied along while between horses on the backstretch, gave way approaching the stretch, KEY TO THE MINT showed nothing.

Owners—1, Meadow Stable; 2, Meadow Stable; 3, Jones Mary F; 4, Hobeau Farm; 5, Blass Patricia; 6, Stollery Mrs. A W; 7, Rokeby Stable.

Trainers—1, Laurin L; 2, Laurin L; 3, Whittingham C; 4, Jerkens H A ; 5, Davis D Jr; 6, Whittingham C; 7, Burch Elliott.

SEVENTH RACE

Belmont

SEPTEMBER 29, 1973

1½ MILES (2.24) 20th Running. **THE WOODWARD** $100,000 Added. 3-Year-Olds and Upward at Weight for Age. By subscription of $200 each, which shall accompany the nomination; $500 to pass the entry box; $500 to start, with $100,000 added. The added money and all fees to be divided 60% to the winner, 22% to second, 12% to third and 6% to fourth. Weight for age, for 3-year-olds, 119 lbs; older, 126 lbs. Starters to be named at the closing time of entries. Mrs. William Woodward, Sr. has donated a trophy to be presented to the owner of the winner and trophies will also be presented to the winner trainer and jockey. (Closed with 11 Nominations Saturday, September 15.)

Value of race $108,200, value to winner $64,920, second $23,604, third $12,984, fourth $6,492. Mutuel pool $209,814, OTB pool $77,296.

Last Raced		Horse	Eqt.	A.	Wt	PP	¼	½	1	1¼	Str	Fin	Jockey	Odds $1
22Sep73	^{8}Bow^{7}	Prove Out		4	126	3	$1^{1\frac{1}{2}}$	$1\frac{1}{2}$	$2\frac{1}{2}$	2^{4}	$1^{1\frac{1}{2}}$	$1^{4\frac{1}{2}}$	Velasquez J	16.20
15Sep73	^{7}Bel^{1}	Secretariat	b	3	119	5	2^{1}	2^{3}	$1^{1\frac{1}{2}}$	1^{hd}	2^{8}	2^{11}	Turcotte R	.30
15Sep73	^{7}Bel^{3}	Cougar II		7	126	4	5	5	3^{1}	4^{8}	4^{10}	$3\frac{1}{2}$	Shoemaker W	2.90
1Sep73	^{7}Bel^{1}	Amen II		3	119	1	3^{1}	3^{hd}	4^{2}	3^{hd}	3^{hd}	4^{12}	Castaneda M	11.70
15Sep73	^{6}Bel^{4}	Summer Guest	b	4	123	2	$4^{1\frac{1}{2}}$	$4^{1\frac{1}{2}}$	5	5	5	5	Vasquez J	13.70

Time, :25, :50, 1:13⅖, 1:37⅖, 2:01⅘, 2:25⅘, (Against wind in backstretch.). Track sloppy.

$2 Mutuel Prices: **5-(E)-PROVE OUT** . . . . **34.40 — —**
(Win Wagering Only)

Ch. c, by Graustark—Equal Venture, by Bold Venture. Trainer Jerkens H A. Bred by King Ranch (Ky).

IN GATE AT 4:48; OFF AT 4:48, EDT Start Good Won Driving

PROVE OUT saved ground after opening a clear lead racing into the first turn, was unhurried when replaced by SECRETARIAT soon after entering the backstretch, moved to that rival while continuing along the inside nearing the stretch and drew off when roused sharply leaving the furlong grounds. SECRETARIAT prompted the early pace, moved to the fore from the outside just before going five furlongs, opened a clear advantage while racing well out from the inside on the backstretch, continued a bit wide into the stretch and was no match for the winner while easily besting the others. COUGAR II, taken in hand after the start, moved through along the inside after entering the backstretch, eased out to continue his rally nearing the far turn but was finished soon after going nine furlongs. AMEN II, reserved behind the early leaders for seven furlongs, made a run from the outside at the far turn but gave way nearing the stretch. SUMMER GUEST wasn't able to keep up after going a mile.

Owners— 1, Hobeau Farm; 2, Meadow Stable; 3, Jones Mary F; 4, Dee-Bob Stable; 5, Rokeby Stable.

Trainers— 1, Jerkens H A; 2, Laurin L; 3, Whittingham C; 4, Johnson P G; 5, Burch Elliott.

Scratched—Riva Ridge (15 Sep73^{7}Bel^{2}); West Coast Scout (4Aug73^{7}Sar^{5}).

SEVENTH RACE

Belmont

OCTOBER 8, 1973

1½ MILES. (turf). (2.25⅖) 15Th Running **MAN O' WAR** $100,000 Added. 3-year-olds and upward at weight for age. By subscription of $200 each, which shall accompany the nominations; $500 to pass the entry box; $500 to start, with $100,000 added. The added money and all fees to be divided 60% to the winner, 22% to second; 12% to third and 6% to fourth. Weights for age, 3-year-olds, 121 lbs.; older, 126 lbs. Starters to be named at the closing time of entried. The N.Y.R.A. to add The Man o' War Bowl to be won three times, not necessarily consecutively by the same owner before becoming his or her property. The owner of the winner will also receive a trophy for permanent possession and trophies to the winning trainer and jockey. The New York Racing Association reserves the right to transfer this race to the main course because of track conditions. (Closed Monday, September 24 with 23 nominations.)

Value of race $113,600, value to winner $63,160, second $24,992, third $13,632, fourth $6,316. Mutuel pool $428,256, OTB pool $188,300.

Last Raced		Horse	Eqt.	A.	Wt	PP	¼	½	1	1¼	Str	Fin	Jockey	Odds $1
29Sep73	^{7}Bel^{2}	Secretariat	b	3	121	3	$1^{1\frac{1}{2}}$	1^{3}	1^{3}	$1^{1\frac{1}{2}}$	1^{3}	1^{5}	Turcotte R	.50
27Sep73	^{8}Atl^{1}	Tentam	b	4	126	1	$3^{1\frac{1}{2}}$	3^{3}	2^{2}	2^{6}	2^{10}	$2^{7\frac{1}{2}}$	Velasquez J	3.60
22Sep73	^{7}Bel^{2}	Big Spruce	b	4	126	7	7	7	7	7	5^{2}	$3\frac{1}{2}$	Santiago A	6.90
22Sep73	^{7}Bel^{3}	Triangular		6	126	4	5^{hd}	6^{5}	6^{2}	$4\frac{1}{2}$	$3\frac{1}{2}$	$4^{2\frac{1}{2}}$	Smith R C	25.40
22Sep73	^{7}Bel^{1}	London Company		3	121	6	6^{4}	5^{1}	5^{1}	$3\frac{1}{2}$	4^{2}	5^{7}	Pincay L Jr	8.40
4Aug73	^{7}Sar^{5}	West Coast Scout	b	5	126	5	4^{2}	4^{2}	$4^{1\frac{1}{2}}$	6^{3}	6^{3}	6^{6}	Cordero A Jr	25.90
21Sep73	^{7}Bel^{1}	Anono	b	3	121	2	2^{1}	$2^{1\frac{1}{2}}$	$3^{1\frac{1}{2}}$	5^{hd}	7	7	Venezia M	38.60

Time, :23⅘, :47, 1:11⅗, 1:36, 2:00, 2:24⅘, (Against wind in backstretch.). Course firm.

New Course Record.

$2 Mutuel Prices:

1-(E)-SECRETARIAT	**3.00**	**2.40**	**2.20**
2-(B)-TENTAM		**3.00**	**2.60**
7-(I)-BIG SPRUCE			**3.20**

Ch. c, by Bold Ruler—Somethingroyal, by Princequillo. Trainer Laurin L. Bred by Meadow Stud Inc (Va).

IN GATE AT 4:48; OFF AT 4:48, EDT Start Good. Won Ridden out.

SECRETARIAT, away in good order, moved to the fore from between horses nearing the finish line the first time, saved ground after opening a clear lead around the first turn, responded readily to shake off a bid from TENTAM after going three-quarters, turned back another bid from that rival approaching the stretch and drew away under a hand ride. TENTAM, never far back while saving ground, eased out to go after SECRETARIAT entering the backstretch, wasn't able to stay with that one after going three-quarters, made another run midway of the far turn but was no match for the winner while besting the others. BIG SPRUCE, outrun to the stretch, passed tired horses. TRIANGULAR was always outrun, as was LONDON COMPANY. WEST COAST SCOUT was finished at the far turn. ANONO showed good early foot but had nothing left after going a mile.

Owners— 1, Meadow Stable; 2, Windfields Farm; 3, Elmendorf; 4, Hobeau Farm; 5, Chance Hill Farm; 6, Oxford Stable; 7, Schefler A D.

Trainers— 1, Laurin L; 2, Miller M; 3, Nickerson V J; 4, Jerkens H A; 5, Jolley L; 6, Marks M; 7, Jacobs E.

Scratched—Dendron (21Sep73^{7}Bel^{2}); Riva Ridge (15Sep73^{7}Bel^{2}); Star Envoy (27Sep73^{8}Atl^{2}); Apollo Nine (28Sep73^{7}Bel^{1}).

Canadian Int'l Championship Chart

EIGHTH RACE

Woodbine

OCTOBER 28, 1973

1⅝ MILES. (turf). (2.41) **CANADIAN INTERNATIONAL CHAMPIONSHIP STAKES.** $125,000 Added. 3-year-olds and upward. By subscription of $150 each which shall accompany the nomination and an additional $750 when making entry. Nomination and entry fees to the winner. With $75,000 added, of which $18,750 to second, $11,250 to third and $7,500 to fourth. 3-year-olds, 117 lbs.; older, 126 lbs. (European Scale). Fillies and Mares, 3 lbs. allowances. (No Canadian Bred Allowance.) Final entries to be made through the entry box at the closing time then in effect for overnight events. A trophy will be presented to the winning owner along with a memento to the groom. Nominations closed Saturday, September 15, 1973.

Value of race $142,700, value to winner $92,755, second $28,540, third $14,270, fourth $7,135. Mutuel pool $181,485.

Last Raced		Horse	Eqt.	A.	Wt	PP	¼	½	1	1⅜	Str	Fin	Jockey	Odds $1
8Oct73	^{7}Bel^{1}	Secretariat	b	3	117	12	$2^{4\frac{1}{2}}$	2^{6}	2^{4}	1^{5}	1^{12}	$1^{5\frac{1}{2}}$	Maple E	.20
8Oct73	^{7}Bel^{3}	Big Spruce	b	4	126	4	12	11^{hd}	10^{6}	5^{hd}	4^{1}	$2^{1\frac{1}{2}}$	Santiago A	13.45
13Oct73	^{8}Spt^{3}	Golden Don	b	3	117	6	11^{1}	9^{hd}	8^{2}	8^{5}	$5^{2\frac{1}{2}}$	$3\frac{3}{4}$	Manganello M	28.90
20Oct73	^{7}WO^{3}	Presidial		4	126	9	$3^{1\frac{1}{2}}$	3^{hd}	$4^{1\frac{1}{2}}$	$3\frac{1}{2}$	3^{hd}	4^{4}	Hawley S	23.15
20Oct73	^{7}WO^{1}	Fabe Count		5	126	8	4^{1}	$5\frac{1}{2}$	6^{5}	6^{hd}	6^{hd}	$5\frac{3}{4}$	Duffy L	24.40
8Oct73	^{7}Bel^{4}	Triangular		6	126	1	8^{1}	8^{4}	5^{1}	7^{2}	8^{3}	6^{hd}	Smith R C	32.55
20Oct73	^{7}WO^{4}	Top Of The Day		3	117	2	10^{1}	12	$11^{1\frac{1}{2}}$	9^{hd}	9^{5}	$7^{1\frac{1}{2}}$	Platts R	85.10
20Oct73	^{7}WO^{2}	Twice Lucky	b	6	126	7	$7\frac{1}{2}$	4^{2}	$3^{2\frac{1}{2}}$	4^{3}	7^{1}	$8\frac{1}{2}$	Dittfach H	45.40
21Oct73	^{8}WO^{1}	Kennedy Road		5	126	5	$1^{1\frac{1}{2}}$	$1^{1\frac{1}{2}}$	$1\frac{1}{2}$	2^{7}	2^{hd}	9^{4}	Gomez A	9.25
21Oct73	^{7}WO^{2}	Tico's Donna		5	123	10	5^{1}	6^{hd}	$7\frac{1}{2}$	10^{6}	10^{3}	$10^{3\frac{1}{2}}$	McMahon W G	57.65
20Oct73	^{7}WO^{5}	Roundhouse	b	5	126	3	9^{1}	10^{hd}	12	11^{4}	11^{3}	11^{11}	Grubb R	121.70
20Oct73	^{7}WO^{6}	Fun Co K	b	4	126	11	6^{hd}	7^{3}	9^{hd}	12	12	12	Vasquez J	90.70

Time, :24, :47⅖, 1:11⅗, 1:37⅗, 2.41⅘ Course firm.

$2 Mutuel Prices:

12-SECRETARIAT	**2.40**	**2.50**	**2.10**
4-BIG SPRUCE		**4.4**	**2.90**
6-GOLDEN DON			**4.50**

Ch. c, by Bold Ruler—Somethingroyal, by Princequillo, Trainer Laurin L. Bred by Meadow Stud Inc (Va).

IN GATE AT 4:52; OFF AT 4:52, EST Start Good Won Ridden out

SECRETARIAT stalked the early pace while under restraint, came outside KENNEDY ROAD in the backstretch, dueled with that one to the far turn, took command thereafter to open up a long lead a furlong out and was under mild intermittent pressure to prevail. BIG SPRUCE, well back early, closed willingly GOLDEN DON came outside into the home lane and outfinished the balance. PRESIDIAL saved ground early while stalking the leaders but never threatened. FABE COUNT could not keep up. TRIANGULAR was never a serious threat. TWICE LUCKY a mile contender at the mile, faded thereafter. KENNEDY ROAD set the early pace under restraint, dueled with SECRETARIAT in the backstretch but could not stay into the far turn.

Owners— 1, Meadow Stable; 2, Elmendorf; 3, Donaldson A & Goldchamp J; 4, Windfields Farm; 5, Parkview Stable; 6, Hobeau Farm; 7, Gardiner Farm; 8, Smythe C; 9, Stollery Mrs A W; 10, Stronach F; 11, Resnick & Walsh; 12, Kelm Mary D.

Trainers— 1, Laurin L; 2, Nickerson V J; 3, Dishman O Jr; 4, Johnson R; 5, Lavigne J G; 6, Jerkens H A; 7, Cavalaris L C Jr; 8, Walker D; 9 Whitaker C D; 10, Gross M W; 11, Sarner J J Jr; 12, Sarner J J Jr.

Exacta 12-4 Paid $7.60. Exacta Pool $129,545.

Glossary

added money Money added by a racing association to the amount paid by owners in nomination, eligibility, and starting fees.

all out When a horse has extended itself to the utmost.

allowance race An event other than a claiming race for which the racing secretary drafts certain conditions.

allowances The weights and other conditions of a race.

backstretch The straightaway part of a track on the far side between turns. Also, the stable area.

bad doer A horse with a poor appetite due to nervousness or other causes.

bearing in (or out) Deviating from a straight course. May be due to punishment, infirmity, weariness, or the inability of a rider to control the mount.

bell A signal that sounds when the starter opens the gate or that marks the close of betting. At some tracks a siren is used for the latter purpose.

bit A metal bar in a horse's mouth by which it is guided and controlled

blinkers A device to limit vision and prevent a horse from swerving away from objects, other horses, etc., on either side.

blow out Exercising a horse for a short distance at a fast pace. Designed to sharpen or maintain a horse's condition.

bolt Suddenly veering from a straight course.

brace (or bracer) A rubdown liniment used on a horse after a race or exercise.

break (a horse) To accustom a young horse to racing equipment and methods and to carrying a rider.

break maiden Horse or rider winning first race of career.

broodmare Female thoroughbred used for breeding.

bush league Small race track. Also called Bull Ring.

canter A slow gallop.

cast A horse in such a position that it cannot rise.

claimer A horse running in a "Claiming" or "Selling" race in which the horse can be claimed by the buyer after the race is run.

club house turn Generally, the turn at the point where the club house is usually located.

colors Racing silks. The jacket and cap worn by riders to denote the ownership of the horse.

come back Relax or slow down temporarily from an all-out pace or training routine.

cooler A thin wool sheet used in cooling out. It absorbs sweat and prevents chills.

cooling out Restoring a horse to normal, usually by walking, after it becomes overheated in a workout or race.

cow kick When a horse kicks forward and to one side with a hind foot. Similar to the way a cow would kick over a milk bucket.

dam Mother of a thoroughbred.

dogs Low wooden portable rails placed a certain distance out from the inside rail. They are used during a workout period when the track is muddy or heavy to prevent horses from churning the footing along the rail. Term is also applied to mediocre horses.

draw out Lengthen a lead in a race.

driving Strong urging by a rider.

easily A horse running or winning without being pressed by its rider or position.

eighth A furlong: 220 yards (660 feet).

entrance fee Money paid to start a horse. Usually required only in stakes or special events.

entry Two or more horses owned by the same stable interest or trained by the same person and running as a unit in the betting.

exercise boy A rider who exercises horses.

fast track Footing at its best: dry, fast, and even.

fence Sometimes called the "outside rail." More properly, the barrier between lawns in front of the stands and the racing strip.

filly A female thoroughbred up to and including four years of age.

firing Applying a searing instrument, hot iron, or electric needle to a horse's leg to correct or cure an injury or infirmity.

first turn   The bend of the track beyond the starting point.

foal   A new-born thoroughbred, from birth until weaned. Male or female.

founder   To contract a disease of the foot known as laminitus.

four furlongs   One-half mile: 880 yards (2,640 feet).

fractional time   Intermediate times made in a race: quarter, half, three-quarters, etc.

freshening   To rest a horse after it becomes jaded from racing or training.

furlong   One-eighth of a mile: 220 yards (660 feet).

gallop   A type of gait; a fast canter. To ride a horse at that gait.

gelding   A male horse that has been castrated.

get   The progeny of a sire.

girth   A band put around the body of a horse to keep the saddle from slipping.

good doer   A horse with a good appetite.

good track   Condition of footing between fast and slow.

grand dam   Grandmother of a horse.

grand sire   Grandfather of a horse.

groom   A person who cares for a horse in the stable.

hack   Easy exercise at a walk with a rider.

half   Half mile: four furlongs, 880 yards (2,640 feet).

halter   Like a bridle, but lacking a bit. Used in handling a horse around the stable and when it is not being ridden.

hand   Four inches. A unit used in measuring the height of a horse from the withers to the ground.

handicap   A race for which a handicapper assigns the weights to be carried. May be an overnight or stake event. The handicapper allots weights or makes selections on the basis of past performances, workouts, etc. A handicap horse is one that races in handicaps or is of that quality.

handicapper   A person who handicaps races, officially or privately. Also, an expert who makes selections for publication.

handicapping   To study all factors in past performances in order to determine the relative qualities of horses in a race. These factors include distance, weight, track conditions, riders, past performances, breeding, idiosyncracies of the horses, etc.

handily   Working or racing with moderate effort; not under the whip.

handle (mutuel)   The amount of money bet on a race or the daily card, or bet during a meeting, season, or year.

hand ride   Urging a horse with the hands and not using whip.

head of stretch   Beginning of the straight run home.

hots   Horses after a workout or race before cooling out.

hot walk   Cooling out a horse by walking.

icing   Standing a horse in a bucket of ice water or applying ice packs to its legs to deaden pain.

in foal   A pregnant mare.

in hand   When a horse is running under moderate control at less than the best pace, but with speed in reserve at the call of the rider.

irons   Stirrups.

jog   A slow, easy gait.

lead pony   A horse or pony that heads a parade of the field from the paddock to the starting gate. Also, a horse or pony that accompanies a starter to the post to quiet it.

lead shank   A rope or strap attached to the halter or bridle, and used to lead a horse.

lean into the bit   When a horse strains its head against the restriction of the bit, indicating to the rider that it wants to run.

leg up   A jockey having a mount. Also, strengthening a horse's legs by exercise. Also, lifting a rider on a horse by the leg.

length   The length of a horse from nose to tail, about 8 feet. The distance between horses in a race.

lug   When a horse tries to bear in or out.

maiden   A horse that has not won a race on the flat in any country. Also applied to a non-winning rider.

mare   A female thoroughbred five years old or older.

morning line   The approximate odds quoted at a track in the morning, after scratches and track conditions are known.

odds-on   The price less than even money in the betting odds.

off track   A track that is not fast.

on the bit   When a horse is eager to run.

paddock   The structure or area where horses are saddled and kept before post time.

pari-mutuels   A form of betting that originated in France. Money bet in win, place, and show pools, less commissions, is divided among those holding tickets on the winner and the second and third horses.

pipe opener   Exercise at moderate speed. Also, a breeze.

pocket   Shut off, boxed in. Running in a position with horses in front and alongside.

pole Markers placed at measured distances around a track: eighth pole, quarter pole, etc.

post parade Horses going from the paddock to the starting gate, past the stands.

post position The position in the starting gate from which a horse breaks. Positions are numbered from the rail outward.

post time The designated time for a race to start.

prep (or prep race) Training. Or, an event preliminary to another usually more important engagement.

purse The money or other prize for a race to which the owners do not contribute.

quarter One quarter of a mile: 440 yards (1,320 feet).

quarter pole A marker placed one-quarter of a mile from the finish.

restraining chain The chain part of a shank. It is looped over a horse's nose or through its mouth for greater control by the handler.

scale of weights Fixed imposts to be carried by horses in a race according to age, sex, season, and distance.

scratch To withdraw a horse from a race. There is a deadline for scratches after which permission must be obtained from the Stewards.

set down Suspension. Generally imposed on riders for a specified period.

set him down When a rider gathers a horse and by use of the hands, legs, and sometimes a whip, urges it to an all-out effort.

seven furlongs Seven-eighths of a mile: 1,540 yards (4,620 feet).

shed row The stable area. A row of barns.

silks The jacket and cap worn by riders.

sire Father of a thoroughbred.

six furlongs Three-quarters of a mile: 1,320 yards (3,960 feet).

sixteenth One-sixteenth of a mile: 110 yards (330 feet).

snug Mild restraining hold on a horse by the rider.

splint An inflamed oval enlargement on the splint bone that may keep a horse out of action for a month or more. It is most commonly found in yearlings and two year olds and is believed to result from a tear in the ligament or a blow to the area from the opposite foot.

starting gate A mechanical device with partitions that confine horses until the starter releases the doors in front to start the race.

stayer A stout-hearted horse; one who can race long distances.

stewards Top officials of a meeting.

stick A jockey's whip.

stretch The straightaway portion of a race track. More particularly, the homestretch.

stride Manner of going. The distance progressed after each foot has touched the ground once. More broadly, a step.

stud A male horse used for breeding. Also, a breeding farm.

stud book The registry and geneological record of the breeding of thoroughbreds that is maintained by The Jockey Club. Only thoroughbreds of accepted lineage are eligible for admission.

tack A riders' racing equipment. Applied also to stable gear.

tacked up All tack or riding equipment set and in place on a horse in preparation for riding.

totalisator An intricate machine that sells betting tickets and records the total of win, place, and show pools and the amount bet on each horse in the three categories. It also shows the odds to win on each horse in the field and the complete pay-off after the finish.

track record The fastest time at various distances made at a particular course.

traps Stable equipment.

triple crown In the United States, the Kentucky Derby, the Preakness, and the Belmont stakes. In England, the Two Thousand Guineas, the Epsom Derby, and the St. Leger.

turf course A grass racing course.

walkover A race that scratches down to only one starter who merely gallops the required distance. A formal gesture required by the rules of racing. Also, an easy win.

warming up Galloping a horse on the way to the post.

watered off When a horse has finished drinking water during cooling out.

weight assignments The weights assigned to be carried by horses in a race. These are determined by such factors as age, sex, and past performance. In "condition" races, these weights are determined by the conditions of the race. In a handicap race, they are decided by the official handicapper. Weights are used to give all entrants as even a chance as possible.

weight-for-age A fixed scale of weights to be carried by horses according to age, sex, distance of the race, and season of the year.

withers The raised area or slight hump at the base of a horse's neck.

The Grayson-Jockey Club Research Foundation

Secretariat's ongoing Legacy to the welfare of the horse through contribution to the Grayson-Jockey Club Research Foundation

The Grayson-Jockey Club Research Foundation is the leading private organization in the field of funding equine research. It operates free of politics, government, and any specific commercial institutions. All of the research underwritten by the foundation is devoted to the sole cause of protecting the health and safety of the horse, and that means your horses as well as others.

The original Grayson Foundation was formed in 1940. A number of leading sportsmen had been discussing for some years a method of supporting research into the health and welfare of the horse, but it was not only the wars of racing which held their attention. Nearly 800,000 horses had been used by German forces in the opening days of World War II, indicating that use of horses, despite the advances of mechanized warfare, promised to be even heavier than in World War I. Thus the founders had the grim realities of their time to consider in evolving aims for their new foundation. However, they were also heavily committed to the sporting use of horses as they looked to the future. The original founders were William Woodward Sr., then chairman of the Jockey Club, and fellow, well-known patrons of Thoroughbreds John Hay (Jock) Whitney and Walter M. Jeffords Sr., Kentucky farm management expert Major Louie Beard, and Dr. George Crile, a founder and director of the Cleveland Clinic Foundation. They set the goals that endure, namely to pursue the funding of research rather than performing the research itself and the public distribution of information growing out of such research. That information would have the primary purpose of reaching as many horse and mule owners as possible. The founders chose the name Grayson Foundation to honor one of the leading figures of the time, thus providing a beneficial tone to the organization. Admiral Cary Grayson, during his career, had been best known as the personal physician of President Woodrow Wilson. In his final years, he had also been chairman of the American Red Cross and president of an organization known as the Gorgas Foundation. Through the latter, he had significant involvement in research relative to the horse, the animal that provided him his greatest pleasure. Dr. Grayson died in 1938, two years before organization of the foundation bearing his name, but he had been one of the first to support equine research as well as being owner of a successful breeding and racing operation at Blue Ridge Farm in Virginia.

In 1989 the Grayson Foundation was merged with another foundation organized by the Jockey Club. Henceforth it became known as the Grayson-Jockey Club Research Foundation, Inc. The areas of research by the foundation are many, but the death of Secretariat brought on by laminitis drew a significant increase of public attention to the work being done by the organization and, along with it, increased support. A special fund was organized whereby individuals could donate to Grayson with the specification that the money go to research into laminitis. Largely because of Secretariat's end under such pitiable circumstances, Penny Chenery became increasingly active in the organization and was its president throughout the 1980s. Laminitis continues to be one of the

219

most serious problems of the horse, and the Foundation in most years funds at least one project on that dreadful affliction. Many veterinarians regard laminitis as the biggest problem they face and also a nightmare enigma by reason that the disease is even more complicated because it stems from so many various causes.

In the first 11 years following the merger of the original Grayson Foundation with The Jockey Club's equine research activities, the increase in broad based support has been gratifying. Whereas once the Grayson Foundation struggled to achieve a goal of $100,000 for equine research in a given year, the merger resulted in support reaching a new average high of $825,000 annually. Even more encouraging is the fact that the figure grows each year.

Such growth came through exceptional generosity of the few, solid support from quite a few, and, of course, competent investment and operational portfolio management. The net worth of the foundation grew to $17.5 million in the year 2000, about six times the total at the time of the merger. Such stability was no accident. It was the result of building on a strong history of achievement. Over the years this has included

- Identification of major diseases and their causes which were once known collectively as "equine influenza."
- Development of a vaccine for equine influenza, improving control of racetrack cough.
- Defining the cause of virus abortion and developing a vaccine against it.
- Discovering the cause of hemolytic icterus in foals and defined many aspects of passive immunity.
- Developing basic knowledge of Equine Infectious Anemia (the dreaded Swamp Fever).

- Leading development of the field of the biomechanics of lameness in horses.
- Defining the cause of Colitis X and beginning investigations of the role of bacterial endotoxin in colic and laminitis.
- Developing vaccines against herpes virus infections in horses.
- Developing use of lights in stalls in encouraging early cycling in broodmares.
- The controlling of the Shaker foal (an equine strain of botulism, primarily in foals, which causes loss of muscle control, shaking and general inability to function).
- Defining the nature of the Wobbler syndrome (a neurological/muscular condition in foals).
- Discovering EVA (equine viral arteritis, an arterial disease primarily affecting the testicles of stallions and other vital organs supplied by arteries) and developed a vaccine for it.

Recently, foundation funding was instrumental in helping owners cope with EPM (Equine protozoal myelitis, a neurological disease affecting the horse causing weakness and general lack of coordination resulting in loss of use of the horse and frequently death). With regard to studies of the human gene map, the Grayson-Jockey Club was ahead by some ten years by cautiously entering funding of this cutting edge research insofar as the horse is concerned. Results of these studies may well benefit many species, including mankind itself. Some other more recent developments include

- Study in long bones of horses which pointed to safer training regimens.
- A project explaining how tendons splitting works.
- Improvement in equine influenza diagnosis and vaccine.

- Conclusion that laryngeal nerve problems can occur at the earliest stages of a horse's life.
- Improved surgical protocol for horses with certain cartilage defects.

Foundation research has succeeded in eliminating the necessity of last resort euthanasia in the case of many catastrophic injuries including many types of fractures. With regard to continuing improvement of medication and drug testing techniques, Grayson-Jockey Club Research Foundation continues to devote its efforts and its funds to the fundamental cause of protecting the horse from wrongful, frequently harmful medications. While strict rules and regulations exist in this regard, enforcement of them depends on the most advanced testing techniques possible.

Constant research and vigilance are critical to the cause of protecting the welfare of the horse and the sport of racing, and, of course, the need for funding is always a pressing necessity. While individual institutions and firms specialize in one or a few things, Grayson-Jockey Club Research Foundation devotes its funding to resources that cover the entire range of research and development for the protection and welfare of the horse.

Secretariat's death was not in vain, and his great gift to the horse and all who love horses continues through his contribution to the work of this devoted foundation.

For those of you readers who might wish to obtain more information about this worthy organization and its fine work, Grayson-Jockey Club welcomes inquiries and donations via its Lexington, KY office at 821 Corporate Drive, Lexington, KY 40503. Phone (859) 224-2850 / Fax (859) 224-2853 / E-mail: *ebowen@jockeyclub.com*. The foundation's Website can be accessed from *www.thejockeyclub.com*.

A Footnote

It seems to be destiny that a special piece of old Virginia known as Meadow Farm near Doswell be rescued by the love of people who revere its history, its accomplishments, and its gifts to our own history.

In December 1992, after having gone through a transition of several owners since the Chenery family, Meadow Farm once again was fated to be on the block and at the mercy of the merciless tide of commercial real estate development. And

once again, at the eleventh hour, Meadow was saved, this time by a young native of Richmond named Ross Sternheimer, president of A&N Stores, itself a Cinderella story of a family business which had risen from humble beginning in 1868 as a simple general store. Ross's family expanded their enterprise after World War I by merchandising military surplus clothing and equipment, thus starting what most of us remember as the old "Army-Navy" store, hence A&N.

Like many young Americans of his generation, Ross Sternheimer loved Secretariat for the hero he was to all of us and to America. When he became aware of the fate of Meadow, he was in the position to purchase it, and so he did. Since his acquisition, he has literally restored the entire farm to its original, labor-of-love state in which it was kept by Christopher Chenery. Only the original residence, unfortunately razed by previous owners, had to be replaced by a new structure. Other than that, the farm has been faithfully preserved, a fitting memorial to the great contributions of Meadow to American racing and to lovers of the Virginia Thoroughbred. Best of all, SECRETARIAT's birthplace, the small, humble white shed in the front field near the house, has been preserved to its smallest detail. Those of you who wish to visit the birthplace of the wonderful horse who became a hero of his time and to us all are welcomed. The only price of your visit is your love of his memory and what he gave to all of us - His great heart.

Raymie Woolfe - April 10, 1998

THE AUTHOR

Raymond G. "Raymie" Woolfe, Jr. is a lifelong horseman. Son of a leading trainer he turned professional at 16, has been a steeplechase jockey, licensed trainer, manager of horse farms and designer of race courses. He still holds the record as the youngest professional jump rider licensed and youngest to win at a major U.S. track .

An alumnus of the University of Virginia and the University of South Carolina School of Journalism, a Marine veteran and long-time career photo-journalist, including 11 years as chief of photography for Daily Racing Form, and author of STEEPLECHASING, Mr. Woolfe lives on his "Hawk's Nest Farm" near Charlottesville, Virginia.